PENGUIN BOOKS

THE RACIST MIND

Rafe Ezekiel is based at the Harvard School of Public Health (Public Health Practice Initiative), where he is studying youth development and youth violence prevention. For thirty-one years he was on the psychology faculty at the University of Michigan. His previous social psychological research has addressed, among other issues, the lives of inner-city African-Americans in Detroit and Peace Corps volunteers in Ghana. He lives near Boston.

Also by the author

VOICES FROM THE CORNER:
POVERTY AND RACISM IN THE INNER CITY

CROSS-NATIONAL ENCOUNTERS
(WITH HERBERT C. KELMAN)

The
RACIST
Mind

Portraits of
American Neo-Nazis
and Klansmen

**RAPHAEL S.
EZEKIEL**

PENGUIN BOOKS

PENGUIN BOOKS
Published by the Penguin Group
Penguin Books USA Inc., 375 Hudson Street, New York, New York 10014, U.S.A.
Penguin Books Ltd, 27 Wrights Lane, London W8 5TZ, England
Penguin Books Australia Ltd, Ringwood, Victoria, Australia
Penguin Books Canada Ltd, 10 Alcorn Avenue, Toronto, Ontario, Canada M4V 3B2
Penguin Books (N.Z.) Ltd, 182–190 Wairau Road, Auckland 10, New Zealand

Penguin Books Ltd, Registered Offices: Harmondsworth, Middlesex, England

First published in the United States of America by Viking Penguin,
a division of Penguin Books USA Inc. 1995
Published in Penguin Books 1996

1   3   5   7   9   10   8   6   4   2

THE LIBRARY OF CONGRESS HAS CATALOGUED THE HARDCOVER AS FOLLOWS:
Ezekiel, Raphael S. [date]
The racist mind: portraits of Neo-Nazis and Klansmen/Raphael S. Ezekiel.
p.   cm.
ISBN 0-670-83958-2 (hc.)
ISBN 0 14 02.3449 7 (pbk.)
1. Racism—United States.   2. White supremacy movements—United States.
3. Ku Klux Klan (1915–).   4. White Aryan Resistance.
5. United States—Race relations.   I. Title.
E184.A1E98   1995
320.5´6´0973—dc20   94–45177

Printed in the United States of America
Set in Adobe Sabon
Designed by Kathryn Parise

To the memory of

James Chaney
Andrew Goodman
Michael Schwerner

Addie Mae Collins
Denise McNair
Carole Robertson
Cynthia Wesley

ACKNOWLEDGMENTS

This work was supported by major grants from the Harry Frank Guggenheim Foundation and the Carnegie Corporation of New York; by grants from the Harris Foundation, the Institute for Pluralism of the American Jewish Committee, and several executive offices of the University of Michigan; and by private support of Mr. Ralph Colton. I am grateful to all those sources. Errors in fact or interpretation are those of the author, not the funders.

I am especially indebted to Karen Colvard at Guggenheim; Susan Smith, Geri Mannion, and David Hamburg at Carnegie; and Susan Lipschutz and Billy Frye at Michigan (Frye is now at Emory).

I have benefited from the comradeship and counsel of Dan Levitas and Leonard Zeskind, both at the Center for Democratic Renewal; Danny Welch at Klanwatch; and Kenneth Stern at the American Jewish Committee.

Bob Beattie at Michigan's research office was a great friend. Pat Gurin made the Michigan psychology department a warm haven. Bill Gamson and Jerry Post said the right things at the right time to the right people, as did Pat. Brewster Smith's wise counsel was a great resource.

Tish O'Dowd insightfully edited early drafts of the second chapter.

Mary Cain transcribed all the tapes from Detroit; she has always been a fine pal, and I wish I could have printed the editorial rejoinders she added to several transcripts.

Mary Jo Beck transcribed all tapes from the second half of the research and handled constant redrafts. I depended on her brains and energy. She met deadlines, no matter how much work it cost, and she believed in this work from the start. They don't come nicer. Thank you, Mary Jo.

Thanks also to Judy and Russ for love and hospitality in Atlanta.

Kathi Paton, my agent, is a tough bargainer, thank goodness. Thanks.

Mindy Werner, my editor at Viking, has high standards, good sense, and fine taste. She kept demanding better work, and I thank her for it.

This work has rested on the cooperation of a number of individuals in the white racist movement, for which I am grateful. They probably will not like this book, but I have kept my promise: To the best of my ability, I have presented the sense they make of their lives, and in their own words.

R.E.
September 1994

CONTENTS

NOTE ON NAMES AND
PSEUDONYMS

Major public figures in the white supremacist movement are presented or referred to by their real names. These include Tom Metzger, Dave Holland, Richard Butler, Robert Miles, James Farrands, Thom Robb, J. B. Stoner, Ed Fields, James Venable, Robert Mathews, Gordon Kahl, Jim Ellison, Glenn Miller, William Pierce, Wesley Swift, Louis Beam, and David Duke. Minor figures, who are often transient, are presented under pseudonyms; this includes all members of the Detroit neo-Nazi group.

With one exception, all organizations are presented under their real names. I have altered the name of the Detroit neo-Nazi group, so that my extensive treatment would not add needlessly to its publicity.

Hospitals and social service institutions in or near Detroit are presented under pseudonyms.

The
RACIST
Mind

INTRODUCTION

Who am I? How do I fit in the world?

We ask this of ourselves, each of us, including the Klansman and the Nazi. For these people, the answer is race: "I am a member of the white race. My people built this civilization, built this country. We have the intelligence and the initiative for the task. Our blood is different and special. Our heritage has been taken from us; inferior races have taken power through their cunning. My race is near destruction. Most of my people are numb and passive, seduced and tranquilized by the enemy. The enemy plans the full destruction of my race's genius—its blood—through racial mixture. Ultimately, we or our enemy will be destroyed."

The core of this statement—that race identifies an essential, defining quality and that the white race is superior—is both similar to and different from the thoughts of most white Americans. It leaves out the many other ways through which people can see a connection to the larger society—through church, profession, occupation, age group, gender, school, or social class. It leaves out wider images of democratic community or religious fellowship that suggest a future beyond race. It does, on the other hand, resemble majority white perception by taking "race"—an idea built over time by a society and having little scientific significance—as a biologically meaningful description of reality, and therefore a fundamental way to categorize people. It further resembles majority white perception by taking for granted the specialness and the entitlement of Americans of European descent.

Most white Americans, however, have little acquaintance with the parts of their psyches that are congruent with the spirit of the acknowledged racists. We do not know, the old joke says, who discovered water, but we do know that it was not a fish. Just so, in a society in which white folk predominate and are seldom challenged in everyday life, white Americans have little conscious awareness of being white or of what that might mean. Only challenge or crisis makes this categorization relevant. The militant white racist movement is composed of people who permanently feel in crisis.

The militant white racists look at a world in which white Americans and nonwhite Americans are treated differently in almost every interaction; they infer that race is a powerful biological construct that identifies essences. (They are unfamiliar with modern genetic research, which has found that "race" identifies only trivial aspects of human genetic variation.) They look at a world in which almost all positions of power are held by men who are white; they infer that whites (and men) have a nature that is superior. The *boss,* the person one must worry about, is white. Everyday experience tells the militant white racist that race is basic and that white is good.

Because most white Americans, *at some level,* share these perceptions, the potential exists at all times for the militant movement to expand its influence. The militant movement keeps these ideas fresh and strong, persistently reinjecting them into the social discourse, ensuring that people stay vulnerable to interested parties who wish to use racism to capture public allegiance.

Many, perhaps most, of the readers of this book are, like the author, white. We in the general European-American public share many beliefs with the militant white racists, but we are not identical to them—it is *not* that "we have met the enemy, and he is us." We whites believe many things; we believe most of them in a dull and muddled and jumbled fashion; many of our beliefs are contradictory. The militant movement takes one of the many jumbled belief sets in our heads and preserves it in sharpened, intense form, adding to it a sense that life is struggle, that the fundamental issue between humans is power, that the world divides into Good and Evil, and that Good and Evil must fight to the death. And that events usually have hidden causes.

Because the movement rests partly on beliefs that *are* a part of us white Americans, but a part that we do not acknowledge and do not deal with, it has enjoyed an extraordinarily long life; it is regenerated again and again, taking new forms as circumstances change. We are astonished by the resurgence of Nazism in Europe. We have already seen large numbers of the American public seduced in the last two decades by racist appeals from mainstream politicians. The situation is going to become worse. Our national economy is grinding through brutal transformation: An enormous number of people can have no confidence that their jobs, wage levels, health care, or pensions are safe. They face *erosion* of their positions. Their fears will become only more acute as the swelling populations of the underdeveloped nations try to save themselves through mass migration. These highly predictable changes are going to make white Americans more and more vulnerable to a movement whose ideas are already a part of their inner life.

The basic propositions about the centrality of race and the superiority of whites pervade interactions in our culture, and institutional forms make those theses part of everyday experience. It is likely that nonwhites internalize these messages to some degree and much against their will, just as women absorb the presumptions of sexism. My research for this book speaks only of the mental and emotional life of whites; I am interested in the relation of acknowledged white racism to its unacknowledged white cousins.

This is a fairly personal book. For a decade I have interviewed followers and leaders in the militant white racist movement, the white supremacist movement, and have observed some of their rallies and get-togethers. I have dealt openly and honestly with these people, making it clear that I am Jewish, a leftist opposed to racism, a professor at the University of Michigan. I have told them, honestly, that I think people build lives that make sense to them, and that my goal is to understand the sense the person's life makes to that person. I tape-record conversations so the person's own words can be used. I listen much more than I talk. I try to ask searching questions. I try to encourage the respondent to give me a full picture of his life. I show him, periodically, how our basic beliefs differ and explore with him the bases of those beliefs. Occasionally I explain myself with passion; if I already know the respondent, I learn a lot from confrontation. Communication rests on my candor, their interest in being heard, my deep interest in understanding the phenomenon, and my background in a particularly racist culture. Until 1944, when I was twelve, I lived in an east Texas town during the years of total segregation; the values inside our family's home were liberal and egalitarian; the values and institutions outside the door were unself-consciously racist. I hate racism, which sunders the world I want to live in and harms great masses; but I have no trouble knowing that the racist is a comprehensible human: We went to school together.

In my research I have tried to understand the life and the thinking of the people I have met. Much comes from the interviews, but the observations of gatherings have also helped; I have been able to watch and listen as the movement members talk to each other and outline the party line for each other. This book, a selection from those experiences, expresses the sense I make of my work. Someone else would have interviewed differently and would have interviewed different people and chosen different excerpts for presentation; moreover, the guardedness of the movement presents many barriers to understanding. The best corrective for distortions produced by my idiosyncrasies would be similar pieces of work by others who had different backgrounds. Unfortunately, fieldwork is not popular in social science and this subject matter is even less popular, so there is extremely little research involving direct experience with the white racist movement. But the reader does need to remember that these are one man's reflections—nothing more—based on a great deal of challenging work out in the real world—nothing less.

The book tries to give an idea of the beliefs at the core of the movement today, the emotions in which those beliefs are drenched, and the life histories that lead to membership. This helps us understand the meaning and significance of the movement, but the reader should also remember that you have not accounted for a movement when you have only described some members. A movement is more than the sum of the psychology of its members. Its history, its structure, its links to other groups, and its ideology also shape a movement. There are more books to be read. But I hope that this introduction to the psychology of the membership will give the reader a useful grounding.

The militant white racist movement, in the latest estimates by reliable groups such as the Center for Democratic Renewal (CDR) and the Southern Poverty Law Center, includes about 23,000 to 25,000 hard-core members. Some 150,000 sympathizers buy movement literature, send contributions to movement groups, or attend rallies, and another 450,000 people who don't actually purchase movement literature do read it. Of the hard core, 5,500 to 6,000 belong to one or another of the Klans; 3,500 are Skinheads; and 500 to 1,000 are in Nazi groups or in groups close to the Nazis. The remainder of the hard core is much less easily identified; the CDR refers to them as the Christian Patriot Movement; they can be found in politically active churches of the Christian Identity sect and in rural groups scattered across the country. (The American Jewish Committee usually endorses the CDR's estimates. The Anti-Defamation League of B'nai B'rith concurs largely but would omit the Christian Patriots from the tally.)

The militant movement is a loose confederation of small groups. Coordination comes from the constant circuit riding of the leaders and their lieutenants and from the rather frequent gatherings at which speech makers lay out the party line, which is taken by minor leaders back to their own groups. Policy evolves in the conversations of leaders with each other, in person and on the phone, and in the argument over tactics between these very competitive organizations.

The media image of a monolithic group is misleading, but a commonality of basic precepts does lead to considerable coherence in action. The Klan itself is not the united organization that it was decades ago; for years it has been made up of some thirty or forty competing organizations, each with a name involving the word *Klan*. At present one wing of the Klan seeks to grow by painting itself as intensely activist, while another wing seeks to grow through seeming respectable; I think of these as the roughneck Klan and the smooth-talk Klan. The roughnecks figure to attract members by showing that they are tough and audacious; the smooth-talkers want to show the world that they are simply interested in white unity and have nothing more radical up the sleeves of their robes. It is all the same old mix, however: white supremacy, male dominance, and homophobia.

The largest of the Klans in recent years have been the Invisible Empire, Knights of the Ku Klux Klan, led by James Farrands from North Carolina; and the Knights of the Ku Klux Klan, led by Thom Robb of Arkansas. Farrands disbanded the Invisible Empire in 1993 when a successful lawsuit stripped it of its assets; some of its former members were reassembled as the Unified Knights of the KKK, while others are drifting. Additional Klan groups bear names such as the Confederate Knights of the Ku Klux Klan, the White Knights of the Ku Klux Klan, and the Southern White Knights of the Ku Klux Klan.

Some thirty neo-Nazi groups compete for membership; important clusters include Aryan Nations, led by Richard Butler of Idaho; White Aryan Resistance, led by Tom Metzger of California; and the American Nazi Party. Over a hundred Skinhead organizations, some with multiple locations, hold names such as Confederate Hammer Skins of Tulsa, Memphis Area Confederate Hammer Skins, Las Vegas Skins, and Southeast Boot Boys. A scattering of organizations aren't readily classified as Klan, Nazi, or Skinhead. Some of the groups, such as the main two Klans, have been national in scope, with cells in ten or twenty cities; most organizations, however, have had a cell in only a few towns.

Membership in the movement is highly fluid. Recruits cycle in and out rapidly; in the words of one Klan chief, the movement is a revolving door. People come in and stay awhile; they see nothing is happening; and they go away. Some fraction of the members—a quarter? a third?—will drift away over the next four years; a more or less equal number will replace them.

The inner circle is permanent. A cadre of leaders and lieutenants —movement activists for life—keep organizations breathing in lean times and rebuild as opportunities arise. Even among the cadre, however, disorder reigns. Would-be leaders split from existing organizations to form new ones; some of those fail, others succeed and bleed membership from their rivals. Leader reputations grow and dwindle. Leaders gossip maliciously about one another, distrustful rivals vie for attention and influence. Trials reveal the presence of informers; arrested leaders quickly turn state's witness; loyalty is shallow.

Despite jealousies and distrust, the movement does not die. Repeatedly it has flickered almost to extinction, only to be reborn. The funeral oration for organized white racism is always premature. The continual rebirth speaks to its deep roots in the national culture.

The movement has a long history of violence, and its recruits do not enter casually. The aura of violence—or at least of serious determination—is part of the basic attraction, even if the individual recruit has no intention of endangering his own skin. Direct movement violence has declined since the era when local authorities were Klan members or at least quiet collaborators. Movement groups piously disown to the media any person who has been arrested in a violent act, and it is hard to know how much of today's racial violence comes directly from the movement. Most serious analysts figure that the bulk of racial violence and homophobic violence is carried out by unaffiliated individuals, but equally believe that the organized groups do a great deal to set the climate for that violence. The groups that monitor racism (CDR, SPLC, AJC, ADL) periodically release tallies of reported race-related violence; their most recent figures (which depend upon very incomplete reporting systems in most jurisdictions) say that murders related to race or to the white supremacy movement came to seven in 1989, twenty in 1990, twenty-seven in 1991, thirty-one in 1992, and thirty in 1993. There have been hundreds of bias-related assaults in those years, and incidents of race-related vandalism rose from 322 in 1992 to 405 in 1993. Arsons directed at religious institutions more than doubled between 1989 and 1991, with synagogues and Jewish schools the most common targets.

The impact of racial and homophobic violence is much greater than simple numbers would suggest. *Targeted* violence carries powerful messages to the targeted populations. If I live in a medium-sized city and hear that there have been five murders during the winter, I feel in the presence of some random violence. If I am a lesbian woman living in that same city and hear that there have been three fatal assaults on lesbians, I feel very much endangered. Especially when the attackers belong to a hidden and continuing organization.

The militant white racist movement is small. Its impact is far greater than its numbers, because of the reputation for violence.

Historically, the Klan had been the anchor of the movement, and it kept some distance from the Nazi groups as they emerged. Since the 1980s, however, a merging of the tendencies has taken place, what some have called the Nazification of the Klan; ideas and stories and symbols have become indiscriminately mixed among the groups. There is a great attraction to images of Hitler's Third Reich and a sense of identification with an unusually powerful armed force that conquered most of Europe. For the white racists, the Wehrmacht was an army of brave, skilled men defeated only by overwhelming numbers. They speak of a Germany in which all classes were brought together in zealous effort by a unique leader, a man who could move great numbers by his voice, a man who brought a pride based on race to a shamed people. These images of strength speak more loudly today to potential recruits than do the older legends of the Confederacy's Lost Cause. The image of the armed night-rider still works, though with less power than the more contemporary images of tank drivers and Stuka pilots. Late-night movies on television have given the relevant public many more images of the Nazi epic than of the Confederacy or of Reconstruction. And I have found that the pictures recruits have in their heads do come precisely from these movies: This is where they have heard of the Third Reich.

Most strikingly, recruits have little in their heads to *inhibit* their adopting these legends. Many have a considerable level of fear about their own survival and their own significance; identification with strength is deeply rewarding. Nothing inhibits this unconventional identification. The legend is scorned by the Establishment, but this only increases its value to young men who feel equally ignored by those in power. Contrary legends are lacking; no alternative myth tells the young man that his life has significance.

The Holocaust plays a paradoxical role in all this. On the one hand, Holocaust denial matters to the movement, and it presses claim insistently that it is debatable whether these systematic murders took place. The white racist movement knows that for most people the immediate association with the word *Nazi* is the word *Holocaust,* an association that hinders broad organizing. At the same time, I sense that the movement's fascination with the Holocaust is exactly that: fascination. The most important thing for members about Hitler's regime is that it was a force so strong and so ruthless that it did not hesitate to murder. I think contemporary white racists *need* to talk endlessly about the Holocaust, need to keep saying over and over that it did not happen—so that they can keep talking about it, can keep thinking about it, can keep reassuring themselves that it *did* happen, that they are a part of a movement so merciless that they are safe.

If they really believed Nazism had not killed, it would bore them.

On occasion I have asked a young militant to imagine, just for a moment, that people like me are telling the truth: that Hitler and his group *did* kill six million Jews, individuals who were in no way guilty of a crime. Would that make any difference to him? Every one answered it would make no difference at all. The Bolsheviks were Jews, they would say, and had killed twenty million Christians themselves, and bad things happen in wartime anyway, and so on. The point is that not one of the young men who has been able to imagine for a moment that I am right was at all bothered. I think that they are fairly sure that Hitler did murder, and they are fairly glad; it reassures them.

Fear is at the center of these groups, fear and a sense of isolation. Belonging to the group affords comradeship within struggle. The mythical "white race" is the larger family for which these spiritual orphans long.

Confrontation is a prime activity of the organized groups. Demonstrations provoke counterdemonstrations. People with a deep inner sense that they may not be real, that they are already shriveled, are reassured by the hostility of counterdemonstrators that they are alive. Provocative symbols—the swastika, the Reb flag, the shaved head and shiny boots—ensure the necessary feedback.

The movement today feels itself a defense organization. White rule in America has ended, members feel. A new world they do not like has pushed aside the traditional one they think they remember. In the old world, the only significant people were white; men struggled as individuals to build a life for their families; good men and dutiful women lived peacefully; somewhere in the background were others. Today, they feel, those others have taken control. The government and high society fawn over the blacks. Blacks are given special privileges and special access to work. Blacks breed recklessly and fill the cities with unloved and illegitimate progeny. Blacks have no feel for honest work; blacks rob or live off welfare; blacks live on drugs. The inner city is the best that the black has constructed in America and shows his character. A conspiracy of wily Jews and their gold-crazed, race-traitor white flunkies has taken control of the churches, the media, the schools, the government, and the corporations. Preaching hypocritical cant about racial equality, they have stripped whites of their rights and are attempting to destroy the white race through forced sexual mingling. All this to ensure Jewish rule. Jewish pornographers debase white moral fiber; Jewish educators attack white pride; Jewish television peddles homosexuality as normalcy. The only good thing that has happened has been the advent of AIDS; *"Praise God for AIDS!"* the white racists cry out at their rallies.

For several decades the major energizing element in the movement has been the theology of Christian Identity. This religion teaches that the whites are the only true children of God, a Being who is white. Identity teaches that the whites are the people described in the Old Testament as Israelites. Moses, the great leader of these first Aryans, led them from Egypt to Canaan, where they conquered and ruled. Dispersed first by the Assyrians and then by the Romans, the Aryans migrated north through the Caucasus (acquiring the name Caucasian) and westward into northern Europe. The tribe of Judah became Germany, the tribe of Dan became Denmark, and so forth. Ultimately the white God in-gathered His people to the United States and Canada, where they are to draw strength and fulfill their destiny to rule the world.

Identity preaches that only whites have been created by God. Only whites are human. The people of color, known as the "mud races," have arisen through the mating of humans with animals. Jews are the children of Satan, born from the coupling of Eve with the Serpent (Satan). The children of God will struggle with the children of Satan until one or the other has been destroyed.

Most groups in the militant movements are involved by now in Christian Identity, and its key concepts reach far. The nonhumanity of nonwhites is an old belief among whites, of course, as is the animal-like nature of Africans and the diabolical nature of Jews.

The imagery employed in the movement is indeed ancient. The black is depicted repeatedly as the Ape, an image that appears in the first European contacts with West Africa before Columbus. And again and again we hear of the Jew as the Serpent or the Spider, the hidden, cunning force, images current since the Middle Ages. The white is the Warrior, a single, beleaguered figure, a straight young man or a bewhiskered Nordic Berserker, laying about himself with some sharp pointed (phallic) object such as a sword or a spear, plunging it into a dragon or a serpent decorated with Jewish stars and Communist hammer and sickle.

The movement—at least the visible, uniformed militant organizations—is almost entirely male. All leaders and most members are men. A few women are around, never as speakers or leaders; usually they are wives, who cook and listen. Highly traditional ideas of sex roles, and fears of losing male dominance, fill the conversation and the speeches.

Recurrent images have a feeling-tone frequent in exclusivist male assemblies; an underlying voice seems to say, "Sure you are a man, you don't have to be so worried about it." There is talk of order, of "strength"; the seductive burrowing enemy is not in your insides but out there in society; we can still achieve purity, we can fend off contamination.

These psychic undercurrents are expressed in macho images that may well be repellent to women. It is even possible, of course, that the fundamental activity is repellent. Women have probably been socialized (and are perhaps predisposed) to value harmony and the building of relationships. This would make them less at home than men at dwelling on the distinctions between people rather than the commonalities, and less prepared to assume that hostility is the basic language between people.

In time the movement may become less exclusively male. In a later chapter I describe a pioneering moment in that process, when women claimed the chance for the first time to participate—at the tail end and with grudging toleration—in a central ritual of the Aryan Nations group. Young women seem to play a more active role in the Skinhead youth gangs than in the traditional Klans.

If most of the members are men, from what economic level do they come? Little objective work has been accomplished on this question. My initial field research in Detroit took place among young men from a very poor sector of the white population, and I assumed as fieldwork broadened that I was looking at a movement of people who were struggling economically. My later observations seemed in line with that presumption, although I seldom saw again the flat-out poverty of the Detroit racists; in general I seemed to be looking at blue-collar workers, some of them skilled, and people of modest middle-class standing. There was lots of variation. At rallies and in conversation, leaders referred to their following as working people with little money; they were jealous of the resources of the Left. Observers have tended to assume that Klansmen and Nazis are fairly poor, but this may not be the case. James Aho of Idaho State University has done the only scientific work that I know of in this regard, and the extremists he has studied come from a representative slice of American society. Leonard Zeskind of CDR, whom I consider the most astute observer of the movement, also sees movement membership as directly reflecting general American society.

Membership in the uniformed groups may draw more heavily from the less monied—people with businesses or careers shy away from visible identification with notorious groups. Behind that frontline group are the Christian Patriots, who probably include many more from the middle classes. And behind all of these, there are the sympathizers who regularly send in contributions and subscribe to movement publications; these legions are white Americans representing every economic level, distinct only in that they do not identify with the values to which the national majority pays at least lip service.

Movement members are not impressed by the majority's verbalization of nonracist values. They believe that most white Americans agree with them at a gut level and can be brought into alignment with them as circumstances worsen; history will turn other whites into their allies. At the same time, they feel a good deal of scorn for the white masses. The average white person today, they feel, is "a vegetable," a dupe tied to "the boob tube." Deep down there is a connection between the movement and the white public, they feel. They are correct, in my estimation, but the real question is *what else* that average white American has in his or her psyche in addition to the primitive constructs that are shared with the militants.

When I began talking to racists, I expected to find that economic fears played a central role. It makes sense to me that economic facts can drive history; I am less used to thinking of ideas as having profound power, and I was surprised to gradually understand that the agreement on basic ideas is the glue that holds the movement together, that the ideas are important to the members. The white racist movement is about an idea.

I had thought that there might be emotional factors that one could find at the center, as well as economic. I think the reader will see some similarities among the members in their sense of self as isolate and threatened. But there is no simple and overpowering psychological "explanation": There are many ways to be a racist, just as there are many ways to be a nurse or a professor or a grocer. I have met members who were dependent and nasty; I also have met men who strongly valued independence, mavericks who bridled at conformity.

Readers may or may not feel by the end of these selections that they see a psychological base to the movement. With hesitation, I will suggest that I hear one voice repeatedly, a voice that puts me in mind of the very early teenager—a rebellious youngster, very frightened about himself, utterly self-absorbed. With one or two ideas in his head.

This does *not* mean that we are dealing with a harmless, misunderstood kid. Lots of members are harmless; the *movement* is not and does not mean to be. Its goal is power and domination; its history, rhetoric, and analysis direct it into violence; its language draws to it people who will be capable of violence, along with many other people. Without periodically re-earning its reputation for violence, the movement would disappear.

Violence is a key to understanding the multiple meanings of the movement for different kinds of members. The six blind men of fable who feel different parts of the elephant variously report the elephant to be shaped like a snake or like a tree and so on, depending on which part of the elephant they touch. The white racist movement is reported in bafflingly different forms, for similar reasons. A journalist sent to cover a killing reports a murder gang; a feature writer speaking at length with the parents of a jailed member reports an assembly of economically deprived peasants straining for hope. The movement holds many different people who are living in many different worlds. All are linked by a central set of beliefs and by adherence to certain leaders who closely share beliefs.

Four kinds of membership can be identified if we look at degrees of involvement and issues of self-control.[1] The national leader and his lieutenants are men with a lifetime of involvement, whose lives are centered on their work as organizers and who keep groups alive. Violence for them is the hidden subtext, as is sex in many other settings; there must always be the almost-unspoken possibility. The organizational dress reinforces the message; the code of secrecy emphasizes it. The hint, the wink, tell the media that the gathering or the march must be covered: Violence is news; the potential for violence can't be ignored. The possibility of violence is the bait that makes the organization visible and that draws members. Much more loosely connected than the leaders and cadre are[2] the ordinary followers, the ordinary members. Most are by no means fanatical, most have no wish at all to be harmed or to spend time in prison or to lose their jobs. More than that, they have no serious wish to personally harm some nonwhite person. They do, however, like the feeling of being part of a serious endeavor, and the Klan group, or the Nazi group, because it does hold the possibility of violence, *is* a serious group. So it is a thrill to have the card in their pockets. But they don't want anything dangerous to happen near them, and people drop out fast when police investigations begin.

A third kind of person in the movement is the[3] loose cannon, the unpredictable fellow who gets drawn in by the language and the history, the fellow who doesn't really get the picture that one is supposed to take everything with a grain of salt and cover his own ass. The loose cannon is tinder, waiting for the spark. He catches fire and does his act; is caught and is put away; but the movement gains immeasurably from his behavior. He will be disavowed by the leadership and the ordinary members, but in fact his action is indispensable, as it keeps alive the aura: This movement *can* be violent. A fourth kind of person in the movement is the [4] potential terrorist, the guerrilla. He believes the ideology literally, word for word—there is an Enemy, the Enemy is Evil. He believes the ideology because he *wants* it: He *wants* the grounds for radical action. He must have radical action. Violence is the language in which he can speak his message; his spirit needs the comradeship of the tight terrorist cell.

For the casual member, the movement is similar in many ways to alternative social groupings to which he might belong; the hint of violence is dramatic, but not much is happening and membership doesn't transform his life. For the member who stays in more than a year or so, the group has much more defined meaning: The ideology has become very large in his mental life; a great deal of his thought has to do with the "conspiracies" and seeing the hidden meaning of events and brooding about the future. The senior members—very longtime members, cadre, leaders—feel thoroughly embedded within a framework: The movement is the world, the progress of the multiple racist organizations is minutely followed, their struggles with the authorities meticulously attended, the rise and fall of their competitive status endlessly tracked. Finally, the potential terrorists construct tiny alternative structures within the surface ones. Underground cells—secret small gangs—form periodically here and there, the "Klan within the Klan," as knowing leaders may call it. Absolute secrecy is sought, but whispers percolate up into the everyday movement. Public, visible national leaders may become fairly sure such a cell is being formed, and work to be able to seem unaware of it, while lending full moral support. For the national leader, the terrorist cell, like the loose cannon's act, is lifeblood, the vital infusion of *violence as possibility* that ensures the reputation. Much more than the loose cannon's act, however, the underground cell's acts can endanger others, especially leaders; prison walls await.

In all these degrees of membership, and all these forms of involvement, violence plays its particular role, as does the ideology, the set of beliefs. The vital function of the movement is to keep the beliefs in an active state. The periodic gatherings insistently repeat the beliefs and give them form, drench them in the language of blood. And the movement, by providing that incessantly recharged machinery, makes sure that there is a *setting that will draw, will enspirit,* the

ordinary member, the senior member, the loose cannon, and the terrorist. Those who need meaning for their lives will find it here; those
who need the spark that will let them explode will find it here; those
who need the framework in which to live conspiracy or violence will
find it here. The elephant is many things.

The movement tries out new forms in new circumstances. In 1993
and 1994 a number of prominent leaders began to preach "leaderless
resistance": The movement should abandon parades for action, but
action should be carried out by very small cells in which no one
knows more than he must about the organization as a whole. The
most recent of the movement's fictionalized versions of the desired
future, the novel *Hunter* by the leader of a faction called the National
Alliance, describes a lone white racist assassin whose murders of interracial couples and of integrationist leaders set an example so dramatic that hundreds of other lone whites carry out spontaneous
assassinations along the same lines, without the need for organizational ties. This suggests a high level of frustration in the white racist
movement at the moment, a feeling that old forms have not worked,
and an emerging organizational climate that is more likely to attract
and nurture potential terrorists.

In a less dramatic development, the movement, especially its Christian Patriot sector, is hitchhiking on gun-enthusiasts' fears of legal
restrictions, just as it hitchhiked on farmers' fears during the farm
foreclosures crisis of the 1980s. So-called militias have sprung up in
a number of states, designed to prevent government seizure of pri-
vately owned weapons; some of these "militias," especially in the
Northwest, have been organized by longtime lieutenants of Aryan
Nations and other white racist groups.

While organizations in the white racist movement come and go, the
basic themes are constant. The particular members and leaders and
groups that appear in these pages may or may not be on the scene
in ten years, but others much like them will be. The people I present
here are quite real; the names are not, unless otherwise noted. The
interviews were tape-recorded and transcribed. The quotations in the
chapters based on interviews (Parts Two and Three) are exact. I did

not tape-record, on the other hand, while observing gatherings. I took almost verbatim notes during speeches and typed them up the same day. The quotes in the chapters about gatherings (Part One) include many of the exact words of the speakers but necessarily leave out many words; the reader can take those quotations as definitely true to the intended meaning of the speaker and largely accurate, but not a transcription.

The actual fieldwork began when I learned that a Nazi bookstore had opened in Detroit and I visited it. My interest was aroused by what I saw. As later chapters detail, I made connections with that group and for about three years observed them and did in-depth interviews with the members of the group. I was increasingly aware of differences between the leader of that group and his members, and decided to try to interview national leaders in the racist movement. An initial contact with Robert Miles in Michigan (a major racist figure, recently deceased) was highly fruitful. We talked many times at his farm forty miles northwest of Detroit, and he helped me assemble a list of leaders I would hope to interview. Miles suggested early on that I attend the Klan's Labor Day rally at Stone Mountain, Georgia, which opened a contact with additional national leaders. During the next few years, I made a series of visits to a number of national leaders and periodically was able to make observations at racist gatherings. The leader interviews and the observations took place in the South, the Midwest, the Northwest, and California. I have had many conversations at gatherings and, when visiting leaders, with their lieutenants and members; these have helped lend depth. Periodically I have revisited respondents from the Detroit group; most recently I have been doing a fair amount of observation with a Klan group in Michigan.

In my work, I am trying to understand the *meaning* that a person's activity has in that person's life. I listen to words, and they tell me a lot; I think about what has not been said; I think about patterns.

Over time, my understanding of this movement has changed. The initial work in Detroit spoke loudly to me of the neediness of the young members as individuals. As I moved on to the broader inquiries—the listening and looking at gatherings, the interviews with leaders—I saw more clearly that we were dealing with a movement, even if its local appearance seemed more like a gang.

In constructing this book, I reverse the sequence of the research.

Part One of the book presents three of the gatherings that I witnessed. The reader can listen to the words of the speeches and feel the emotions of the crowd, as well as visit a trial. We meet national leaders in Part Two. I present three of the eight or ten whom I have come to know well. The three case studies present three distinct and important styles. Part Three presents the Detroit group. The university's location only thirty-five miles away allowed visits two or three times a week and interviewing late into the night. Here are detailed portraits from one setting; the culture and the personalities we look at recur at many places in the movement. I hope that this picture of one group will not long stand alone, that I or others can soon add similar case histories from other groups, illuminating additional styles.

In the book, I usually employ the term *white racist*, but occasionally employ the term *racist*. Let me say, for clarity, that there is no analysis here of any group but the extremists who come out of white American culture.

One further point about language: The movement includes few women, so I usually employ the masculine form of pronouns.

Several terms must be explained. Speakers refer to the *Northwest Republic*. Movement leaders advocate the migration of white racists to the northwestern United States and adjoining parts of Canada, where they might become a majority and set up a white world separate from the rest of the country. Speakers rail at *ZOG*, the *Zionist Occupation Government*. This is a label for the group that they believe truly controls and governs America, the conspiratorial cabal of Jews and their flunkies.

People sometimes ask me why I have studied these groups. My previous book grew from similarly depth-oriented interviews with African-American men and women who lived on a small inner-city street in Detroit; there, too, I wanted to understand the meaning of lives. The issue of race is absolutely central to American life. Our lives are deeply affected by the conceptions that segments of our society have of one another and by the institutions that have grown up over the years to embody these conceptions. It is necessary to explore these conceptions. The militant racist groups are worth studying in their own right; they have impact. But they are especially worth study because they let us see white racism in its unfiltered, unguarded form.

The history, the experiences, and the cultural lore that operate on the white racist operate on each white American; and each of us, regardless of origin, has internalized at least a part of the set of beliefs and emotions that predominate in the white racist. We who are mostly nonracist, whose minds and spirits are 70 or 80 percent non-racist, cannot act in a way that can be trusted until we have become familiar with our own inner parts that do speak in a racist voice. We need to come to know our own racism, so that it does not trip us when we are trying to behave responsibly. The energy we have spent in hiding that part of ourselves from our awareness is energy we can *use* in trustworthy acts to build coalitions.

Finally, this book presents detailed portraits in which white racists appear as individuals with real lives. It would be simpler—and pointless—to simply reinforce the reader's stereotypes and pander to the reader's preexisting images. It takes no effort to speak glibly about a stereotype.

Nothing more befogs the critical relationships of wealth, power, poverty, and the common good than the racism of our culture. We need desperately to understand that racism at a deep level. One piece of that process—pointless without learning economics and history, but vital to understanding them—is to comprehend the experienced world of the people who are involved. That is much the task of this book.

To present white racists as humans is not to approve their ideas or their actions. But to picture them only in stereotype is to foolishly deny ourselves knowledge. Effective action to combat racism requires honest inquiry.

Part One

GATHERINGS

Over the years I have gone to a small number of racist con-claves and rallies. Most have involved indoctrination speeches in the daytime and robed ceremonials at night, usually around a flaming cross. Gatherings will be publicized through movement newsletters and by word of mouth. Some are very local, drawing from a small region; others are meant to be national and draw middle-level and top leaders from across the country.

I had not especially thought of going to this sort of gathering when I began this work; my attention was on getting to know individuals well. But observing gatherings turned out to be as valuable as any-thing I had done.

I did not come to a gathering unannounced or in disguise; I would first check with some national leader to let him know I wanted to be on hand. While at the gathering, I would listen and watch. Most of the people present would know, by word of mouth, who and what I was. Sometimes I would start short conversations with strangers, explaining myself and asking questions; other times I just listened.

The gatherings gave me a completely different window on the movement than the interviews gave. I could hear how members talked to one another, the kind of language they used, the sorts of trust and mistrust they showed. I could hear the kinds of words that came up in their conversations. I could watch how tense their bodies were when they stood talking with a stranger from another racist group. I could see the wide variety of people in attendance. I could see ordinary-looking folk and tense, desperate-looking folk; I could hear quiet drawls and loudmouths. Crucial to my work is that, in the speeches, I heard the ideas that were influential; in the way the ideas were presented, I could see the *kind* of education and followership that was involved; and, most important of all, I would hear the great similarity between the speeches and the overheard snatches of conversation. I learned a lot by hanging around.

The next three chapters deal with three gatherings—two voluntary and one involuntary. All came within the first year and a half of my interviews with national leaders.

ONE

Klan Rally at
Stone Mountain, Georgia

This chapter describes a rally at Stone Mountain, Georgia. One or more of the Klans has hosted this rally every year; speakers are leaders from across the country; attendees include highly active members of supremacist groups in Georgia, the Carolinas, and Tennessee (mostly Klan groups), and curiosity-seekers from the immediate vicinity. This was my first view of the organized supremacist movement beyond the one group of young Nazis in Detroit whom I had been interviewing. More important, as I will relate, the *experience* of being seen only as *a Jew*—not as a person who had a name, a history, friends, children—produced powerful feelings of sadness and loneliness. To experience the emotions firsthand was to visit briefly, under temporary and artificial conditions, the inner world of individuals assaulted by social contexts on the basis of a group label only: those assaulted by racism, by the hatred and fear of women, or by the hatred and fear of homosexuals.

Three years after I had begun interviewing members of a neo-Nazi group in Detroit, I began the work with national leaders through conversations with the late Robert Miles at his farm in Cahoctah, Michigan. Miles had once headed the Klan in Michigan and now held unity meetings for far-flung racist groups at his farm twice a year, as well as publishing a monthly newsletter. His phone rang incessantly when we talked. The calls came from across the country; he was one of the main figures holding the white racist movement together and supplying it with ideas.

As we were talking one afternoon in July, he suggested that I go down to the Labor Day rally at Stone Mountain, Georgia, if I really wanted to know what the Klan was about. He gave me the names of several leaders who lived in Atlanta so that I could make arrangements. Late in August I decided this was a good idea. Other than Miles, I had never known anyone who openly discussed any connection to the Klan. I could observe a large group of Klansmen; it would be a good way to start this leg of the work. I called several people whom Miles had suggested; they were noncommittal but said to call them if I came down.

I flew down with misgivings. It was a long, long time since my boyhood in Texas. I had spent two years as a draftee in Georgia during the Korean War; in the 1970s I had once driven through North Carolina to the ocean. Other than that, I had not been in the South since 1944. But I had ideas: The South was where they killed people.

At the airport terminal in Detroit, I heard Southern accents. *This is nuts,* an inner voice said. But I did need to meet the South again, and, more, I needed to walk as a human among some Klanspeople and gain a sense of them as humans. A friend had suggested that for my safety I should let the FBI know what I was planning and where I was going to be. I had turned the suggestion down. My work has always depended on building an atmosphere of trust; I want respondents to be open with me, and I have to earn that openness by treating the respondents with honesty. I also thought it would be dangerous to have a police contact that I was trying to hide, and I have avoided contact with police agencies throughout this work. It looked like a very lonely three days coming up, and I had managed to contact an old student of mine who lived in Atlanta, and we hoped to see each other while I was down there.

The Atlanta terminal was a shock. The gleaming metals and sophisticated lighting in the hallways screamed the distance that this cosmopolitan center of the New South had moved since the mid-fifties. Much more impressive, and significant, were the self-confident faces, the brisk walk, the expensive, lustrous shoes, the crisp suit jackets, the narrow ties of the small army of African-American professionals and businessmen who marched through the terminal, with equally well-dressed and confident black women at their sides. Memories welled up: the misery of black life in my hometown, the rags and the dust. Obviously Atlanta must include the same poverty-filled stretches that Detroit did and the towns of my youth, but I was excited to see evidence of a healthy black middle class that was not minuscule. I looked with awe.

I phoned several of the people I had previously talked to long-distance; the first was evasive, but the second, an elderly leader named James Venable, told me to come on over. I bought maps and went looking for him. The village of Stone Mountain showed up okay, some ten miles east of Atlanta and at the foot of a massive block of granite rising abruptly from the plain—Stone Mountain itself. Finding Venable's house took a great deal longer; his directions didn't correspond to landmarks I could find, but after exploration I found the street and the right number. An old gray wooden farmhouse stood far in the back of a huge lot. No one answered the door; no one seemed to be about. I waited an hour in the silent, empty yard beneath the huge pecan trees, the quiet afternoon sky.

Then, morose and lonely, I drove to the little motel at the edge of Atlanta. I called Judy, my old student, and we arranged to have breakfast in the morning.

After a depressed supper, I drove back to Venable's house. I was getting nowhere; it was probably a waste of time to drive back out, but what else was there to do? The miles of ticky-tack did not cheer me up, nor the deepening dusk.

Venable was in. He led me from the door into a kitchen filled with steam. Four great cauldrons were bubbling on the stove. He was preparing soup for the rally, he told me.

Venable and the house were both old. The house recalled those of my home town: an aging country home, with stacks of old newspapers, old paper bags, scraps of this and that against the ancient wood. Cats wandered about.

Venable talked at length. He didn't especially understand who I was, but he wanted to teach me Klan lore. He gave me old newspapers from his branch of the Klan; he had been its national leader for many years. He went upstairs and got me a copy of the handbook with rules for initiation to the first degree—there seemed to be successive degrees, as in Freemasonry. The handbook was known as the *Kloran*. The *Kloran* listed the Klan's labels: The local cell is called a Klavern; its head is the Exalted Cyclops; officers below the Cyclops included the Klaliff, the Klokard, the Kludd, the Kligrapp, the Kladd, the Kliabee, the Klexter, and the Klarogo. The national head of a Klan, Venable told me, is known as an Imperial Wizard; a state director is a Grand Dragon.

Venable talked about how things had been in the olden days. Great crowds used to come to rallies, he said, great numbers to parades—there used to be ten thousand at the Labor Day rally, he said. There was much secret lore and special ways. You could always find another Klansman: When you pulled up to a gas station in a strange town, you would ask the attendant, "Do you know Mr. *Ayak?*" *Ayak* stood for *Are You A Klansman?* The attendant would answer, "Well, I know Mr. *Akia.*" And *Akia* stood for *A Klansman I Am.*

Venable's stories went on and on. He talked about huge cavalcades of Klan cars roaring through the black sections ("niggertown") to keep the black people ("niggers") in line. He talked about internal Klan politics; he talked about ceremonies, rituals, and fellowships—the Klan as a fraternal order. He seemed close to senility.

It was getting dark, and I wondered how I was going to find the rally ground the next day. Where should I park? Venable said we should drive down right then, so he could show me the way.

We drove through town toward the mountain, to a huge meadow at its foot. I saw little knots of men by small fires. We walked to a fire and met Dave Holland, a young leader who was organizing the rally, and two of his lieutenants. I walked across to four young men who leaned on a truck. They were hesitant and careful, but soon got interested in talking. I talked at length with two of them. They were friends, trying to keep a North Carolina Klan alive after the arrest of its leader, worried about how to do that work without seeming to try to take over the group. Both were twenty-two years old; both came from blue-collar families. They believed in the Aryan Jesus, the Aryan Israelites.

Men were setting up their sleeping bags around the fires. People had driven in from a distance. It felt like a camping trip, a kids' gang.

Later I talked more with Venable at the house, wrote some field notes in my motel room, and slept.

Saturday morning was cold with light rain. I had breakfasted with my former student, who wanted to join me in a brief morning reconnaissance. Raised in Chicago, Jewish, very thoughtful and very bright, Judy has lived in the South for some time, and I value her reactions. Back at the rally field we saw flags snapping in the wind: Masses of Reb flags lined the great stage that had been erected at the far edge of the meadow; flags flew from many of the dozens of vans and trucks that had by now accumulated—there were rattlesnake DON'T TREAD ON ME flags, Nazi battle flags with swastikas, and many more Reb flags.

We walked through the meadow. Additional vehicles arrived steadily. At four or five places, wooden booths set up beneath tents held books, buttons, and stickers for sale—WHITE BY BIRTH, SOUTHERN BY THE GRACE OF GOD, PRAISE GOD FOR AIDS. Judy chatted with an older woman who talked of her own childhood in Michigan's Upper Peninsula. I listened to the conversations; I looked at the mass of Confederate flags up at the speaker stand—the racists had taken over the handsome symbol. I listened to the lively country-western music coming over the loudspeaker. I started to be able to understand the words in the lyrics: Again and again the lyrics used the word "nigger." They had their own music, their own songs, and they were getting joy by being able to say "nigger" out loud.

I drove Judy back to the city. She talked about her work in nearby towns with country people. They are independent, she said; they are warm when they have accepted you; they are cautious, defensive, and secretive, afraid of being patronized by city people. This crowd at the rally ground had seemed familiar to her. My own mood was dark. I was getting a headache and feeling the strain: It is important for my goal to let a real sense of the stranger come into me, not to block it or distort it. At the same time I need to keep my own sense of myself. It would be less effort just to reject the stranger. But I would gain no understanding.

I thanked Judy and ate lunch. Wool socks made my feet warmer and I was happier. I returned to the rally field. The rain was lightening. Knots of men spread across the meadow; I walked past conversations:

". . . What I can't understand—any white woman, I can look at any white woman, no matter how ugly-looking she is, and I can find something to admire. But what I can't understand, how anyone can take some bush monkey, some ape, and crown her Miss Mississippi." (The man talking was a squat creature from Galveston.)

". . . What is the worst, to see a couple—to see some white woman and some black man—ugh! It just turns my stomach!"

". . . They don't tell you about the sixty-six million white Christians the Russians killed. The Bolshevik Jews created the Russian Revolution."

". . . They don't tell you, Trotsky, his real name was Bernstein, he was a New York Jew. They don't tell you, the three men who made the Russian Revolution, they were in New York, they were trained in sabotage and revolution by a team of Rabbis."

". . . The Jew is the seed of Cain. The Canaanite Jews are the children of the serpent."

". . . Talmud is their holy book. And I don't even have to tell you about the Kol Nidre. As I understand it, a man could go out and lie and cheat all the rest of the year."

So the comments went, so the conversations flowed. The good folk took comfort, as they do at these meetings, passing tidbits on to one another, having their wisdom confirmed.

I soon found myself alongside a cluster engaged in picture taking, another favored pastime—souvenir photos of oneself in uniform or robe at the gathering. A tall fellow aimed his camera at two of the security guards, young men posed side by side in black T-shirts and black boots, Klan logo on the T-shirts, arms raised in Hitler salute.

The guard nearest me, a young man with short hair and blue eyes, asked me to be in the picture with him. I thought useful conversation might result and went to stand next to him.

He leaned close to me and said, "Hey, are you kosherish?"

I was surprised. "What?" I asked. "Excuse me?"

"You wouldn't happen to be Jewish, would you?" he asked.

"Well, yes," I said, "I do happen to be Jewish."

"*Out!*" he cried. "Out the gate! Let's go!"

"Are you serious?" I asked.

The older, lean, taller man who had been taking the pictures said to him, "Wait, Arthur, I know that. That's why I said you would want the picture to throw darts at. It's all right, Venable brought him in last night."

"We'll *see*," Arthur Prone said grimly, and stalked off to see Dave Holland.

The lean man, Lennie, and I waited, side by side. It was a longish wait.

The young man returned, very put out. Lennie said, "It's all right." Young Arthur yelled back toward Holland, "You're asking for some mighty hard decisions."

Arthur stared at me. He ground his jaw. He looked hard into my face and said, "I don't give a damn for kikes." He said, "Keep the dream alive. Kill a Jew. Keep Hitler's dream alive."

Hatred hardened his voice. His eyes blazed. There was no way to communicate. I turned and walked off; I was not going to get into a macho contest.

I paced around, much agitated. He followed me with his eyes constantly. My stomach was rolling. I walked over to one of the guys from North Carolina, who stood by his truck, and spoke of what had just happened. That fellow said, "He doesn't mean anything personal."

"Well," I said, "I am here to learn. I don't like upsetting the man. I thought it was obvious I was a Jew."

"You're not an Orthodox Jew, are you?" the North Carolinian youth asked. When I said no, he went on: "Well, then. I take it you're here in a professional capacity, not as representing Jews. If you were here *that* way, *I* might have problems."

I walked about for ten or twenty minutes. The incident raised problems for me. As a thin and nervous child, I had learned with great difficulty the necessity of standing up to intimidation. At the same time, I truly hate rudeness, and I felt that Arthur had a right to be startled that an agent of the arch-fiend had wandered into his gathering. I needed, for my dignity, to confront him; I felt that I needed, at the same time, to acknowledge his right to his own responses. These things had to be done, and perhaps good would come of it.

I walked back up to Arthur, who had been eyeing me steadily. I stood in front of him. I told him that, speaking as one man to another, it had not been my intention to upset him. I looked squarely at him.

"I told you what I mean," he said. "I don't like a kike."

He stared at me. "I have no use for a Jew. Keep Hitler's dream alive: Kill a Jew."

He was still trying to provoke me.

He said again that he had no use for a Jew.

I said, "Well, that's you."

I had already told him I was studying the movement; I now said, truthfully, that I would like to hear more about what he was saying—that this wasn't the time or place, but if it were, I would want to hear more about this.

He said, "If it were the time and the place, I would *show* you."

"That's you," I said in a level voice. I walked off.

I realize now, some years later and after much more interaction, that I must have been conspicuous since my first appearance. I had felt rather casual, strolling among the folk, nodding and saying "howdy" now and then. I was dressed in no particular manner. I had supposed I seemed out of place, but not especially noteworthy. I much misunderstood, I now can see, the amount of fear in which these people live, and their belief that a Jewish power base was out to endanger them. There had undoubtedly been bits of gossip following me all morning and afternoon as I walked about. The incident with Arthur ignited that tinder; a strange few hours, harmless, deeply frightening, and deeply educational, followed.

As I experienced it, tentacles of hostility seemed to snake out from the encounter, seemed to spread through the meadow the rest of the afternoon. I was talking first with the North Carolina men, and someone called across from an enclosure, "He's a Jew!" Soon, as I was asking one of the attendees where the afternoon's street parade was to be held, another called across, "Don't tell the fucking Jew!" As I walked about the meadow, I picked up pieces of conversation: "Jew," "Jewboy." There were periodic catcalls. As I passed near a row of parked vehicles, one of the Klansmen hidden in a van called over a speaker system in a metallic, loud, and nasty voice, "*Yeah,* just move your niggerized self along, Jewboy! Just *move along.*" More catcalls; more frozen stares as I passed; more hard, hostile faces.

I talked then a long time with the men from North Carolina about Jews: What was the deal? I heard deep enmity. The Klan was profoundly anti-Semitic. I left that little group and continued to walk about; the catcalls followed, the nasty stares.

I talked after a while with a blond, bearded young fellow over by some cars. He talked to me about the Federal Reserve, about the conspiracies, about the Jews. The Jews are children of the Serpent.

"Look," I said, thinking to myself that I must not answer in the terms of his delusion but as a real person, must see the effect, "in real life, I get my ideas about people by what really happens, day by day what really happens with them. Now you, you're from a little town in North Carolina, I reckon."

"No," he answered. "Tennessee."

"Okay," I said. "But the point is, how many Jews were in your town?"

"None," he said. "None. But all I need to know about Jews—" He was shouting by now; he had grabbed his Bible and sprung it open, he thumped it, he lifted it into the air above his head, he slashed the air with it. "All I need to know about Jews, I get it *right here!*" He slammed his hand onto the Good Word. "All I need to know, *the Book* tells me!"

I stood near a tent, quietly. I was not willing to be driven away. More catcalls came. I understood: I would not be safe here if it were dark: If someone moved to hurt me, no one would stop him.

I had been defined. I was not "Rafe," not Raphael Ezekiel; I was not the individual my friends knew, my students knew, I knew. I was Alien, stripped of my particular history.

I was Jew.

It was incredibly lonesome.

I wandered quietly along the meadow, tasting the strange sense of isolation. People were stirring, thinking about getting ready for their parade. Venable arrived and we talked a moment, then he reached into the car for his robe and pulled it over his street clothes. Other old men followed suit. Soon men all over the meadow were pulling folded robes from the cabs of their trucks—robes of all designs, all manner of trim on the sleeves, one even reading KLAN BOAT SQUAD. Dressed now, the men—there may have been one or two women on the grounds—drove off, headed to a nearby schoolyard where they were to park their vehicles and line up for the march down the village main street.

I walked up the hill from the meadow to the village. The deep loneliness persisted. I walked silently an hour down the main street and the little side streets. The village shops are set up to attract the visitors who come to see the Confederate memorials atop the mountain. Very few people were about. I felt numb and sad. There was no one to speak to me as the person I really am, the self built from experiences that I really have lived. The word *stripped* came constantly to me. This experience, I thought, must resemble the experience of American black folks, this kind of getting shoved out of your real identity. Shoved by someone else. Becoming invisible as a real human. Becoming a thing.

What it must have been, I thought, to have been a black man or woman and to have worked here for civil rights. To have been stripped in this way, to have no identity—*and* to be marked: TARGET. What incredible courage, I thought, to have persevered.

The Klan procession arrived and came down the main street. The street is short—a few blocks; I counted only twelve spectators. The Klan has paraded here every year for decades, and I suspect the village is sick of it. One of the spectators was a black man. I wondered at the thoughts of a black American waiting to look at a Klan parade; he explained that he was a state policeman in plain clothes assigned to watch the Klan.

The procession proceeded down the street. The members avoided my eyes—when a man would see me at the side of the street, he would turn his head so as not to make eye contact. Twenty or so men at the front of the parade wore camouflage fatigue uniforms and marched in step; there followed three or four groups of robed men, and then various children and preteens. They came by quite fast. There had been seventy-one cars in the meadow; I saw about two hundred people in the march.

I returned to the meadow in the evening for the speeches, staying fairly late. I spent a lot of time at the gate area, watching and listening to a group of men in their twenties and thirties who were on duty checking cars in. Each driver was asked: "Do you have any liquor or guns? Are you working for any police system?"

I did not want to leave my rental car on the grounds and risk its tires being slashed in the darkness. I parked on the town street fifty yards up from the gate. I figured I could get to it in a hurry if I had to.

A lot of people were driving in. By dark, the meadow held between 150 and 200 cars and about 700 people. They were of all ages, and about fifteen percent were women. I had many brief conversations, some easy and some hostile; even the easy ones were heavily charged. One fellow said, when I told him that I was studying the movement, "You know what's funny about this movement? Nothing. Ain't nothing funny about the Klan. This is dead serious."

After dark the speeches began. Dave Holland, as host, began. "You know," he said, "before this rally I talked to that fat little cop, that black police chief, and *he* said, 'Now, David, I don't want to hear the word *nigger*.' Well, Sheriff, hear this: *Nigger, nigger, nigger, nigger!*"

A good friend of Holland's, a black-uniformed Nazi, gave the next speech, a vile compendium of slogans. And there were many more speeches: Klansmen, Knights of the White Camelia, guests from other organizations. Each would exhort the crowd to cry out *"White Power!"* They cried out, most with arms raised in the Hitler salute.

In Chapter Three you will read the text of typical speeches. Let us say for now, the speeches were: Humorless. Unsubtle. Inaccurate. Self-congratulatory. All were about: The fight. The struggle. Continuing the struggle.

I was watching from the edge of the crowd. It had been dark for several hours. I knew cross burnings would follow, higher on the hill. I thought it would be dangerous in this day's atmosphere to join that ceremony without invitation and left, as the speeches wore on.

I drove through the dark night to the motel, a bare-bones little spot at the edge of town run by two men who had fled the factional violence in Lebanon. I typed field notes for two hours. My chair and table were next to the window. The window was open to catch the breeze; I felt much too visible framed in it at my type-writer.

Sunday morning, I returned in a light rain to the rally grounds, now empty, the vehicles departed. Lennie, the lean older man, motioned to me to come sit with him under the tarp—"You might as well come out of the rain." He was guarding the site while the last pieces of equipment were removed. An old man was working over pieces of wiring while his wife sat in their car. Lennie and I talked for several hours.

He told me his stories. He began with much talk about "the niggers," and "the money masters," and "the oh point four percenters" (the 0.4 percent at the top of the income distribution). He spoke of Rockefeller and Warburg, who had built and controlled communism, who had stirred up the blacks.

Lennie had been hurt at his job and had gotten nothing in compensation. He had hurt his neck twice. Then, coming home from physical therapy, his car had been hit and his back damaged. He worked now as an independent welding contractor.

He had, he told me, a boy who was super at math—you could read him a line of figures and he would add them in his head. The kid had been in a gifted children's program. Lennie had been for a time vice chair of the metro Atlanta Head Start program, but he realized after a while that it was "a damn socialist program." His daughter had "a nigger principal." Lennie had asked the principal whether he would want to live in Atlanta.

"Hell, no," the principal had answered.

"Well," Lennie had told him, "that's what people out here are concerned about; they don't want Atlanta to come up here."

Sitting under the tarp, Lennie seemed a familiar sort, a somewhat older version of some of the laconic noncoms I had known in the Army, fairly independent men with dry wit. The sensible talk we were sharing was interrupted at intervals by recitations of his harsh racist mythology:

"What started it, in the First World War, Rockefeller paid to have three battalions, these three nigger battalions that got sent over to Europe. These niggers got a taste for white meat. Come back and said, 'I want me some.' In 1919 New York burned, in 1919 Philadelphia burned, in 1919 Chicago burned. They don't teach you *that*.

That was the cities the three battalions were from. They went home.
Had a taste for white meat now and wanted some. Them cities
burned. . . .

"What some people don't realize, when the Klan, the old Klan,
when they took some nigger and hanged him, most times, damn near
every time, this was someone who was guilty. They just saved the
town the cost of electrocuting the man. Most towns didn't have the
money to have an electric chair, they just saved them the money.
Send the sheriff on a fishing trip; sheriffs, mayors, in those days they
was all Klansmen. Not today. But they took men who were guilty.
They made sure of their facts; they had their ways to know."

Lennie gave me his card. He was an Exalted Cyclops.

I returned to Venable's house, met several visiting Grand Dragons
breakfasting under the pecan trees, and went to the airport. A few
hours later, one of my sons and his wife came for me at Detroit
Metro. I was a real person with a family. As we got into their car,
they slid pillowcases over their heads in a Klan imitation and sang a
silly song they had made up. They were relieved. So was I.

POSTSCRIPT

The chance to speak further with Arthur Prone came eventually. I
had begun a series of interviews with Dave Holland near Atlanta;
each time I told him I would like to speak again with Lennie and
with Arthur. I kept reminding Dave of this desire, and at last the two
showed up for one of the sessions at Holland's house. Holland had
spoken often of both of them, presenting Arthur in particular as the
kind of man who was important to him—Arthur had served prison
time for assault on a black man, but immediately upon release had
swung back fearlessly into full participation in Holland's Southern
White Knights. Arthur, Dave would say, was a real Klansman, not
a hollow talker.

At this meeting, Dave and I settled down at the dining room table,
Dave a bit to my right, Lennie at the end of the table to my left, and
Arthur directly across from me. I reintroduced myself and explained
the project again. Arthur stared without expression, while Lennie
asked to whom I was going to feed the information.

Arthur had smooth pale skin against which his short hair was a
dramatic black. He wore an olive-drab T-shirt with a paratroops logo

and the slogan FACE U.S. PARATROOPERS/FACE DEATH. I asked whether he had been a paratrooper. He said, quietly, "No. I like shirts, so I bought it." He is not a veteran. He had tattoos on his arm below the T-shirt's sleeves: a swastika, the letters SS, and the generic Klan design of the cross in a circle. He held a small child, two or three years old, on his lap; I could not tell the child's gender, but Arthur cuddled him or her nicely.

The discussion, first with Dave and then with Lennie, went on for several hours. Arthur's eyes bored into me steadily the entire time. He sat, smoldering and angry. Several times he took a knife from his pocket, being sure that I noticed, and stroked its long blade. When I asked Lennie what he would do if the movement came to power, Arthur suddenly erupted with words of deep violence: *"Castrate all the men, sterilize all the women, and chain them in the backyard like dogs!"*

His voice had been sudden, guttural, and level. "What I'd like to do," he went on, "whites ever once get into power, that would be the thing to do: Castrate the males, Jewish and nigger males, castrate them and sterilize the females, chain them in the yard like dogs."

Dave Holland grinned and said, "Nice man."

I laughed and said, "Arthur and I have a friendly relationship."

Holland added, "That's one thing about it, buddy, he lets you know where you stand."

"Yeah," I said, "that was kind of subtle. Now, quite what did that mean?"

"I sit here," Arthur said, "and thought about it a little bit, that's what I'd like to do."

"Well," I said, "I guess I'll have to ask you, Arthur, how come?"

"How come what? How come the way I feel about Jews?"

"Yeah," I said. "That's a fairly strong statement you're making."

"That's the way I feel it personally," he said.

"Since you were little?" I asked.

"Yeah," he answered. "I think they're behind communism and I think the Holocaust is a hoax. They're out to destroy the Aryan race. Like Dave said and like Lennie said, they're backing the niggers because niggers aren't smart enough, aren't wealthy enough, to back the communist movement in America. Which I think started, the nigger part of it started with Martin Luther King, and now continues with Jesse Jackson, Hosea Williams. And what it says in the Bible, in Saint John, chapter eight, I think it starts in verse thirty-six, it says, you are of your father the devil and of him you will do, he was a murderer from the beginning, abide not in the truth because there is no truth in it. And it goes on to say, the Jews. And Jesus was speaking to the Jews. And I think they're the children of the Devil."

"Literally?"

"Yeah. Literally."

"So," I asked, "like, you and I are just absolutely different?"

"Absolutely different! As different as Karl Marx and Adolf Hitler."

"Well," I pointed out, "they were both human beings, that's all."

"I don't know," Arthur said. "I don't feel the Jews are a race. I don't feel that the Jews are a race of human beings."

"Another species of animal?" I asked.

"Lot more along the lines of a *leech*," he answered. "Or a *maggot*."

"How long," I asked, "have you rejoiced in this belief?"

"I guess most of my adult life. As long as I can remember, from a small child."

"Did your daddy and mommy teach you that?"

He said no—said that he just woke up and realized what was going on in the world. I asked whether he had ever seen a Jew, and Arthur said he had seen plenty of them. I asked where, and he replied, "Sitting around, they're around—oh, not that many, quite a few, they're around. I saw them in delis and bakeries, in Atlanta."

"And you looked," I inquired, "and you said, 'Wow, you're a devil'?"

"No," he said, "I just believe in the Bible, what the Bible says about Jews."

My questions took him around the bush a couple of times. He had not learned this from a preacher, it turned out. He felt that most preachers avoided what the Bible clearly said, just took up collections "so they can drive new cars around." He said, "I believe it's just what I came to believe. I think God instilled me with it, the feelings I feel and the beliefs I feel toward Jews."

I expressed doubt—how could one just wake up one morning with this insight? He said it had come to him over a period of time. Again

I asked how could this be. What would he think if I told him that I woke up one morning and thought, *Good Heavens, the people of Iceland are children of the Devil.* Wouldn't that seem odd to him?

This drove him to bedrock: "I got it from the Bible. Like I told you, I believe in the Bible."

Was he a Bible reader? Had he read it as a child? "Well," he replied, "I studied it for quite a while when I was incarcerated. I could show it to you."

I had Holland supply us with a Bible. ("The new English version, modern-day English," Arthur specified, "nobody can understand where *thee* takes the place of *thou* and all that. It's easier to understand.")

Arthur made his way to the chapter he wanted. He began to quote: "You are doing the deeds of your father—"

I made him stop; where were we? We were in John, chapter 8, verse 42. He read aloud for me, slowly, haltingly:

" 'If God were your father, you would love me, for I proceeded forth and have come from God, for I have not even come on my own initiative, but He sent me.

" 'Why do you not understand what I am saying? It is because you cannot hear my word, you are of your father, the devil. And you want to do the desires of your father.

" 'He was a murderer from the beginning, and does not stand for the truth, because there is no truth in him. Whenever he speaks a lie, he speaks from his own nature, for he is a liar and the father of lies.

" 'But because I speak the truth you do not believe me. Which one of you convicts me of sin if I speak truth? Why do you not believe me?

" 'He who is of God hears the words of God. For this reason you do not hear them because you are not of God.' And then the Jews answered him and said to him . . ."

He quit reading here. I had been unacquainted with most of the New Testament and had not heard these passages before; it was educational. Lennie explained that "the Jews infiltrated religious organizations, supposed to be so dog Christians, and they wound up being, still working for the devil. Installed [he meant "infiltrated"] the Christian religion, just about any and every which way they could, for the last hundred years. You can't find a Bible that's not revised today."

I agreed that the passage in John seemed straightforward: Jesus was mad at these Jews. Arthur again pointed out that "anybody knows Jesus wouldn't have said something that he didn't mean in the first place."

Lennie joined in again: "*Now* you wonder why the Catholics will not accept the state of Israel? Because they are considered Christ-killers."

"Yeah," Arthur said, "you was saying that you was very proud of the Jewish history."

"By and large, yes," I affirmed.

"You proud of that part of the Jewish history?" he asked.

When I asked which part, he replied, "The crucifixing of Christ."

I told him I had the strong impression that the Romans had crucified Jesus, and the discussion wandered around the Bible for a while longer. Lennie dominated the discussion. Arthur rejoined a few minutes later, as we spoke of comparative white and black incomes. Arthur insisted that "blacks don't make as much 'cause they are all out raping and robbing white people." He pointed out that the bulk of the population in his prison had been black.

I said I wasn't talking about the prison population. What proportion, I asked, of the general black population was busy raping and robbing white people?

"I think maybe thirty or forty percent," he answered. "Probably a lot more, because they can get jobs over white people, easy, any time, because they have to hire and have a quota. My ex-boss where I used to work, the government came in and made him lay off several white people to hire blacks because they say he didn't have enough blacks and he had to hire black, like twice as many minorities as he did white men. They even made him lay off some white women so he could replace them with blacks."

I asked what kind of business the boss had been in. "It was automotive parts," he said, "and he was Jewish as a matter of fact, and he didn't like it very much."

Blacks, Arthur felt, "were too sorry to work when they do get jobs." He bossed a crew of four at his current job in a yarn-baling shop. "And I seen them come and go, and they usually last two or three months, and they are usually too strung out on drugs, or just don't want to work, too sorry to work half the time, they will lay out of work half the time, the ones I've worked around, they lay out of work, they come and go, and they usually hire back blacks again 'cause the government makes them, you know; you got to have like a steady quota. And they usually last a few months, long enough to get a little money in their pocket, and they can't stand to work anymore, cry and complain all the time about working, they'll find a place to hide and find a place to sit down so they won't have to work, and they're all the time selling stolen goods, trying to sell stolen goods, taking their dope, you know.

"I think it's like I said, at least thirty to forty percent, you know, if not more. Of the young, I think, it's the most violent ones are between the ages of maybe fifteen and twenty-five."

I told them I was curious about something. "When you talk about black people," I pointed out, you say 'nigger.' When you talk about Jews when I'm not in the room, what do you call them?"

Arthur answered at once and in a flat voice: " 'Kike.' " Then he spat out: " 'Finks!' 'Leech!' 'Maggot!' "

I asked what kind of word he would use ninety percent of the time.

"Just 'Jew' or 'kike,' you know; simple as that."

We talked awhile about a theory Lennie offered, that Jews were related to goats. A bit later I tried out on them my observation that Jews, whom they hated, committed few violent crimes. Arthur croaked out: "They crucified Christ! They crucified Christ. In my opinion, Jews did it. And if we only knew how many babies have been aborted since abortion was invented, then we would know practically how many Jews in modern day, you know. History for murders! In my opinion, Jews engineered and invented abortion from the very beginning, when it was first invented. And if we only then, then we'd know, I'm sure there's a lot more Jews that's murderers than there are whites. And the Jews also crucified Christ!"

I wanted to check a few things out with the pair of them—just which crimes had the Jews committed? Lennie quickly added the two World Wars to the crucifixion. I asked whether the Jews had created the American Revolution, and he became unsure of himself. I felt we might be getting past the party line. Eagerly I asked whether the Jews had created the Civil War.

"The treasurer of the Confederacy!" Arthur cried out.

"Judah Benjamin," I supplied for him.

"He was Jewish," Arthur went on. "He ran off and went up north with the money, and that's what caused them to lose the Civil War."

I knew Arthur was badly misinformed here. But it is rare to get a Klansman trying to talk logically about stuff he hasn't been taught, so I asked some more questions about history. Lennie, sure of most things, just didn't know about the American Revolution and thought that by the War of 1812 I was referring to the 1898 war with Spain. "No," I told him, "the war with England in 1812."

"No," Lennie said, "I don't know about that."

"Was Andrew Jackson a Jew?" I asked him.

"I really don't know that, either," Lennie said.

I persevered: "Was Abraham Lincoln a Jew?"

Lennie said that he was assassinated by a Jew. Arthur leaped in. "Was Abraham Lincoln a Jew? No, I think he was an Aryan, I'm not sure, that's my personal belief, and I was under the impression that John Wilkes Booth was one of the original founders of B'nai B'rith." (As it happens, B'nai B'rith was founded in 1843; Booth was born in 1838. Arthur was probably wrong.) "And when Abraham Lincoln first freed the blacks, he said, once he said they would be no more than chattel property, you know, ever. And I think he was going to send them back home. He was going to send all of them back to Africa and all where they came from. When he freed them.

"I think John Wilkes Booth, I think it was a Jewish conspiracy, even way back then. And they assassinated Lincoln so he couldn't send them back. Because they knew then how it was going to be today. They had it planned out, and perceived in their minds."

We were almost done by this time. Lennie asked about my synagogue affiliations; I don't have any. Arthur asked who was the beneficiary on my death policy. He wondered whether it might not be Morris Dees, leader of the Southern Poverty Law Center.

Lennie, who had been teasing me for an hour about being "some kind of a sociologist or something like that," closed our interview. "What you going to do with all this material, besides publish a so-called book?" (He had accused me from the start of being an agent for Dees.)

I was indeed going to publish a book, I told him. "Yeah," he said, "but who's going to benefit from the book? I can see it now, be all kinds of innuendos about this and innuendos about that, you know.

You all [the Jews, the universities, the foundations] think you can make this a think tank on everything we say, and you all scrap and distort it, you all have two thirds of the book in just distortion."

We closed with that. I had been impressed mightily by the volcanic fury I felt from Arthur throughout. Even at the end he had stood with his arms folded tight, making sure we did not shake hands—which I didn't begin to offer. Driving to my motel, I thought about Arthur. It had pained him to have me sitting there. I had felt strongly that the wrong word could have sent him catapulting across the table for my throat.

I was intrigued that he was Dave Holland's chosen companion. It was my first, but not my last, experience finding that leaders tend to have a pet crazy.

I was a little frightened as I drove home, felt I had been pushing my luck. How close to the edge did I need to come? On the street, I avoid people like Arthur, give them wide berth—I don't want to be next to a smoldering man when he blows up.

And then I thought about our confrontation from their point of view. Here they sat with *Satan!* Satan was tape-recording evidence for future court cases. How scary and hateful that must have felt. How needful for Arthur to take out the knife to peel his apple. To brandish the big-bladed buck knife, as he looked sideways at me.

I knew little of Arthur's life, only what I had seen—that he was at home with surges of energy that frightened those next to him. I knew nothing of the reasons or the history. He was essentially inarticulate, much in contrast to Lennie. He lived in a very small world; his mind ranged very little; he hated Jews and blacks; he clung to his Bible passages. He was a man of abrupt, violent thought, seething, unsure of himself, brooding, muscular, short. Deeply ignorant. Fueling Dave Holland.

Several years later, Holland, under pressure from Morris Dees and the Southern Poverty Law Center, resigned his leadership of the Southern White Knights and turned the group over to Arthur. Predictably, the group splintered under Arthur's impulsivity. Arthur soon left the group, wandered alone for a while, and then decided to go to Chicago to start a new life with a girlfriend. He called Dees to tell him that he wanted to stop in Montgomery on the way, to tell the SPLC everything he knew about the Klan. Investigators met with him and found he had nothing new to tell them. His present whereabouts are not known.

This left me wondering about Lennie. Informants at the Center for Democratic Renewal told me a bit later that he also had turned; he had appeared at a trial as a hostile witness against Holland.

I will say several times in this book: As an old leftist with ties and friendships in peace groups and groups of the left, I am startled by the shallowness of loyalty in the world of the white supremacists. It is tempting to think that it may have significance. Leftist groups tend to focus on the commonality of humans and the need to help one another; perhaps it is fair to imagine that rightist groups stem from a fundamental self-centeredness in which loyalty to one's comrades is not important. I have sometimes asked right-wing leaders whether this makes any sense to them; they usually feel I am being parochial and seeing what I want to see. At the same time, they speak invariably of other leaders in a highly disparaging manner: No one but the man with whom I am speaking has the correct insight or is to be trusted. Obviously, I enjoy perceiving this crew as a batch with poor capacity to feel trust or commitment, but I think there is more to this than my own bias. Particular ideologies, I suggest, draw to themselves particular character types.

Years ago writers spoke glibly of the likeness of the extreme right and the extreme left. I have observed both closely, and I think this generalization is largely inaccurate. Left and right attract different character types; there is a distinction that has to do with openness and closedness, with inclusion and exclusion. (On the left, equally, ideologies centered on violence draw different character types than those that are not.) A right-wing sociologist probably would write otherwise, as indeed middle-of-the-road sociologists have.

TWO

Breakfast in Arkansas—
Sedition Trial

The second gathering I will describe took place in 1988. It was not planned by the white racists but by the U.S. Department of Justice. Hoping apparently to amputate the leadership of the white supremacist movement, the Justice Department mounted a major trial in Fort Smith, Arkansas. The charge was conspiracy to commit sedition—the principal allegation was that the defendants, during a gathering hosted by the Aryan Nations organization at their compound in Hayden Lake, Idaho, had met with some twenty other people in the living room of the organization's chief and plotted together to overthrow the U.S. government. The defendants included three of the movement's most important leaders: Robert Miles of Michigan (who died five years later), Richard Butler of Idaho, and Louis Beam of Texas, along with a set of members of the terrorist cell known as the Order. The Order members were brought to Fort Smith from the penitentiaries in which they were serving long sentences for involvement in murder and armed robbery. They and Beam, who with his wife had tried to avoid arrest by fleeing to Mexico, spent their time in Fort Smith in jail when not in court; they entered and exited court in handcuffs that had to be unlocked to begin the day's proceedings. Miles and Butler were free on their own recognizance and had rented apartments in Fort Smith with their wives. I came to Fort Smith for two extended weekends, watched the trial, and had long talks with Miles and Butler.

On my return from the second visit to Fort Smith, I wrote the notes that follow, which began with a breakfast in the restaurant at my motel.

The blessing nearly catches me with a biscuit in my mouth.

I have forgotten that both Robert Miles and Richard Butler are reverends. The food has arrived and I need my oatmeal; I am fiddling with the coffee jug, getting ready to dig in, when I notice that Miles has fallen silent. Pastor Butler has closed his eyes. He thanks Jesus quietly for the food.

I look at Butler's worn face; cardiac problems and six weeks of the trial here at Fort Smith are taking their toll. Head of Aryan Nations, Butler is sixty-nine; Miles, a former Grand Dragon of the Klan in Michigan and now a major theoretician of the far right, is sixty-three. Like Butler, he has had serious health problems. He previously served seven years in Marion, a tough prison; he is fairly sure he would not survive a second prison term. The present trial will end in a few days; Butler and Miles face long terms if convicted.

Miles is a husky man with a lively face. His beard is thick, white, and well-trimmed; his eyes are bright. He is not lean. He lives on a small farm northwest of Detroit and looks much like a vigorous farmer; actually, like Butler, he is a former engineer. We joke that their ideas are the nonsense you can expect when engineers try to deal with social issues. Miles has a fast tongue and says outrageous things for effect. Butler, who speaks in a less dramatic fashion, had quadruple bypass surgery not long before the trial. His walk is slow. His wife, Betty, worries about him.

I have known Miles and his wife, Dot (Dorothy), now for over a year; we have taped interviews on a regular basis. My contact with Butler has been more limited, but we have done some interviewing at the Aryan Nations compound in Idaho.

Prayers done, we begin to eat, while the reverends fill me in on the weeks of the trial that have gone by since my earlier visit to Fort Smith. The other defendants in the trial had chosen either to argue their own cases or to work as co-counsel with their lawyers; the other defendants thus have been active in the courtroom, rising to make objections, rising to cross-examine government witnesses. Miles and Butler, who had chosen first-rate lawyers, have had to sit still, watching others. Passivity has quickly gone sour.

The other defendants include Louis Beam and eleven men who took part in the brief violent life of the underground gang called the Order. The reverends discuss the court appearance of Glenn Miller, the recent head of the White Patriot Party in North Carolina. Miller had been a bright star of the white racist movement, an emerging leader able to draw large numbers to his marches and demonstrations. Free on bail pending appeal after a conviction for running a paramilitary training camp, he had fled North Carolina and later been apprehended at a remote spot and in a drunken stupor. Now he has been brought from prison to Fort Smith to testify against his colleagues.

I had already watched one of these turncoat witnesses during my first visit to Fort Smith. He had told the court that he had now seen the light, that he planned to write a book explaining how evil his former racist views were, that he regretted using for his own ends the counterfeit money that the Order had provided him, and that he would never do anything like that again. Like most of the government's witnesses, he was trading testimony for favors; some have had sentences reduced, some have had charges dropped.

The scene in the third-floor courtroom on that earlier day had been somber and striking: the long, wood-framed windows descending from an unusually high ceiling to shoulder height, their blinds shut so that sun could not come in and no one could look out to the Arkansas sky; the fourteen defendants and their lawyers ranged around tables that formed a great U; the Justice Department lawyers in serious gray suits at their table; the rows of earnest jurors in their box; the laconic judge in black robes. Twelve federal marshals in business suits had stood impassively along the perimeter of the room.

In the morning, observers had been passed through unusually sensitive metal detectors on the ground floor and again at the door to the courtroom. Linked by handcuffs wrist to wrist in groups of three, the jailed defendants (that is, everyone but Miles and Butler) had made their entry. Some of these men were serving long terms—forty years, sixty years, a hundred years—for their involvement with the

Order. They spoke with contempt as they cross-examined the witnesses who had previously worked with them and who now appeared for the government.

The jury looked on, puzzled, studying, hoping to make sense of the kaleidoscope that was being assembled for them. The jurors were all white. Most were men, looking to be between twenty and forty years old. They were dressed informally. Many had moustaches; three had beards. The several women were quietly attired. The youngest chewed gum. She studied the defendants very closely.

After the testimony on that first visit, Miles and his wife and I had gone to their apartment to talk. He had shucked his courtroom clothes and reappeared in a bathrobe for a shower; he struck karate poses. "Hai!" he called out. "The dragon strikes!" His wife had grinned, her ever-present cigarette burning in the ashtray by her coffee cup. "They should see you now," Dot had said. All of this had been hard on her, too, and she was less able to escape into humor and theater than her husband.

The Justice Department's case would have it that Miles and Butler actively plotted the immediate overthrow of the government, and that the Order's actions sprang from the plotting. Miles and Butler, in truth, have devoted their lives rather openly to the attempt to undermine the present set of power relations. They certainly would welcome the chance to overthrow the government. But neither is ignorant or foolish. It is not plausible that they plotted, directly and openly and out loud, at meetings of twenty or thirty people at a time, actions to assault the government. Had they wanted to do some planning, they would not have done so sitting in Butler's living room along with a crowd of strangers, knowing well that any gathering of racist extremists includes hidden FBI agents and paid informants.

The impending indictments and trial had preoccupied Miles throughout our previous months of interviews in Michigan. Finally, one very cold April night at nine o'clock, he had phoned me at my home to say that he had just received a tip that the FBI was planning to raid his place at one in the morning. Several right-wing people had died during attempted arrests in the previous few years. Miles was shaken—why would the FBI be coming for him in the middle of the night?

After some thought, I told Miles that I would drive out to the farm, thirty miles away, and sit with him, so that there would be a neutral witness on hand. We spent a long night in the old farmhouse, he and Dot and I and a couple of their friends. We sat at the dining-room table most of the evening, with lights on everywhere to reassure any federal agents who might be outside. Resting his head on his arm periodically, Miles was tired and somber. The arrest he had been awaiting was at hand; he was sure that another prison term would kill him; he didn't know whether he would ever again after this night be in this room or with his wife as a free man. We sat through the night.

Just before dawn I drove back home to Ann Arbor to teach my classes. I called his wife at about ten. The FBI had arrived at eight; the arrest had been uneventful.

Before driving out that evening, I had asked myself whether there was anything to fear from people at the farm. I could imagine several bad scenarios but decided they were unlikely. Though I got into my car with some misgivings, I was certain that I should trust my instincts.

"We work with the losers," Miles tells me now, as we tape-record up in the motel room after our breakfast. Butler sits near us in a rocker.

We talk of Miller's testimony. What does it mean for the movement, I ask, that the leaders recant in such haste, the followers in such numbers—that the attachment is so shallow?

"I can have respect for FBI agents on the stand," Miles says, "for witnesses, if they are being honest—but for these dogs, this *filth*, to be sitting up there as paragons of virtue all of a sudden. 'All my friends are black,' or 'I found that all my thoughts about the Jews or the Communists, I've foreswore those and now I'm holier than thou.' Then when the winds change again, you decide to be back to what you were before."

"They are scum," Butler adds.

"We are looking at the death of the far right," Miles tells me, as he has before, "the death of the 'racialist' movement."

Butler sighs. "You try to accomplish something, you know, in your lifetime, and pretty soon it's over and you haven't got anything accomplished."

"If you get sprung," I ask Miles, "what are you going to do when you get back home?"

"Teach people to be themselves and not to trust heroes, to think for themselves. I don't think that you'll find me any different than before the trial."

"That sounds good," I tell him, "and you and I talk about some things we agree about, like economic decentralization. But I look at your newsletter that goes out from your farm to prisoners and thousands of people, and all it's about is—"

"Martial struggle," he completes my sentence for me. "Yes, we could have talked about a cripple overcoming his handicap, but you have to remember that martial struggle is the kind of heroism that Dick and I know about." He is reminding me that he fought with the Free French in World War II. He was a radio man on small planes that landed operatives at night in Occupied France.

"But all the images you present," I repeat, "only talk of struggle, only appeal to fantasies of heroism."

"Don't forget," Miles says, *who we are working with.*

"We elected to take people from a certain income class primarily. We elected to be their champions, like it or not, and they are the lower income people. They're not the middle class, they aren't the achievers, they aren't the winners.

"Unfortunately," he goes on, "most of the people who follow in the right wing are the losers. They're the ones who have been dealt a bad hand to play with in the first place in the game of life. And we can't change their cards. But maybe we can do a little to teach them how to get the maximum out of a very poor hand.

"Because they are *our* people, we are concerned about them. We represent them, whether anyone else understands it or not."

Miles glances out the window, then at me. "They aren't the winners."

Miles is an adventurer. A born organizer, he must struggle; he must also believe in the struggle.

Miles has led a life of considerable adventure. He spins romantic stories of his involvement with several underground organizations and intelligence services. In the late sixties he adopted the rough-and-ready population whom he described as his present base. He had moved into the campaign of George Wallace, a populist campaign with congenial values. With some friends, he wrested control of the Michigan branch of the United Klans from Birchers in order to use the Klansmen as campaign workers and to divert the dues money to the Wallace campaign instead of the John Birch organization.

For Miles, Butler, and others, the ready pool of whites who will respond to the racist signal has posed an enticement. This population, always hungry for activity—or for the talk of activity—that promises dignity and meaning to lives that are working poorly in a highly competitive world, constitutes an alluring prize. The people are needy, and they respond quickly to the signal flag of race.

Much as I don't want to believe it, Miles's movement brings a sense of meaning—at least for a while—to some of the discontented. To struggle in a cause that transcends the individual lends meaning to a life, no matter how ill-founded or narrowing the cause. For young men in the neo-Nazi group that I had studied in Detroit, membership was an alternative to atomization and drift; within the group they worked for a cause and took direct risks in the company of comrades. Similarly, many people whom Miles's newsletter reaches derive a degree of self-confidence and dignity from the suggestion that they are engaged in a heroic struggle for the sake of a larger entity, the reborn family of Whites.

Having accepted a people particularly predisposed to racism as their base, the trap for the leaders is quite real. To animate this base, the leaders must put most of their energy into a particular kind of theater. The movement lives on demonstrations, rallies, and counterrallies; on marches and countermarches; on rabid speeches at twilight; on cross-burnings with Gothic ritual by moonlight.

By their nature those actions guarantee failure and bear little relation to the issues of these lives. When interviewing the young neo-

Nazis in Detroit, I have often found myself driving with them past the closed factories, the idled plants of our shrinking manufacturing base. The fewer and fewer plants that remain can demand better educated and more highly skilled workers. These fatherless Nazi youths, these high-school dropouts, will find little place in the emerging economy. Enacting the charade of white struggle only buys a wasteful time-out. The current economy has little use for overt racist drama; labor is surplus; a permanently underemployed white underclass is taking its place alongside the permanent black underclass. The struggle over race merely diverts youth from confronting the real issues of their lives. Not many seats are left on the train, and the train is leaving the station.

Stirred for a time by the emotions, but soon finding that nothing has changed in their lives, many waves of membership will pass through these movements. The symbols that are used by the movements touch them; the ape-beast, the Serpent, reflect deep human fears. But eventually the symbols lose their power, as the individual asks, *What is happening to my life?*

The weary cycle drains even the organizer. Butler ponders what it means to have accomplished nothing. Miles alludes to his own weariness. What is he to do, though? he asks. He has done this all his life. His wife is annoyed that he talks this way when he speaks with me. "You make him talk about things he doesn't think about normally," Dot charges.

Returning to the courtroom the next morning, I pass through the metal detectors, watch the seating of the jury, the entry of the manacled prisoners, the warm, dry-witted judge. The defense is presenting its witnesses. A sister appears for a young fellow who is already serving a long term for involvement in the Order's robbery of an armored car. She attests that she and her brother were closer than most siblings. She says that nothing he had ever said would lead her to think that he advocated the overthrow of the government. She speaks plainly and clearly. Entering the court, she touched her brother's arm, quietly, as she passed him.

To prove seditious conspiracy, the government must demonstrate that an agreement had been made to commit acts aimed at the violent overthrow of the government. Earlier in the trial, the government's witnesses have claimed that such planning occurred and that such an agreement was reached during a specific morning-and-afternoon informal leadership meeting of some thirty people in Butler's living room on the Aryan Nations compound in Idaho during the July 1983 "Congress." The primary government witness telling this story has been Jim Ellison, who had ruled his own compound in Arkansas as leader of the racist CSA (Covenant, Sword, and Arm of the Lord). Ellison, serving a twenty-year term on other charges since 1985, apparently began presenting this version of the leadership meeting shortly after being denied parole in 1986. Ellison, who at one point had declared himself a descendant of King David and had had himself anointed King of the Ozarks, reportedly had taken himself an extra wife from among his flock on the compound; some said that he first had the husband declared "spiritually dead."

The defense now is presenting a series of witnesses who attended those critical leadership meetings in July 1983. Louis Beam, leading his own defense, quizzes a sequence of those men and women.

"At that meeting," Beam asks, "did you hear any discussion of bombings?"

"No."

"At that meeting, at either of those meetings, did you hear any discussion of assassination of political leaders?"

"No."

"Of poisoning of water supplies?"

"No."

"Of destruction of public utilities?"

"No."

"Of establishing of paramilitary training bases?"

"No."

"Of procuring false identification?"

"No."

Beam conducts each witness through this series of items from the indictment; each witness answers no to every item. Each testifies that the meetings dealt in a general way with the concept of whites moving to the Northwest and with problems involved in getting movement literature across the border to Canada. All of Beam's witnesses found the meetings unremarkable, much like many previous meetings in their political lives.

Beam's string of witnesses, among them several organizers from Canada and the West, and a national Klan leader and his daughter from Arkansas, all walk freely out on the streets; they have nothing to gain from their testimony. Most of the government's witnesses face charges or are in prison, and hope to benefit from their appearances in court.

The government's cross-examination is not impressive. Witnesses are queried about their racial views in great detail as though their positions were in doubt. Action, however, not belief, is the issue. Several times witnesses are asked whether they have read *The Turner Diaries* and whether that book does not outline the steps that might occur in a racist seizure of power. *The Turner Diaries* presents a clumsy but in places chilling fantasy about such a seizure. The novel was written by William Pierce, a prominent racist, and journalists like to present it as the Order's blueprint for the revolution. In this court of law, its relevance seems scanty. The prosecution apparently hopes that jurors will discount defense witnesses on the grounds of their beliefs.

At forty-one, Beam is relatively young; dressed neatly in shades of brown, he looks self-possessed, glad to be on the offensive. He and his young new wife make frequent eye contact across the room. She had been the Sunday school teacher of Beam's daughter. A reporter ungraciously described her to me as "a Yahweh freak." Here in court she wears a frilled white blouse; during Beam's arrest in Mexico, she shot an armed *Federale* who had failed to identify himself.

During breaks and at lunch I meet people I have seen before in Idaho and Michigan; I introduce myself to several whom I need to work with in later stages of the study.

After the day of court, I drive to the airport. Miles and Butler are old men and tired. The government may well succeed in putting them away. On the drive I see an old cat standing by the side of the road. It has been sideswiped and is retching into the gutter.

I am concerned. At home, next to my typewriter, I keep a photo that was reproduced in *The New York Times* in 1980. The photo shows a ten-year-old boy and his eight-year-old brother. They are in coats and caps. A woman holding an infant stands in the background. Six-pointed stars are sewn to the coats of one of the boys and the woman. An officer of the SS snapped this photo of Selig Jacob and Zrilu Jacob minutes after they had arrived at Auschwitz, moments before they were marched into the gas chamber. In the photo, Selig's eyes are fixed. Zrilu's are puzzled, his mouth is twisted, he is near tears. The boys cannot tell what is happening. They are uncertain and frightened.

Their sister, who somehow survived Auschwitz, came upon the photo in an SS barracks the day after liberation.

This photo is my talisman; it reminds me why I study racism.

For four years I conducted interviews with black men and women on a terribly poor corner in Detroit. My respondents were all migrants from Alabama and Mississippi. Almost every one had stories of relatives or townspeople who had been tortured and killed by hooded men in the night.

The Klan, across time, has been a nesting ground for murder, whatever else it has been. Members of the Order did kill, as well as rob; properly, they are jailed. The present trial for sedition, however, is troubling. The charge is odd; the government's case violates common sense.

The defendants, in the end, are acquitted.

THREE

Aryan Nations Congress— Northern Idaho

The third gathering I will describe was the most dramatic, presenting the movement's beliefs starkly. I had met several times with Richard Butler, leader of Aryan Nations, an organization that has been one of the most influential supremacist forces, at the compound in Hayden Lake, Idaho, and had talked several times with him and his wife in Arkansas during the Fort Smith trial. Aryan Nations had quit admitting journalists to their annual summer Congress, but Butler agreed to let me come and sit in for the two-day affair the summer after Fort Smith. This took place, as the speeches imply, several years before the collapse of the Soviet Union, so details of a speech would differ today; the themes would not.

I took almost verbatim notes during the speeches; I transcribed those notes each night. I composed the following description a bit later.

The talks begin in the middle of the morning—a few hours after I have made my drive north from the motel, have driven the country road, enjoying the crisp northern air, the conifers, the hills, but have driven with a considerable taste of apprehension in my mouth. Strong emotions alternate as I drive. I am eager and curious; the annual

Aryan Nations Congress is a major event in the racist calendar nationally, and I am sure two days of observation will teach me much about the movement and its leadership ranks. I am edgy, a little afraid that I won't really be allowed in. And, finally, there is that edge of hesitation; I will be the only outsider in this secluded compound, the only non-"Aryan."

The sign at the bottom of the hill reads ARYANS ONLY; also the sign at the top, where the entry drive ends. The guards accept my explanation that the leader has invited me; they check my name on their sheet; I am waved to a meadow to park among the rows of dusty vans and pickups. Little tents dot the ground from there back to the compound proper, back to the church building which will be our auditorium, back to the wooden platform on which we are asked to stand for the flag raisings. Throughout this first hour, throughout in fact the entire weekend, the "Horst Wessel Lied" sounds from the loudspeakers in the wooden watchtower that has been constructed atop the main building. I know this song, the marching song of Hitler's party, have heard the somewhat sanitized version that is sung in English at meetings of American racists, have often heard on record or in films the German of the original, appreciate the song for its raw quality, know the opening: *Die Fahne hoch! Die Reihen dicht geschlossen!*—"The flag high! The ranks tightly closed!" The song continues: *SA marschiert*—"The SA [the storm troop] marches." A similar party song, similarly popular, comes to the point: *Wenn's JudenBlut vom Messer spritzt!*—"When Jew blood spurts from the knife!"

For two days the party anthem plays from the watchtower. I am filled with it. Are German marching songs truly more harsh than others, or is it my associations? Why are they so compelling? The party anthem does not cease, not even on the second day, when there are christenings and a wedding; even then this is the music at hand. It is played slowly, a dirge, at the ritual section of the program; at this slower pace it is strangely melancholy and stirring, like those other German marching songs—*Ich hatt' einen Kameraden* . . . So much emotion is wrapped up in the imagery of soldiering for this culture. The sentimentality of the male world. I remember the barrenness of my two years of service. (The mess sergeant, deeply drunk, cries out to us KPs, one arm on my shoulder, the other holding the bottle high—it is Christmas night, we Jews have volunteered for this shift; it is midnight, we sit exhausted on the mess hall steps, his to torment or bore in the Georgia night; he is regular Army, over the hill, drunk, lonesome, weepy—"If only," he cries, "If only we can all be together next year!" "Yes, Sergeant," we draftees answer, thinking quietly: *God fucking forbid!*)

The world of men! The lifeless world of men only! I have worked there: the Army, prison, reform school. Now Naziland. Male bonding and other horseshit.

And here, the compound in Idaho, is a world of men. Women are present, as wives, as girlfriends, as supportive people. Women serve the meals. Men lead the rituals; men give the speeches. No woman addresses the group.

The ceremonies begin shortly after my arrival. I have had time only to walk about a little, noting the hand-clasping, the greetings. I nod hello to several people I have met at gatherings before. But I am one of the few who is not in a cluster of friends. Pastor Butler has us mount the wooden platform that faces the flagpoles. Butler is the founder, has created both Aryan Nations and its religious identical twin, the Church of Jesus Christ, Christian. (I have queried him a lot about the Christian Identity theology of the church, but have never dared to ask about the name—should we distinguish it from the Church of Jesus Christ, Moslem?) I am nervous, jammed among the attendees on this platform.

Pastor Butler drones an invocation. Now the Aryan Nations flag is raised as the party anthem increases in volume; everyone but me lifts an arm in the Nazi salute as the flag climbs up the pole. (We are far from my childhood: the classes lined up for the flag raising at Jim Bowie Grade School.) The Aryan Nations flag is black, red, white, a sword crossing an almost horizontal N to suggest strongly a swastika; adjacent poles support an American flag and a red Nazi flag with its grim black swastika.

Now come other flag raisings. In string tie and black riverboat gambler suit, a Texas lawyer—newly fashionable in this movement for his defense of Louis Beam—leads a squad of Texans from behind the barn. Smartly they march to the poles at his commands; smartly they clip the flag of Texas to a line, raise it as he sings the state anthem, "Texas Our Texas." Arms are raised for the Heil. (Heil

Texas? Heil the Alamo? Heil the Texas Aggies?) Flags are raised for
other groups, for other states. The Canadian contingent appears.
True Canada: The shoes are not shined; none marches to the cadence
of the others; at "Right turn!" most turn right, several turn left, one
pauses, puzzled. Canada at last is lined up, the standard clipped to
the line (not, Butler points out, the maple leaf flag Trudeau had introduced, but the *old* standard, the *real* standard), the old flag is
raised as one sings not the new anthem, but the old and real one,
which I had not before heard. All but this Jew raise arms to heil.
(Heil Canada? The mind reels: Heil Canadian civility, Canadian tolerance? Heil loons? Heil beavers?) The Canadians stumble off, the
pastor orients us once more, we shuffle in for the speeches.

We enter the anteroom with its hanging flags of the Northern
European nations; most of the militants in attendance use the
peculiar Christian Identity religion as a major organizing tool,
and Identity preaches that the true Israelites (the "Aryans") founded
the Northern European nations after their expulsion from Palestine. It preaches that the Aryans are called now by their heavenly
white Father to world domination, to rule over the dark subhuman
races, and to a struggle to death with Satan's nonhuman children,
the Jews.

The Northern European flags hang from poles mounted diagonally
near the ceiling; a row of banners is achieved, most handsomely. The
colors are joined by several additional flags—that of Spain, chosen
perhaps for its former Fascist government; that of British Columbia,
chosen as part of the new homeland to come, the Northwest; and
for the same reason, the flags of Washington and Idaho. Our walk
down this path of banners takes us alongside walls of Aryan Nations
art, pictures drawn perhaps by prisoners and mailed in (the organization and most like it maintain a highly active correspondence with
prison populations). In each drawing, a youth of Nordic bearing, a
young man with high cheekbones, plunges a spear or a sword into
the belly of a serpent or a dragon; each of the impaled animals is
identified by a six-pointed Star of David and the hammer-and-sickle
of Communism. Between two of these pictures hangs a framed, ide-
alized portrait of the face of Adolf Hitler. He is noble and suffering;
shining black hair and strong cheekbones surround deep, gleaming
eyes. The intent eyes demand our attention.

We walk from the anteroom into the church itself, a hall perhaps as long as three or four ordinary garages, perhaps half that wide. Windows with a thin border of stained glass give views of the green trees, a meadow, and a hill. Up front are a banner and a lectern. The lectern, the altar, is dominated by an upright Roman sword, the symbol of the organization and its version of the Cross. This sword, this Cross, bears a swastika at its hilt. A memorial wreath to Rudolf Hess, Hitler's lieutenant who had died not long before, stands beside the altar.

The speeches begin and run through the day. I sit quietly at first; soon take a couple of notes, in astonishment; then begin to scribble an all-but-verbatim record. The material is too dramatic to be lost, regardless of the ill will that note taking may cause. Butler and I had made no agreement about my activities, but I had not expected or wanted to play so visible a role; all the same, the real words—more or less—mattered too much to trust to unaided memory.

The first speaker complains about the ads in his city's transport system advocating "the ultimate lifestyle," that is, the use of condoms. He attacks what he called "AIDS groups." The second speaker, a retired military man, sixtyish, round-faced, and vigorous, a stocky man with a big chest, tells us early in his talk that he had become involved in Korea before the war there, that he had been in a community that was the subject of a Communist-attempted coup. That he had seen a nun bayoneted to a wall; he had seen, he says, a baby grabbed and its head smashed against the wall. He had seen soldiers seize a baby and toss it from one to another, catching it on bayonet tips at each toss. He had seen forty beautiful young girls taken from a mission school and stripped and raped. He had seen a beautiful young woman stripped and attached to a tree by bayonets through her breasts, with a rice bowl of oil placed between her thighs and set aflame. This, he tells us, was not an isolated event; since the Russian Revolution, 140 million people had been slain "by the Jew Talmudic Communists."

Every evil, he tells us, comes from money. "And behind money is the Zionist Talmudic Jew." The Federal Reserve system, he tells us, is a private system owned by eight banks, all of them Jewish, four of them foreign; his list includes Warburg, Lazard Fréres, Rothschild, Kuhn-Loeb, and Chase Manhattan. We must get rid of the Federal

Reserve system and of the income tax. We must repudiate the national debt.

"We must," he goes on, "tell the people at the top: *There will be treason trials! You will be strung from the trees!*"

The room explodes in loud applause. Cries of *"Hail Victory!"* Cries of *"White Power!"*

The immigration since 1900 has been alien, he tells us, alien in every way, not Christian. The country was not set up to be pluralistic. He tells us "nigger jokes"—jokes about "nigger preachers," "nigger churches." Americans, he notes, are lazy in their thinking, apathetic, listening to TV, but awakening, beginning to awaken to the dangers of Zionism. Back in 1902, he tells us, the international Zionists decided to destroy the four nations that must be destroyed if the Jews are to control the world: Russia, Germany, the United States, and Canada. They set aside $2 billion for that purpose, the financing coming from Jews in America. Lenin's plan is on schedule, the encirclement of the United States. In 1943, forty-seven U.S. students, forty-five of them Jews, were sent to Russian schools and came back charged to infiltrate American schools; the results, he points out, are visible in the Vietnam protests.

We need, he tells us, free enterprise, respect for the family, and the end of integration. We see around us treason. "The men behind the Iron Curtain would not be afraid to fight, those who have seen their families slaughtered by the Jew Talmudic Communists."

He recites for us much of a heroic ode by Byron, winding up at its dramatic description of one man's sacrifice: "We need men at the gap! *Who will stand at the gap with me?*"

The crowd explodes in cries of *"Hail Victory! Hail Victory! Hail Victory! White Power! White Power!"*

The old officer is followed to the pulpit by a Canadian organizer who has been observing the trial in Canada of a Canadian white racist who disseminates claims that the Holocaust did not occur. The strangest part of his talk comes at the beginning. Details of the Holocaust, for this movement, are lies invented by the Jews to gain leverage over non-Jews. To help set a lighthearted mood and to show the duplicity of the Jewish tricksters, he reports that a Jewish witness had said that "on the first day they burned German Jews, and the chimney gave yellow smoke; on the second day they burned Polish Jews, and the chimney gave gray smoke; on the third day they burned Hungarian Jews, and the chimney gave green smoke." The racist audience seated around me bursts into laughter. I don't know whether the laughter means that the lie was a foolish one, easy to penetrate, or whether the laughter means that it is just kind of fun to think about Jews burning. Having looked at more than enough photographs of naked women trying to cover their bodies with their hands while being herded into the gas chambers, I don't share the general amusement.

The speaker goes through his notes recounting testimony of twenty witnesses who had appeared at the trial. He speaks poorly and his notes are badly organized, but his point comes across: His listeners should be reassured that there are multiple grounds for knowing that the Holocaust story is a lie. The gas chambers were just delousing chambers. As one witness, a Jew, had pointed out, he tells us, there were no exterminations and 99.5 percent of the stories would be retracted if there could be a rabbi at court who could administer a binding oath, since Jews are not bound by court oaths—the Kol Nidre prayer of Yom Kippur, he reminds the listeners, frees Jews from all oaths to non-Jews so that they can lie and cheat all the next year. (He assumes, like most anti-Semites, that rabbis have magical powers. Needless to say, he misunderstands the Kol Nidre.)

As he finishes the trial notes, he points out that twenty-one Jews were behind the French Revolution, the Russian Revolution, and both world wars. What is to be done? "The Order chaps . . ." he says, referring to the terrorist cell that assassinated Alan Berg and robbed armored cars, "the Order chaps were very *sincere* men. They *tried*." There is loud applause. "They lacked security," he goes on, "but they tried and that's what we all should do. Our vision must be Victory. *Hail Victory!*"

The audience cries its echo: *"Hail Victory!"*

A Klan leader speaks next. He is neatly dressed, as usual, and his thin mustache is neatly trimmed. A prissy fellow, he pastors at an Identity church in the South and leads one of the largest Klans.

He asks that we join him in singing "My Country 'Tis of Thee . . ." and after we do, he asks rhetorically why there have been so many attacks at this point on the Christian Identity movement; he lists books, articles, movies. *Why* is there this hatred? There is a real war in the world, he tells us; the seed of the white race is at war with the seed of the Serpent, the Bolshevik. "We will win or we will bend our backs for all eternity." The Jew has a natural propensity to destroy the morals and the children we love, he tells us. There is eternal warfare between the offspring of the Lord and the offspring of the Serpent. "They hate us, they hate our Father, they hate our culture, they hate our music, they hate our children." They are the Antichrist, he declares. The hatred will not go away just because we ignore it; it will go on until Christ returns.

The Jews, he goes on, are a people with one goal: to destroy our faith, to destroy our children. A few years ago a survey was made of the members of the American Jewish Congress, he reports. On every question, the members responded the opposite of the traditions of our fathers—ninety percent favored abortion; ninety percent said homosexuality was okay. It was the same on gun control and on race mixing. "They are a different people that think differently from us. Their sole object is to change our form of thinking."

The children of Satan, he reports, are in rebellion against Christ. They want to change us. They hate us because we love our nation, our morals, our families. We look at what has happened in the last twenty-five or thirty years—the abortions, the homosexuality, the race mixing. We can see that the idea of the Jews is to change us; that the United States will be ruled by God or by tyrants.

We in the United States, he goes on, have joined the rebellion against God, have joined the evil empire. The average church at this time sees nothing wrong with race mixing, with homosexuality. But the Bible, he reminds us, "does not say *convert* the homos, have *dialogue* with the queers. The Bible says to *execute* them!"

Loud applause greets this statement.

The good Christian pastor continues, as the applause tapers. Recently in San Francisco, he reminds us, two hundred thousand gays marched, led by the mayor. "But a new AIDS victim comes down with AIDS every fourteen minutes"—very loud applause—"the mercy of God has reached down to us despite our shortcomings.

"How quickly," he cries, "our dream has become a nightmare." The evil empire rules over the media, over entertainment, over the schools. Over the churches. The National Council of Churches and the ADL cooperate in writing for churches; rabbis write the Sunday school pamphlets.

The pastor holds aloft a leftist newspaper he had exhibited a few moments before. "This paper," he tells us, "this paper, I forgot to tell you, the second half is printed in Spanish." There is derisive laughter from the audience. "The only Spanish I know," he goes on, "is *Up Against the Wall.*" Wide smiles greet his wit.

America, he tells us, is seeking deliverance. "Even those of our people who hate you. They hate you because they do not know you. They don't know where to turn.

"What is our responsibility? We love them, even if they don't love us. America will be delivered because we will get the message to them.

"Repentance," he continues, "does not mean to sit. It does not mean to let them in the gate. It means: *We shall push the enemy out of the gates, out of the churches, out of the schools, out of America!*"

There is loud and sustained applause. *"Hail Victory!"*

The Jewish parasites and their lackeys, he continues, dominate in the schools, in the churches. The nation needs to be cleansed. We must turn back to God. America must be revived. "It is a white man's revival. This is why they try to destroy us, why they need so many books, so many films: They are faced by a *movement.*"

Before national revival comes personal revival, he concludes. "Our people will have to have a personal revival in our lives."

The pastor stands at the podium. He has been impassioned and stirring; he has awoken great applause.

The next speaker wears a bandanna on his forehead and is in shorts, a contrast to the minister's suit. Even more in contrast, he speaks quietly at first, looking down at his paper. "This," he tells us, "will be the Gospel of the Holy Spirit and the Gospel of the Sword." The Mexican invasion, he tells us, is real; the Chicanos have their own word, Aztlan, for the Southwest, and their own manifesto. More than that, he points out, Soviet officers are even now in his own southern California, supervising the destruction of cruise missiles. We are closing bases, we are exchanging military personnel, there is talk of the reduction of conventional forces, of the elimination of nuclear weapons. It is the fusion of the internal and external threats. Unless we are effective, we face *genocide,* we face our extinction. Our first need is to identify the opposition. Our main obstacle is that we do not contact our Holy Spirit.

"The doctrine that interferes," he tells us, "is that there is no Satan. If there is no Satan, then there can be no descendants of Satan, no seed lines." Then we can not distinguish the enemy from ourselves, and cannot fight.

"The people who say there is no Satan are obsessed by their own carnality. They are annexed to Talmudism." Yahweh, he reminds us, is infinite. We can experience only a part of Yahweh, a part of the Holy Spirit. We do this by repenting. We must look in ourselves for Yashuah. We must find the Spirit.

(He uses the terminology of Identity: *Yahweh* is the favored form of name for God the Father, YHWH; *Yashuah,* for Jesus.)

"The Spirit"—his voice begins to rise—"is power. Israel [by which he means the Aryans] used power. This is the story of Gideon. The Holy Spirit is our energizer, your sword arm. The Holy Spirit is now our secret weapon."

Satan rebelled, he reminds all, with one third of the host. He is now the earth's ruler. But Yahweh made man with free will. *"They shall all fall by our swords!"*

The audience resounds with applause. "Hail Victory! Hail Victory! White Power!"

The speaker cries out, *"Hallelujah!"*

He goes on: "Yashuah said he is coming. He will come. The Serpent, Satan, fears Israel's reacquisition of the Holy Spirit [that is, the reacquisition by the Aryans]. The potency is in us to destroy Satan. We then are given immortality.

"First we must pay back the Devil for all the harm that has been done. We must perform acts. In secret.

"There is war on four fronts: against the carnal self, against the Jew, against the lack of spirit, against Satan.

"We must first acquire the Holy Spirit. We must then *execute judgment* on those deserving of it!

"The government has three legs: the political, the economic, and the media. The media is the weakest. We must execute the false."

His voice now becomes still and level: *"If you imagine you can win without shedding valleys of blood, you are naive."* There is a pregnant pause. *"All the speeches have been made—it is time to get to work!"*

The room explodes: "Hail Victory! Hail Victory! White Power! Hail Victory!"

The plan, he concludes, is twofold: Love Yahweh, love your kindred. "We will win if we remember four words: *Spirit. Race. Faith. . . . Sword!*

Cries: "Hail Victory! Hail Victory! White Power! Hail Victory!"

The speaker who follows reduces the emotional tone. He is a small man, perhaps in his fifties, with a middle-European accent. He is in a terribly serious mood, very absorbed in his message, trying to lay out what he sees as a complex and long argument. He feels the task may be too much; he asks the listeners to pay close attention, as he is trying to cram five or six hours of information into his hour and a half. "The pen is mightier than the sword—until we go to the final fighting." He must give us, he says, the understanding of the new doctrine, newly revealed. The new doctrine, he says, is the Seedline Doctrine, the doctrine most feared by the Jews because it is so hard core, because it identifies Satan in the flesh.

One cannot understand the Bible, he intones, without understanding the Seedline Doctrine of Identity. The Bible is the Book of Israel. But Israel is not the Jew. The Jews have the Talmud, that is their bible, just as the Koran is for the Moslems, and voodoo is for the blacks. The Bible is *our* Book. We will look at Genesis, chapters 1 through 10, especially chapters 1 and 2. "This is the Genesis for white people; there is no Genesis for red or black. Monkeys do not turn into people, even to this day."

(The reader might take a quick look at the first two chapters of Genesis, noticing that the story of creation is told twice. Modern scholars see the Torah as the weaving together of the work of a variety of writers or editors, with Genesis 1 and 2 having been compiled by separate editors ("P" and "J") whose dates are at least some five hundred years apart. Fundamentalist interpretations, of course,

have little truck with such finagling, and see each word as a literal
and direct expression of God's message. Within Christian Identity
and other theologies of the racist right, the two stories of creation
are taken as a history of two separate creations.)

The speaker describes the two separate creations, the first being
that of those beings—the black and the yellow races—who would
have dominion over the beasts, but would not have the intelligence
to till the ground, and the second being that of the first white man,
Adam, from whom came Eve. Adam and Eve were the first of God's
true children.

Satan, in the form of the Serpent, beguiles Eve to eat of the fruit.
God, discovering that transgression, curses Satan and puts enmity
forever between the Seed of Eve and the Seed of Satan. The curses
that God invoked on that day still hold. Thus, he told Eve that "in
pain thou shalt bring forth children"; to this day, women of the white
race find giving birth painful, "while the blacks do it easily in the
field."

Later, the speaker tells the group, Eve conceived Cain under the
impression that the conception had been performed with the aid of
the Lord. In fact, however, Cain was the child of Satan.

The speaker is reminded now of a recent occurrence. A woman
had been married to a black man. Fortunately, she had become divorced. Three years later she had married a white man—only to bear
a child that was black!

The audience gasps: the primal nightmare.

The speaker continues at length. We deal with Cain's need to
marry, with none being available but the bestial women from the
first creation. We talk of the Book of Jude; we talk of angels; we talk
of demons. The speaker goes on to prove through endless detail that
the Flood was not worldwide, but local. (One proof: The dove came
back with an olive branch. But a bird cannot fly more than five
hundred miles and a bird cannot land on water. His listeners accept
this; perhaps they've never noticed a gull nor heard of migratory
terns.) With these proofs, he asserts, we can reject the translation
that says there was a worldwide flood, which would have implied
that Cain's seed had been destroyed.

Satan, the speaker cries out, is the Serpent, Satan is the Devil. The
speaker has become impassioned: "People are trying to say there is
no Satan—because if it is so, he can have no children. But the

Kennites—Cain's children, the Jews—*are the seed of Satan. Are alive! Are powerful! This is what Identity is about!*"

There are two seedlines, in short: the seed of God and the seed of Satan. He closes with a warning: "The churches talk of an all-loving God. But God says, in Judges, 'You have deserted me, therefore I will deliver you no more.' He says in Jeremiah, 'I will destroy my people.' He calls for destruction in Judges. In Deuteronomy he tells us that the bastard, the one not of your race, should not enter the congregation of God. In Joel he says, 'I will cleanse this blood.' He is *not all-loving!*"

He leaves the podium, giving a last plug for survivalism, and I look around at these people who have sat patiently through so much and find myself thinking about the antiquated teaching style of the white racist movement. The whole day continues as a succession of uninterrupted speeches; there are no questions, no workshops, no opportunities for interaction. The listeners must sit and be spoken at. Periodically men get up and go outside to gossip with friends, but the speeches roll relentlessly on. The movement is not about the nurturance of intellectual curiosity, nor about creativity. Good members listen.

One more Californian comes to the podium, a bearded Klansman in a straw hat. He begins, to loud applause, by telling the group he hasn't paid federal tax for three years. We are going to patrol the California border against the mud people, the scum, he tells them. You've heard, he says, about the blacks. "But the problem is the *Hebe Jew*, the *hooknose kike. The Jew must be run out of the country!*" We've got to have fighters, warriors, as well as religious people, he tells us. He was born a Klansman, he goes on, has been in the Klan for twenty years. His father was a Klan leader: "*I was born white, I will die white.* I have the right to defend myself." He closes by reminding the group that "it isn't the blacks who bring dope into the country, it is *the Hebe Jew, the hooknose kike.*"

The next man begins somberly, telling the group, "We are on our own." Our job, he reminds us, is to keep it going. We must keep informing our people, telling them *who* the enemy is: *It is the Jew.*

It has always been the Jew. In one of the missing books of the Bible, Nicodemus, Satan says: "my own people, the Jew." The Jew is afraid, the speaker tells us, very much afraid. The Jew knows Identity is growing.

We must bring more people here to the Northwest, he cries out. He retells an old joke: He had moved from one mountain state to another; in two days a rumor had spread that his restaurant was an Aryan Nations headquarters, a Klan headquarters. People then asked him whether he served blacks at the restaurant, and he told them, yes, he served blacks, but that they were awfully hard to get on the grill.

The audience laughs.

Yahweh will provide, he goes on, if you really want it. But we have to help. "God has provided AIDS for us!" Loud applause and shouts of victory and power.

"God will provide more. Victory is coming!" He cries out "Hail Victory! Hail Victory! Hail Victory!" The audience joins.

The final seasoned speaker of the daytime program comes up, another Klan leader. He is of medium height, wears a black T-shirt and a sailor hat. He has a rugged air. His words are rough.

"I feel like a real white man here," he begins, "away from the nigger scum back where we are organizing. I have been in the Klan eight years." He lists areas in the South and in the Midwest where he has lived and organized. "We believe in the Northwest Territory; it is the only way to give our children a future away from the cesspool." If you totally trust God, he tells us, you'll see the miracles you want. He tells how he had come alone to his new location, had distributed literature, had worked at this for three or four months before making his first contacts. "One of my greatest desires," he says, "is to recruit a man like Bob Mathews or Adolf Hitler." (Mathews created the Order.)

He tells how he had tied up his town by trying to get onto the cable public access channel with the white racist videos distributed by Tom Metzger's White Aryan Resistance; the story had burst into the newspapers "on the birthday of Martin Lucifer Coon." A great hassle had ensued over issues of freedom of speech, and he still has the city tangled up. "We come across," he tells us, "as professionals. We wear our three-piece suits. We say 'Negro.' We say 'Jew.'"

It only takes two or three people to do so much, he tells us. "The sedition trial at Fort Smith put new fire in my blood. I don't know what the movement would do without Robert Miles or Richard Butler or Louis Beam. But we would step in." Necessity would guide us. "If we can survive the traitors, the Ellisons, we are going to win." (As mentioned, Jim Ellison had testified against the other leaders at Fort Smith, in hopes of reducing his sentence.) "The Jews are on the run! They are panicking. They are going to go to South America.

"The people are brainwashed. It is like Farrakhan said, ninety percent of white people ninety percent of the time have their mind on their pocketbook, their mouth, or their genitals."

This man has a strong physical presence; he holds the audience. "ZOG [the Zionist Occupation Government] is coming apart at the seams!"

We preach survivalism, he tells us. Store your food, store your AK47s. We know you informers are out there, he adds, his eyes scanning the audience.

"Be careful. They will try to entrap you. Keep your weapons legal: semiautomatic. Be ready. Get ready. Move to the Northwest, you can live off this land. My fight is in my city. I love the fight! I love turning the city inside out!

"We love the white people," he continues. "There has been forty years of brainwashing, but they will come to us. And then," he thunders, *"We are going to drive these Jews out of the country! Into the sea!"* The audience erupts: "Hail Victory! White Power!"

"When I see what the Jews are doing to our people, what the Jews are doing to Germany . . . when I see what they are doing to our women—turning them into men, sending them to go to work, turning their heads— The blacks will be sent back to Africa. BUT THE JEWS? *The sword to THEM! Put tote bags on their heads!"* He finishes to thunderous applause.

I have been sitting somewhat inconspicuously, with no one near me, in the last row of seats. The afternoon has become more and more uncomfortable.

The emotional temperature cools as two inexperienced speakers close the afternoon; they lack presence. First is a young man who has come several times before as a "delegate" from the Detroit group that I study. (He is the only one in that neo-Nazi group who has had any money for the trip.) He tells them that there is good news and bad. The bad is that "the worst has happened—Director Madden has been arrested on drug possession." (Paul Madden was leader of this group and created it.) The good news is that Madden's former co-leader had returned and led the group back to another of the annual Ann Arbor demonstrations. "Four Reds were arrested there, seven windows broken at the federal building, giving thirty thousand dollars in expenses to ZOG." One member (whom I know well) had been able in the fracas to take his helmet and smash a Red on the head. The young man then tells of another allegedly successful rally in a Detroit suburb and talks of plans for two future rallies. One will be an appearance at a new Holocaust Memorial in West Bloomfield (a rich and heavily Jewish suburb). He knows, he says, that his group will be able to stay but a minute. But they will notify all the opposition, in order to stir up a hornets' nest. (That appearance never takes place; the group cannot get it together.)

The group has been working actively with local Skinheads, he reports. He closes, raising his arm in the Hitler salute, intoning: "For Paul, for myself, God bless you, *Heil Hitler!*"

The final speaker, also young, tells how he has been passing out literature at his college. How the Anti-Defamation League set a fire next to his parents' house and sent them death threats. How detectives tried to have "a friend of mine set me up, to sell me hot guns." He had become alarmed and moved South. Now he is putting out literature at gun shows. "Gun shows are a good setting."

The speeches close, and I walk out into the slanting sun of very late afternoon. I walk about, nod to a few people, pay for a Styrofoam cup of coffee, listen a bit to conversations, and leave; I will not wander there in the dark to hear the nighttime speeches; prudence forbids. I return to the Day's Inn and spend some hours typing the notes

I have scribbled all afternoon, anxious to transcribe them while my memory is fresh.

I then type immediate reactions for my journal:

Reactions

Amazed. Here they let their hair down. Jews are it! Hardly a word the whole day about blacks, or others. Again and again: The Jew is the enemy, the Jew is Satan, the Jew is the Satan seed. We shall drive them to the sea.

Scary by the end of the afternoon. More and more vigor by the speakers as the day wears on. More and more into the spirit. People with energy talking. (Schizo moment: The neat little fellow with the mustache doesn't meet my eye at the end when we go out for a break right after his talk. Then a few hours later, he is willing to. We shake hands. I say, "Powerful speech." He says, "I have been known to give a strong speech." This is what we say as we shake hands. Crazy.)

Definitely scary. Would not want to have someone in the room suddenly say: That guy there is a Jew. I am sitting and writing on folded paper, but writing steadily, no attempt to conceal it. I have no idea how it seemed.

They did care a fair amount about what they were saying. Is sort of a mid-rung set: younger, serious. Identity is sure as hell the core these days, and sure as hell is centrally anti-Semitic. They have forgotten blacks. Their desire? Reunion with whites, as I have suggested. Less that, however, than the specialness of the beleaguered tiny minority, training and struggling. Terribly powerful minority. Secret army, Gideon's warriors. Secret army—Identity—special.

Quite scary by end.

I jog by the river the next morning and then return to the compound. There is a church service to open the day. Pastor Butler preaches a sermon based on Ezekiel 37—God takes the prophet to the valley of dry bones, God states that He will bring Israel from the nations where it has been scattered and draw the tribes together in one land. The sermon dwells obsessively with Germany—its travails, its future. Judah, "the royal line," is Germany. The pastor holds his arm out in the Nazi salute for his prayers. Within the sermon, he alludes to the split that took place between Israel and Judah; he attributes it to "the Jew advisers" who were around at the time. (For Identity, while most actors mentioned in the Torah were proto-Aryans, there was also a rabble that hung out at the fringes. This rabble was Jews. One of their acts was the building of the golden calf while Moses was on the mountain.) The sermon resounds with the words *Yahweh* and *Yashuah*.

The hymns are led by the Texan lawyer, who has a very good voice. The children who are present—and there are many—are led in song by a young Klan leader's wife.

The centerpiece of the day begins, the Soldiers' Ransom, a ritual based, it is said, on an ancient Hebrew custom. Each who wishes to participate—and this means almost everyone—will pass through the church, making a vow. A number line up; the line extends out of the building and onto the meadow; as the line moves forward, fresh participants join at the back of the line. Slowly the line works its way forward; throughout the hours that this takes, the Klan wife plays the "Horst Wessel Lied" on the piano, slowly, slowly, a melancholy cry. Each oath-taker moves forward, making his way from the anteroom to the church aisle, adds a little bag of symbolic coins that he has been given to the ransom hoard now growing on a table, then passes slowly up the aisle, arriving at last to the front. The man ahead in line hands the man behind him the great sword. Each, in turn, lifts the sword, kisses the hilt, holds it before him, and recites such oath as he has constructed for the occasion. Most say: "To Yahweh, Yashuah, and to my race, I pledge my life and my sacred honor."

It is hushed and still as each makes his oath.

The oath-taker hands the sword to the man behind him. He steps to the left or right and stands in front of the Aryan Nations chief or a Klan chief, both of them pastors. The pastor has dipped his thumb in oil, makes a cross on the man's forehead, and blesses him.

The oath-taker walks a few steps to the side, turns around. He walks slowly along the wall to the back of the room, then out.

I study the faces as the men walk to the back of the room. The party anthem sounds sadly. The men are solemn. The faces are set.

Each man has sworn, in seriousness, alone. It is a moment of taking on risk.

They are not dummies. They know chances are good that prison can come from this involvement. They imagine worse.

They make individual, public commitment. Each hears his own oath in that sober silence.

I walk outside, cross the long meadow. A young man from Winnipeg leans his gangly body against a fence post. He stares somberly across the fields, alone.

I wander in and out of the church. I sit for long spells, watching this solemnity. One time I sit by accident in the pew where Robert Mathews's widow sits; she quickly moves to another pew. The FBI caused Mathews to burn to death at the end of a furious shoot-out. I assume she believes I am part of the machinery of his death; I move farther back in the building.

The men have finished after several hours. A group of women appear; they announce that they are for the first time going to join this ceremony. The Klan leader with the pencil mustache makes all the men in earshot come in. "This is a warriors' pledge," he tells them. "Women are not warriors. Men," he says, "you should be ashamed, that women must step into the gap." He holds the sword over the head of the first of the women. He announces that he is honoring them. "Men," he cries, "let us pray that the women will never have to lift the sword." He leads the men in a salute, with arms outstretched: "*Heil* the Women! *Heil* the Women! *Heil* the Women! *Heil* Victory!"

The women quietly carry out the ritual with the sword. When they are finished, he again gives a little speech. He is unable to permit the women to act without male sponsorship.

We pass to new ceremonials. There are christenings. To the tune of the "Horst Wessel," two infants and two kindergartners are christened. All rise and Heil each of them. *Heil* Kirstie, *Heil* Kevin. Next there is a wedding ceremony. When it is concluded, the couple exits—again to the tune of the "Horst Wessel." All *heil*.

I wander the meadows. I talk with Skinheads from Portland and Las Vegas. They believe everything they have heard. That they are Israelites. That Christ was white, not a Jew. That this is a Christian Republic, this is Christian Territory. God gave the Bible to us, the Christians.

On all sides, among the Skins, Klansmen, "Aryans," the word *Jew* is heard. The Jew can be an Indian, he can be anything. He is greed. The Jew is the enemy; he pushes us. The Jew is attacking, coming closer and closer. Something has to break.

I try to make estimates. Perhaps a third of the people are over fifty years old, perhaps a quarter in their twenties. About half look a little twitchy; the rest look quite ordinary. Many people are in uniforms.

As I am talking with a Skinhead by their tents, the rugged Klansman who had called for the killing of the Jews joins me. We walk off together. He asks my name. He asks whether I am religious. I assume he means am I Jewish, and assure him that I am a Jew. He knows what I am doing, he says; Butler had explained the research. I say, "That was quite a speech you gave yesterday." He agrees. I say, "It was pretty hard on the Jews, wasn't it?" He says that sometimes you get carried away. We stroll on. I explain the research further; I tell him that I would probably want to come down to his city and interview him. "Yeah, come on," he says. "You'd be welcome, Rafe."

I thank Butler and depart. I drive through foothills and prairie to Spokane; I watch cloud and conifer, hill and grass. I am dazed.

Behind me, the participants make their good-byes to one another, plan new meetings. The "Horst Wessel," presumably, continues.

A year or two later, Portland Skinheads instigated by Tom Metzger's agents have assaulted a young Ethiopian man on the street, killing him with blows to the head from a baseball bat. Between 1990 and

1993, Skinheads—courted and fed dogma by supremacist groups—kill twenty-two people, most of them nonwhites, gays, homeless, or suspected turncoats from their own ranks.

Quite recently I see the rugged Klan leader ("Yeah, come on. You'd be welcome, Rafe") on network TV news. He is in Germany, making links with the resurgent neo-Nazis who have been firebombing the homes of Turkish workers. He is showing them how to hold cross burnings.

Part Two

NATIONAL LEADERS

FOUR

Introduction

The movement does not exist without its leaders. I came to know eight or ten of them well, in most cases holding three or more interviewing sessions of two or three hours each, as well as watching the men in operation. Those interviews usually took place in the leader's house. This chapter discusses national leaders in general; the following three chapters are portraits of three individual leaders who illuminate different styles.

The leaders create the organization. Like a magnet giving shape and pattern to a random scattering of iron filings, the leader exudes a force that gives coherence to a random scattering of alienated people. The leader's great function is to play this orienting role. His home is a place the cadre men can come, sit with him over the kitchen table, and hear agreement to their exotic concepts. He orates to these lieutenants, agrees with them, and gives them wider theories into which to fit their perceptions and ways to think of their own lives. He lets them feel his self-confidence. They can trust that a competent and loving figure is at the very front of the march—a father.

The leader builds the group. His personality gives it its character. He provides a secure setting, a place where valued interaction can go on, a place in which the members can go through feelings that are important to them; for the cadre, this may be the leader's house; for the ordinary member, it may be at rallies.

For the member, the white racist movement today is most impor-

tantly a setting in which he can savor certain sensations: he can feel
that he is a victim, unjustly being victimized; and he can feel that he
is part of a group that is taking significant action in the name of a
higher good. Organized white racism today is much more about getting the chance to have the feelings than it is about an actual program. The leader is a man who serves those needs. He provides words
that elaborate on the victimization in a context that makes it non-
shameful. He provides words and emotions and melodrama that let
members feel they are a part of something in motion, whether or not
anything really is being done. He arranges theatrical events that gain
maximum media attention with minimal risk to the members, large
numbers of whom drift away if real risk arises. There is a delicate
balance between giving members the sense that they run risk and
making members fearful.

The leader must have the gift of acting as well as the gift of words.
He must be able to enact, on the rally stage, the anger that the member would like to be able to express. He must be able to enact the
anger at the injustices that members feel they suffer, the rage at the
conspiracy and at the placid dupes of the conspiracy, and he must
be able to enact contempt regarding individuals from the "subhuman" races. The member wants to feel all these things; the words,
gestures, postures, and tones of the leader help him to do so.

Everywhere there are people who could be organized into the
movement: people with some hunger or some lack, people who do
not have a more compelling attachment to society that would inter-
fere. Maybe ten or twenty percent of the white population is in that
state of spiritual need, and probably at least half of those have
enough simple faith in white specialness to be recruited if someone
approached them. It is the approach of the organized group, led ultimately at the national level by its leader, that triggers the conversion
from among the pool of potential recruits. It is pretty much a matter
of chance who from the pool will get recruited—who happens to live
in an area where recruitment is going on. Once one has joined, three
or four friends will probably follow.

There is an inherent resistance to risk taking, and someone who
has enlisted once in a racist group is much easier to recruit to another
group than someone who has never yet enlisted. More effort is ex-
pended by leaders in trying to draw members from competing
brother groups than in trying to enroll the inexperienced.

As in almost any organization, the primary goal of the supremacist organization is its own perpetuation. Most activity is geared at keeping the group going, and national elders work to this goal as much as local leaders. The primary focus is keeping the organization healthy—a difficult task for a secret organization without a real program. Most activity is geared toward feeding the members' needs for emotional satisfaction; the members are given theatrical events that allow them to experience the feelings that temporarily feed them.

Leaders must win their positions. The movement draws some people who are happy as followers, but, like most politically active elements, it draws many who hunger for some power and quickly feel they could do the job as well or better than those now at work. The pool of potential recruits means that power is quickly attainable if one is talented. But competition is stiff. Those who win in the competition typically are intelligent, competent, and cynical. The discovery that one can sway people with one's words probably helps build that cynicism.

What do the leaders believe? Whatever they last heard themselves say. Whatever has the power to motivate followers.

They are experienced organizers, always alert for an opening—an incident that can be exploited to embarrass the opposition, an instance of establishment hypocrisy that can be publicized. There is a constant readiness to *react* in a tactically profitable way. Words leap to their lips that put the needed spin on an event in the nonracist world—they don't have to stop for reflection. The way to make an event of the opposition seem sickening to one of their followers is immediately obvious to them, and organizationally useful phrases come to the tongue at once.

I would stand on the side and listen to the interchanges a leader had on the phone or with some fellow who had come over for instructions. A very practiced man was at work. He never had to think about what was going on. Years of apprenticeship had produced him, years of learning what works. And very clearly *what works* was the only question that mattered.

Listening to the interchanges between the white racist leader and his followers is to listen to a man who is only trying to create an effect and who is appealing to a very shallow level of his listener. The goal is to induce the follower to feel contempt about something, to feel outraged virtue by comparison to someone, and to feel an anxious superiority to someone. It is a cheap goal. It demands no serious self-questioning by the leader. He needs only to draw on a bag of tricks accumulated in his lifetime.

We do not adequately comprehend the degree to which white racist organizing is a kind of political organizing. Because we have been caught up in our emotional responses to the white racists and the theatrical pieces that they create, we tend to believe in their self-presentation. But they are not what they seem. They are *not* simple legions of hate-filled whites led by even more hate-filled leaders. The mixture of hate, fear, contempt, and anxiety felt by the followers is a damnably complex problem which I only begin to understand—but I do know for certain that the leaders do not fit our image of them. *The leader is a political organizer;* that is his essence. His goal is power; his motivation is the desire for power; his pleasure is the pleasure of moving people to emotion, of being paid attention in society.

His organization is his tool. The defensive fear felt by his potential followers, their readiness to feel terror about their lives at a deep level, their readiness to temporarily alleviate their terror by feeling excitement, contempt, and outraged virtue—all those vulnerabilities among his followers are the resources upon which he counts. Those vulnerabilities are his medium, his raw material. Building his organization is the action, the daily behavior, that yields him his pleasure. Addicts refer to their substance as their "jones." Organizing is the leader's jones. He has to have it. Like every jones, it is his world, his lover, his identity. Without it he is nothing; when engaged, he is God.

So—given that the organizing white racist leader is cynical, what do we make of his racism? Is he someone beset by an extreme hatred for blacks and other nonwhites? Is he at an extreme as a hater?

That is not what I hear or sense. Watching what is going on, I pick up a high degree of contempt and fear and dislike, but not an extreme. He would not stand out if you plucked a random sample of white Americans from the street—he would be there among the more anti-black, but he wouldn't be among those with the strongest feelings.

I may have a less optimistic view of American racial feelings than the reader. I habitually try to catch the emotional climate about race relations wherever I am, and I spend a lot of time in fieldwork, running into people from every walk of life. Listening hard to what people say and what they show with their bodies, I end up feeling that most of us whites feel a terribly great distance from black Americans and a good deal of fear. I pick up a range from slight warmth to strong hostility, and to my perception something like half of us feel at least a fair amount of hostility. It is in this distribution that I am placing the leaders I have watched, and I am saying that they would fall among the half of us who are more negative, but not at an extreme position in that group.

I have been talking about feelings toward black people, although the greater part of the speeches I have quoted had to do with Jews more than with blacks, and the leader portraits will similarly center on Jews. I have focused here on the feelings regarding African-Americans because fear of and hostility toward black people has been the deep center of white American racial feelings throughout our history and is still the base on which the white racist movement is founded. Distrust and dislike of Jews has never been nearly as intense in the general population, and is much less a simple building tool for the organizers. But is the organizer an extreme hater of Jews? The answer is not obvious. I start to say no, because I don't think the organizer has much of an idea who any Jews are—after all, almost everyone I asked for an interview gave me one, and they tended to become fairly warm. As I think about it, I see that by "the Jew," the organizer means the construct he carries in his head, a rather medieval figure who lurks behind the scenes and secretly makes conspiracy. That figure he does fear and hate with an extreme intensity. That figure is blurred in his mind with all Establishment figures in general—the heads of corporations, the heads of publishing companies, the heads of political parties, the heads of mainline churches—and he fears and hates the Establishment with passion.

So then I tell myself that the leader doesn't really hate Jews, since the figure he has called "Jews" is an imaginary one. And there we see my blindness, since the figure he is calling "black man" equally has nothing to do with real black people.

The leader, then, holds a moderately high position as a hater of black Americans and an extreme position as a hater of Jews. He hopes to build on a white base of mass dislike and fear of African-Americans; he hopes to build on mass anxiety about economic security and on popular tendencies to see an Establishment as the cause of the economic threat; he hopes to teach people to identify that Establishment as the puppets of a conspiracy of Jews.

I have been asking about the racist leader's emotional stance in relation to his target communities, and saying that it is more complicated than seeing him as simply an extreme hater. But now I want to turn from the question of emotion to a dimension on which we do find him at quite an extreme position, and that is the belief in exclusive categories. For the white racist leader, it is profoundly true (and for the general population it is fairly true) that the socially defined collections we call races represent fundamental categories. A man is black or a man is white; there are no in-betweens. Every human belongs to a racial category, and all the members of one category are radically different from all the members of other categories. Moreover, race represents the *essence* of the person. A truck is a truck, a car is a car, a cat is a cat, a dog is a dog, a black is a black, a white is a white.

This categorizing is fairly widespread in our particular culture, and daily experience tends to reinforce it. We see black and white people living in different neighborhoods and holding different kinds of jobs. We see them being treated differently, and this reinforces the culture's suggestion that they are different. Categorizing by racial category is a pretty basic habit of the mind in our society, and we do tend to feel that a great deal is implied by the categorization (even if we don't often become conscious of *how much*).

The white racist leaders do fall at an extreme on this habit of thought. Racial labels, for them, express profound differences in the nature of the person. A black is not a white; a white is not a black. These axioms have a rock-hard quality in the leaders' minds; *the world is made up of racial groups.* That is what exists for them.

Two further basic beliefs play a major role in the minds of leaders. First, life is war. The world is made of distinct racial groups; life is about the war between those groups. Second, events have secret causes, are never what they seem superficially. Events are caused by the complex scheming of tricksters. No event is random; no explanation should be rejected just because it is unlikely.

Still I am missing a key point. The preceding paragraph brings us almost there, but somehow we have to be able to say: For the leader, as for the follower, absurd and intricate fairy tales make perfect sense. Any myth is plausible, as long as it involves intricate plotting.

The leader, like the follower, is *ungrounded*. Nothing keeps him pinned to the lessons of common sense. The world of everyday reality doesn't matter. Daily experience doesn't matter.

The leader, like the follower, is uneducated in a basic sense, although he has almost always had much more schooling than his following. In his self-guided reading, he has taken on none of the mental discipline of any of the reality-based professions. He has begun at an early age to decide what is true. It does not matter to him what others say. He is much more caught up in his own *ideas* than he is in ordinary *experience*. He lives in his ideas and in the little world he has created where they are taken seriously. He is victim of his deep lack of common sense, his deep disrespect for the reported experience of others. Gold can be made from the tongues of frogs; Yahweh's call can be heard in the flapping of the swastika banner.

Finally: The white racist leader thinks men are fools. (He has no thoughts about women.) He divides humans into two groups: those with power and those without. He responds sensitively and deeply to the scent of power. His following comes, as he knows, from those without power. He has deep contempt for them, but works with them, since their membership will provide him power. He has contempt as well for the vast bulk of other whites, the apathetic non-politicals, whom he considers vegetables. His respect is reserved for terrorists from his side—the men of the Order who robbed and murdered; Hitler, who destroyed and murdered. He is close to respect for terrorists from the other side. He respects Satan, for his power.

The bedrock of the leader's mentality persists: There is a conspiracy. The details change without strain. Recall all the speeches in Idaho about the organized Soviet menace. Yet when I asked Richard Butler in September of 1994 for his response to the collapse of the USSR, he responded airily that it meant only that "a branch office that was not doing well had been closed."

Does the leader think that he will win? I would say not. I think he feels that there is enough work and enough support to keep him occupied for his lifetime. He has some hope that chaos and disintegration may truly come about, that events may truly flow toward chaos, that his influence then will increase considerably. But I don't pick up the feeling that he seriously expects victory within his time. Yet organizing goes forward: Organizing is pleasure, and there is enough to do at this time and rewards are real enough that the work goes forward. Better to carry out the work, which might possibly bear fruit, than to hold still and have a life of nothingness. Without the work of organizing, what is there for this man?

The leaders I have met seemed to live rather simply and didn't have much materially to show for their involvement. The several marriages I got to know were good ones; husband and wife had shared a lifetime of risk, respected each other, and treated each other well. I saw little sign of sexual adventuring; I think their emotions were elsewhere.

In the succeeding three chapters I will present portraits of three of these leaders: first, Tom Metzger, a dangerous middle-aged organizer in southern California; second, Dave Holland, a young Klan leader in the South; and third, Richard Butler, a cold elder of great influence who operates in the Northwest. We have met several of them briefly in earlier chapters.

FIVE

Tom Metzger:
White Aryan Resistance

Tom Metzger leads a strident organization named White Aryan Resistance. With units in southern California and scattered other locations, it publishes a violent paper named *WAR!* and prides itself on its determination. Metzger and his close associates have mastered videotaping and have put together a series of "educational" videos with racist leaders; they sell these tapes to supremacist groups around the country who show them, or try to show them, on public-access cable television channels. Like many groups, they try to organize among white prison inmates, playing on their fears of black inmates. Over the years, Metzger has devised a variety of provocative actions that could be easily publicized and that embarrassed conventional authorities and made them choose between being embarrassed or acting unconstitutionally. The provocations included mounting an impromptu jeep patrol on the border with Mexico to harass illegal immigrants; running for elective office, uninvited, on a major party ticket; and defending the rights of Marine recruits to maintain a Klan cell in their barracks. Metzger's publicity has won him a number of appearances on network television talk shows, where his contentious behavior has ensured return visits. His most dangerous activity has been a continuing outreach to racist Skinhead groups; in person and through his workers he has pulled them into closer links to the White

Aryan Resistance and to each other, deepened their commitment to white racist beliefs, and brought them nearer to street violence.

At present, the whole supremacist movement is going through a period of transition as old leaders pass on. Metzger, despite recent legal setbacks and the death of his wife, will be a major force for many years. He is relatively young, highly energetic, and quite intelligent; his mind is free of mystical nonsense; and he is the most cynical of the leaders I have met and the least deterred by conscience or social conventions. Metzger knows himself. He has no doubts that others are like him: People look out for themselves; any claim to unselfishness is hypocritical and self-serving. Judging from himself, Metzger has concluded that life is a war pitting man against man. He is sure that people who claim to have a conscience are pretending.

Tom Metzger works out of a modest home in a small town north of San Diego. I reached the town by a drive up through the foothills— I left the sprawl of crisp white condominiums that surrounds San Diego and drove north through the sparsely settled hills with light brush, semiarid hills. After about fifty miles, a little road led through dense groves of orange trees. Oranges shone in the southern California sun, the deep green leaves glistened, irrigation had done wonders. I was into the small city, a tidy town with neat streets and white buildings. You could live here happily; it would be a good place to be a schoolteacher.

In the evening I walked from the motel over to Metzger's place. The neighborhood, mixed Anglo and Hispanic, was far from affluent; the homes were small, but seemed open to the street—in contrast to Metzger's, which was surrounded by a six- or eight-foot fence of flexible wooden slats woven into wire mesh. Next to the fence were signs for his TV and appliance repair business. A sloping and tricky path led down an incline along the fence to what seemed to be a basement door. Metzger met me there; it was indeed a basement with bare cinder-block walls; he led me past a room with old and sparse furniture, where several cronies sat and brooded, and took me into a corner room, walled off from the rest of the basement—his personal office for movement work—a room filled with stacks of publications, various tools along the wall, desks and a telephone, chairs for working at the desk and for sitting back and reading publications, piles of mail, and waist-high bookcases filled with movement-related books. Among hardware atop one bookcase I noticed a knife and cartridges about the size of those that went with my old .45-caliber pistol from the service.

Metzger fit that Army mood. He engaged with me directly; sat solidly in his wooden chair, faced me, listened carefully to my introduction. He reminded me of the old sergeants or warrant officers. He had the look and feel of a career military man with twenty or twenty-five years behind him of rough duty and disciplined time, much of it outdoors. His manner said that he would rather be doing something else just then, but that he had agreed to do this and he would do it honestly and as thoroughly as he could. He would try to keep from going off on tangents. He would be polite. He would not want to build any closer connection than direct response calls for.

He was not tall. But he sat so erect and had such bristly, aggressive energy that he seemed trim. I could easily imagine him as a tough police lieutenant who had worked his way up through the ranks.

He was a hard, tough man. Much more than anyone else I interviewed, he felt like someone who could be dangerous: a really intelligent man, an aggressive man driven by intense energy—this was a man you easily could envision building an underground.

All the same, he responded ultimately with some warmth as we proceeded. I had presented myself accurately as someone fascinated by political organizing, thoroughly interested in what made some efforts work and others fail, and thoroughly interested in the personal biographies of the men who were making themselves careers in this movement. When my questions and my responses to his statements made it clear that I had some professional knowledge and experience around organizing, even if under very different banners, he began to treat our discussion with some respect and to relax into telling stories about himself. He began to enjoy himself and to loosen up a bit, while never losing track of our respective and very different agendas.

Metzger had a gift for language; his images worked. When I had asked about the time frame in which he imagined the movement coming to power, he spoke of unpredictability, the number of variables involved. Things might happen in a second or over fifty years. But, he said, he told his people, "If you're standing at a railroad platform and you know that the train is not going to come to a complete halt, you don't stand there with your arm out so when you grab the train it pulls it out of the socket; you have to be running in place so you're ready to pick up the train. You never know when that time's going to be." Given the right frame of mind and ideology, it didn't matter when the time came, but what you did at the time. "I believe in politics of the deed," he said. "There's only one politics, really, that's politics of the deed." You could not force events—had he ten thousand people in the streets, things might not change—but "the events, the coming together of events . . . all of a sudden, the door, the window of opportunity . . ." You could not say when things were going to happen, he continued. "We do know that we don't like what is going on now, and we do know we don't have any future. As social power decreases faster and faster, state power increases faster and faster. And we see ourselves, if you will pardon the expression, as the new niggers."

Metzger was fifty at our first interview, married then to a very supportive wife (since deceased) and father of a flock of children. He began by explaining that he was nonreligious or anti-religious and that he stood for a "Third Force," a racism that was centered on the white working class and was anti-capitalist. He saw it as continuing the spirit of the earliest, pre-Hitler years of the German Nazi party.

In his trek through the right wing, he had been involved with religion, including Christian Identity, for some time, but by about 1980 had come to atheism. Until then, he said, he had thought that there must be an answer to his social questions in formal religion. "I remember one day," he said, "I came into this very room, turned off the lights, and sat here in the dark." He had realized, as he sat and brooded in the darkness, "that the answer isn't in formalized religion, that's where all the garbage is coming from. So that now we have to look for another alternative." He had begun a search. "I've read a lot of Bertrand Russell, *Why I'm Not a Christian*, many of the atheist books, agnostics, and was very impressed. And began to relate man more to animal than to, you know, angels. And we better solve the problems by ourselves, because there's nobody going to come down here and magically do it for us. So if you're going to make a change, make it; don't depend on some deity to do it, and don't waste your time in a lot of mysticism, that are only theories that can't be proved." He went on at length about his deep skepticism, certainly including the theories of Christian Identity. ("There was no way," he said, "that one could connect the white Caucasians to the Hebrew people.") The answers he saw lay in social biology, in the social Darwinism so rampant in the racist movement.

He also talked, from the beginning, about his "Third Force," the successor to both monopoly capitalism and communism. He saw it as a worker-based nationalist movement that targeted major capitalists as the central enemy. These capitalists were mostly white, although deeply influenced by Jews. White workers were to be rallied into a cohesive force. "The goal," he said, "is a radical change in the system of the United States, a national-socialist system." This would mean "the straitjacketing of the supercorporations so that they could only do things as long as they served the country they are in. If it was found that their profits were interfering with the best interests of the people and the ecology, the top ones go to jail; if the crime is too bad, they are executed to bring them under control." When I asked how race was relevant to this, he had no real answer; when I asked how it could be imagined as possible, he was definite: "You stop them by whatever methods it takes to stop them. If you have the will or the imagination, whatever you can imagine can be done. If you have the collective will, you can do anything you want. Arrest them, high crimes against the state. If that doesn't work, kill them. Crimes against the people. I mean, if you're going to talk, hey, talk turkey; they're never going to give up like gentlemen, so either you're ready to go all the way or you don't go at all.

"It doesn't come," he replied to my skepticism, "without a struggle. Sacrifice. Nobody's going to *give* you anything. And nobody is going to give the power that they've got."

The same vigor had appeared in an earlier remark—he had spoken of partitioning the country so that most minorities had sectors of their own, but with Asians forced to leave, as a plague that could not be tolerated at all. When I had asked how the Asians would be forced onto the boats, he replied, "We make our laws and then we force them. Isn't that the way they do, isn't that the way it's done? You draw up a plan, you have the laws, you say this is what we're going to do, and then you do it."

Metzger saw the Holocaust as a rhetorical device, "a club, a guilt club over people" that "the Zionists" used. Unlike most white racist leaders, he did believe that "a lot of Jews died in the war" but doubted the numbers. Moreover, he pointed out, millions of others died in that war. "Genocide happens in war," he pontificated. "If you don't want genocide, don't have wars. There wouldn't have been a war if it had been up to me." In a racial state there would have been no need for genocide, since there would have been no Jews to persecute. Did that mean, I asked, that in the country of his goal the Jews would be sent away, the blacks, the Chicanos? "Either that," he said, "or we'll disappear. There is no middle ground. Ultimately we will be driven out." Whites had too low a birthrate; the white population was aging; the nonwhites were becoming younger and more prolific. "Anybody with a pocket calculator can figure it out."

And so? I asked.

"Whatever has to be done will be done. You know, you just have to be honest."

"So what would happen?" I pursued. He believed in negotiation, he said, but neither blacks nor Hispanics had ever answered his invitations to negotiate. Thus, he said, you have to have the struggle, and then whoever wins, there is a winner-take-all situation.

What was there to negotiate? I asked.

"The partitioning of the continent." But, he complained again, no one would come to negotiate.

Why would they, I asked, given how little power his movement had?

"If we had a lot of power," he answered, "we might not even need them to come to the table."

Metzger, like so many of the people in this movement, lives in a crude concept of social biology. People seemed to need to believe in something, he allowed, but "I think it's a sad state of affairs if man has to have a mythological religion to keep going. If we can't rise above that . . . I think it weakens us, I think that we get too far from nature and we lose—I think that too much compassion is just as dangerous as too little. I believe in the betterment of the species and breeding and genetic improvement, striving for the best, and if religion gets in the way, that's pretty bad."

Something about this brought the Jews to mind again: "But Jews —I think the bulk of Jews are very psychotic people." He began a long, strange rap about the Jews. "I think they love to be aided," he said. "I'm not saying all Jews, I know a lot of Jews, I've worked for Jews who treated me great. But, I think I've studied the idea of why the Jews are so attracted, can't leave go of, the Hitler thing, I think the Jews in general have this love/hate relationship with Nazi ideas. I think they're jealous that they didn't develop the power and I think that now they are using the same methods in Israel that are a copycat of the SS and so forth, and I just think that there's some kind of neurosis that is catching and it seems to be passed around among the Jews. Maybe even more than some other people. I mean, I found so many Jews, and even when nobody was giving them any trouble they thought they were being persecuted, they're always looking for somebody to persecute them, and I think that many times they end up getting persecuted because of it. But Jews are not Aryans or Caucasians as far as I'm concerned."

I noted that the movement seemed as hostile to Jews as to blacks. He agreed that there was deep animosity, explaining that "movers and shakers, within Jewry, and I don't think it's any secret, do tend to be sharp, intelligent, sometimes Machiavellian, and move in beside the seats of power, to be the advisers and so forth and so on. They always have. And so, when that power becomes unpopular, the Jews are going to get painted with the same brush. And that's what, a lot of it is happening now. Some people, it's a religious thing, they say Jews are from Satan. Well, I don't believe in the Devil or God or any of that stuff. So I'm not saying that, but due to the floating nationalism of many Jews, the nation within a nation, the perception of an allegiance to even a foreign power, tremendous financing of a foreign power, which could not even exist without the tremendous sums of money from this country and organized Jewry.

"They make themselves more disliked, more suspicious, and if they are going to cleave unto the corrupt people of our race, then when the corrupt people of our race get it, they are going to get it. I mean, this story has been told many times throughout Europe.

"I've always said that the corrupt leaders of our own race, when we really start getting hot on their heels, they are going to throw the Jews to us, to try to get us off them. I know that's what they'll do; this time I don't want to be fooled, I don't want the people to be the fool."

Who are the corrupt leaders of the white race? I asked.

"The corporate structure of this country, the churches, the media moguls. All those entities that are working together to keep power consolidated against the bulk of the people's best interest, and that is black or any other race." The civil rights movement, he said, was a mirage that had been constructed to convince the emerging nations of Africa "how much we love black people, so they could do more business with them. . . . It's all a cynical creation by these money powers."

"Money powers" does not necessarily mean Jews. "You cannot blame Jews for everything in this country. You can't say the Jews run everything, there are not enough of them. So you are going to have to finally admit that you've been betrayed by your own people. And if the Jews do have this disproportionate power, it's because your leaders have given it to them. And for that reason your number one enemy are of your own household."

He had admired the late Meir Kahane: "He's an honest Jew. He has one line, he sticks to it. Now, whether I agree with him or not, I can respect that. I can't stand all this devious crap. The false humanitarianism that we love everybody but stab them in the back. And you know that's the way most things are run, whether you agree with Meir Kahane or me or who."

As he continued, one could hear his certainty that most people were shams, his anger at the establishment, and the deep contempt for Jews that seeped into statements that he meant to utter as dispassionate. "I wouldn't want people in power in Jewry to think that I believe that that in totality is that much of a problem. The Fifth Column is always your own people, whether you're a black country or white country, Asian country or what. The only reason your country can go shitty is because of your own people, and if you have a healthy society, you don't have to worry about catching diseases, but if you have a decadent society, then you're open to diseases. And I believe the cosmopolitan mercantilism, the hyper-mercantilism that is promoted by a lot of Jews is that type of thing, and we don't need it.

"Too bad," he continued, "there's Jews that don't fit into that. When things go—you know how things go when shit hits the fan, man. When the shit hits the fan, it always happens. See, if I'd have been in Germany—see, where I don't trust Hitler was, he didn't go after the big-shot Jews, the banker Jews, he went after poor Jews and left the big bankers out. I don't trust that man. You don't start on poor people; you go after the big criminals. Then a lot of the others will leave, as far as I'm concerned.

"But once it breaks out in the social upheaval, we know how this crowd mentality is. They don't start checking around, what have you done good. Mass hysteria. Once that's started, it can't be controlled."

This long train of ramblings about Jews says much about the thoughts that are magnets to a white racist mind—the images he keeps being drawn to and disavows briefly, only to revisit them at once. If you reread his words, you will see how thin his tissue of self-deception is. Violence lay beneath almost every line. He has elaborated with "sorrow" *his own fantasy* of the undeserved but unavoidable killings that would take place—how sad he was that the Jews were going to be killed although it wasn't really right, only a mistake—how sad he was—how much he enjoyed talking about it. I could not resist pointing out to him that his own newspaper printed unusually vile cartoons caricaturing Jews. And that when he helped to feed those vicious stereotypes, he was helping to build the problem.

This comment did not produce an instant conversion. Metzger talked about threats he had received from Jews, and then about a great connection between Jews and crime. By now I was tired of the white racist movement's allegations of criminality toward my own all-too-repressed community. (Jews, in my experience, control their emotions and behavior too much, not too little. Guilt is our specialty, not sin.) I pointed out to him how closely Jews fit the standards of decency the movement claimed to champion—I spoke of their low crime rate, their low divorce rate.

"I think," he replied, "Jewish males tend to stick it out with overbearing Jewish women while they play around with Aryan girls on the side. Just because they are still married doesn't mean too much."

It was, I thought to myself, another interesting fantasy.

Metzger, however, persevered. The issue was that "Jews believe in miscegenation for other people but not for themselves. They were behind, very strongly, the civil rights movement. They always ran the NAACP until a few years ago. What they do is, they take their persecution, and they're always wearing it on their sleeve, and then anybody that they perceive being persecuted, they jump into things, and sometimes there's more to the struggle than what they perceive. In other words," he concluded—and now we were talking clearly— "they meddle a lot."

Metzger is a fairly frightening man. He is energetic and extremely hard-driving. His mind is tough; he has little interest in the fairy tales, the Dungeons and Dragons baloney of the movement. He is much more to the point: a plain flat-out racist, looking to organize white racists in as tough a program as possible in a world that is all about power and violence.

Deep into our final interview, I asked Metzger to talk about the Order, the group that arose in the Northwest, and—before the leader, Robert Mathews, was killed and the others imprisoned—assassinated Denver radio commentator Alan Berg and successfully staged several armored car robberies. Metzger's discussion is worth study. "From where you sit," I had asked, "from what you can see, what actually was going on?"

"What was going on?" he responded. "Well, it was, I think, the first stage of many others. Frustrated, racially conscious young white people. Some were religious, some were not religious. The chemistry was just right; they came together and they decided this was their time. And they declared war on the government and went from there.

"I respect every one of them," he continued. "Not because I would say go out and do it the way they did it. But they weren't hypocrites. They decided what they wanted to do and they didn't make any excuses, they went out and did it. And I put people like Robert Mathews in high esteem. Because I would anyone who is willing to die for their belief. There's very few people that are.

"So, it was good for the movement, because a lot of the camp followers [the less-motivated members] split, and only the hard core stuck around, attracted more hard-core people. Unfortunately, now, I think it's been enough time now, where a lot of the camp followers are starting to try to come back in again. Try to set up the same old crap [that is, engage in empty talk], and that I don't like. So that's why I want to do everything I can to keep the Order in the public's eye, and have vigils for Robert Mathews, going up there in December [to the island in Puget Sound, where he was killed], have an all-night vigil, and like that. Because there's going to be a lot more of those kinds of things from all kinds of groups, races in this country, it's just begun and the government knows it. As far as terrorism, the government can't stop terrorism, that's the biggest myth in the world."

I asked, "If some folks came to you tomorrow and said they were thinking of trying to become active in that fashion . . . ?"

"That wouldn't work," he said, "because I'm too high a profile."

"No," I explained, "I'm not saying they wanted you to do it with them."

"No, even then," he said, "there's no way I could—there's plenty of people out there that know what has to be done, they don't need a book or a letter from me or anything. There's more now than there ever were. They don't need to go to anybody, they don't need to go to Dick Butler or Robert Miles or anybody."

I persisted, wanting to get his views on terrorism. "Would you think it was wise for them to follow that kind of course?"

"Personally, it's not wise," he answered. "Collectively, it may be wise. It depends on the people. If they know everything that's involved in the problems that go along with it. And the revolutionaries usually don't make it. Don't live long. [Metzger distinguishes here between revolutionaries—active underground fighters, whom we on the other side would call terrorists—and people like himself who can live above-ground and build the visible movement that supports the revolutionaries.] And if they want to cut their ties with family, with friends, and everyone, and become a true revolutionary—if that's the road they want to take, they are free to take it. I wouldn't discourage them or encourage them."

I asked, "Would it be likely to be good or bad for the movement?"

"There is not good or bad," he said. "There's only, you're going forward or you're going backwards. The only thing bad for the movement is nothing happening. Stagnation.

"But those people have to decide what was effective, too. I mean, Mr. Berg wasn't a very effective target, if you ask me. That don't quite make sense. Berg may be a symbol, but really Berg was really nothing. I mean I could go in and debate with a guy like Berg, and he would scream and yell at me, I'd laugh at him."

I asked Metzger whether he thought that Berg really had been shot by the Order people; he claimed not to know for sure. Then he went on: "I mean, I don't know what people want to hear, but if there is a will to power or a will to change, there is going to be violence, people should not be shocked. I'm not shocked when blacks strike out to try to help themselves in a revolutionary manner—because to me that's natural—against a system that they feel they have no control over. I understand it completely. Even though we're on different sides of the fence. But that's a lonely road for people to get in, that kind of activity. It's a very lonely life. If you're effective.

"That was one of the things with the Order people, they tried to keep their families and everything together, traveling across the country with their family, their pets and everything. I mean, they didn't quite understand that that ain't the way it worked."

Metzger is a direct person. He prefers to paint himself in strong colors. In one conversation I was saying to him that I felt he was to some extent trapped by his own racism, limited in what he could do. While he might claim, I said, to have multiple goals, his publication was "ninety-five percent race talk, and not very elegant race talk. Like every racialist I've ever talked with," I said, "you would tell me that what you're about is 'pro-white,' not about anti-anything. But the product that comes out—"

"Oh, no!" he quickly interrupted. "I'm anti. Sure, I'm anti things."

"The product that comes out," I said, "is expressed in terms that are much more crude than most."

"What you're talking about," he said, "is hatred. Hate is a central emotion, and emotion is a very strong driving force which is implemented by all kinds of people. Many times in a weaker position you have emotion and, if you will, even hatred, in lieu of the power and money to do it otherwise."

You must use the weapon you have, he said; with less power and less money, you cannot afford smooth approaches. Moreover, he said, he was not embarrassed about what he used. The material in his paper did not vary that much from the truth, he said, "at least in most cases. I believe what I put in my paper. Now, sure, there is rhetoric that maybe, you know, amplifies it to a degree." Nevertheless, he claimed, the cartoons he had put in the paper that I might see as crude would bring his reader to the more substantive articles —a claim that struck me as too absurd to discuss. I scarcely imagined that the Skinheads drawn to the vile, sadistic, and scatological cartoons would move on to read the wooden, dense columns of his version of labor history. I was only interested that for Metzger himself there was psychic income in presenting himself as learned in social history. There are pages in his paper devoted to astonishingly dull labor histories, told in a whites-only voice, but the paper itself is one of the most vulgar in the movement and fairly reeks of race hatred.

For all of this, one wonders what reward there was for Metzger in thinking of himself as more than a race theorist. My own best guess is that white racist organizing is at its core intellectually dull. The theory at hand has almost no detail to it, and a bright mind would soon be bored. Once you have said that whites are inherently different and inherently better, there is little more to say. There is only the task of explaining why a superior race is losing, but the available theories have little texture, only axioms, and leave the mind hungry—they are empty-calorie theories of conspiracy. Metzger's social theorizing, I am suggesting, is the work of a good mind with too little to think about.

When I asked Metzger to discuss any of his organizing campaigns that had gone badly, he could think of none—not anything "where I've sat down and actually mapped it out that it's gone badly. I've been in several riots; I've never had a man jailed or seriously hurt." Why not? Because, he said, "I carefully map it out like a military action."

He told me several stories of such encounters. They rang with the courage of the small group, the beastly behavior of the opposition, and the wisdom of the leader. I heard in them the world that lives in this leader's mind, the self-image as an active, competent, military commander.

The most engaging was a long story of a vast riot that supposedly occurred when Metzger had operated as a Klan leader. A young white woman had been brutalized in an interracial incident. The Klan group announced that they were coming up to hold a meeting and give a benefit showing of the film *Birth of a Nation;* the Progressive Labor Party (a Maoist group) announced that they would prevent this. Metzger and aides went to the police to warn them of the violent record of the PLP, but found the police uninterested. Metzger trained his people in riot tactics. During the morning of the Klan meeting, PLP members could be seen drifting into a nearby park carrying lead pipes wrapped in newspapers. The Klan contingent arrived in a truck and disembarked at the hall where the meeting was to be held. The mob of PLP members attacked the Klansmen but could not prevent them from getting into the hall. The PLP mob then attacked the police who guarded the hall's doors. The Klansmen rescued the police from the mob, using pipe from the bathrooms, fire hoses, and broom handles. The Klansmen barricaded the entrance with tables and chairs, throwing back the one leftist who managed to come over the top. The leftists then "went nuts" and rampaged through the neighborhood, going through people's houses and attacking cops. All this worked, he said, because of his careful planning.

The story is apparently distorted. I later talked with a police officer who had been present at this incident. This officer recalled the incident clearly and checked his memory against the police files. The Klansmen had indeed arrived—rather unnecessarily, since the culprits had all been arrested by then and were soon tried and convicted. The Klansmen, when they arrived at the hall, were indeed pounced upon by a mob. The mob heavily punished the last two of the eight or nine Klansmen who ran from the van to the hall's door. "You might have thought the Klansmen in front would have gone to help their fellows," the officer said, "but all we saw was assholes and elbows! They were terrified!" The Klansmen made it into the hall, as the police rescued these last few members and sent them in as well. The police then took the Klansmen into an interior room and locked them in for safety, then held back the large crowd that tried to enter the hall. The police had to use nightsticks to repel the group, which did include some members of PLP but was for the most part made up of townspeople. The Klansmen waited inside their room, along with several officers. "They didn't think they were going to get out of there alive," the police officer continued. "They would have done anything we asked them to. You have never seen frightened people like this. If we had asked them to sit on the ground and bark like dogs, they would have done it." A black command officer was sent back to reassure them.

For half an hour the townspeople tried to push the policemen aside. Police reinforcements arrived, and the crowd finally was dispersed. No homes were broken into. Toward evening, the police were able to spirit the Klansmen out of the hall through a side entrance and get them out of town.

The officer who told me this story happens to be black; he had accepted it as his duty to protect the Klansmen, regardless of their ideology. One of the leaders of the town crowd that had tried to push him aside had been his own brother.

The Klansmen did not make a barricade of chairs, did not bloody a PLP activist, did not rescue the policemen. The Klansmen waited, terrified, in a room while a small detachment of police officers fought to protect them. In his memory or in the telling, Metzger has transformed a rout into a heroic stand. It pleases him to see himself in this pose. The movement in general speaks of itself as a warrior group, although in fact its real history of warfare is one of ambush at night, anonymous bombing, and petty vandalism hidden by darkness.

Metzger loves questions of tactics. You don't need many people, he said, to have a lot of effect. "My motto is always use the weight of your enemy against him. His problem is he is big; with bigness comes sloppiness. And mistakes. And bureaucracy. If one is fairly sharp, you can find that little niche, that little opening, and you go for it. Try to put your opposition in a no-win situation where either way you win."

In this fashion Metzger has worked a lot with television, preparing programs to be shown on public access channels and reveling in the no-win position into which this places the opposition. Similarly, he was able to embarrass local Democrats by becoming their uninvited nominee for a minor position in a thoroughly Republican district. These things lead people to "not have confidence in their institutions. We're going to change the institutions. First you have to make them understand you can't have confidence in it."

This deeply cynical man sees hypocrisy everywhere; it enrages him and provides him with ammunition. "I just want people—if there was one thing I would want to outlaw and make the death penalty, it's hypocrisy. Because it's the hypocrisy that causes all the crap, or so much of it.

"So they tell you that you're free, but then they close up every hole to express the freedom, so you have to . . . it's guerrilla warfare. Only it's not with guns—I mean, I used to tell my guys, I said, look, the way you do it is, you got a piano and you just keep thumping on the keys until you hit a note and the system goes nuts, and then you just keep hitting that note. And after a while they will figure a way of solving that and you start plinking on the piano again until you find another note that drives them up the wall."

He seeks tactics that will make the Establishment eat its words. "See, I believe that most of what people say is bullshit. They lie to themselves and they lie to everybody else. And believe they are telling the truth. They say they believe in free speech. But when you ask them on the street, they say, well, not for these guys. You put it up to a vote, the Bill of Rights would be out the window in a week."

Metzger has loved his appearances on network TV talk shows; they give him access to a mass public, from which will emerge the special few with whom he can work. The talk shows are "really the pits of television," he says. "But even out of that dogfight you reach people. And so I like a hostile audience. A lot of my friends in the movement don't understand, in fact some of them get really discouraged because of these hostile audiences.

"Well, I thrive on hostile audiences. I understand that many audiences are actually stacked. Or they're a misrepresentation of a broader percentage of people around the country. Because people live in Podunk, Indiana, or Tennessee, don't think like people that live in urban areas of New York or Chicago and so forth.

"And it always helps to be the underdog, too. And I'm glad when they scream and spit and yell and cuss at me. Because the mail I get shows it, this gets people up off their ass enough to even write a letter. If it was just sort of a calm discourse, they wouldn't do it.

"So, my method seems to work for me, and I try to get across to these people. I mean, when the red light comes on a camera, you're talking to millions of Americans out there in their own home. Don't worry about the audience or the moderator. I don't try to please them, many times I even try to agitate them. Because I know they've come in, many of them, or most of them, with a mind-set, and they get the herd instinct and the crowd psychology, and then even if there are some in the audience that might be sort of inclined your way, they are afraid to say anything, afraid of the rest of them—the crowd, you get all these people and they sink to the lowest common denominator. On the show, it becomes sort of a collective thing. I mean, even people who have some very intelligent things to say, and I think I do sometimes. Once in a while, even, we all sort of, you know, it just gets down into a dogfight. I mean, when people call you really bad names, insult you, it just gets into a big thing."

I asked how it feels, being in the show with all this going on.

"Well, you feel as a professional that no matter what happens, you have to be prepared for it. You don't allow things to make you totally lose your cool, because if you do, you lose. But also, you have to rise to that aggression, and not allow it to shout you down, either. So it's a tricky thing."

Metzger holds deep contempt for the bulk of the white population, the politically inactive. "Most of the white people around here are against me. Brain-dead. I can talk to a Mexican down the street who can agree with me more. I can talk to an American Indian who will say, 'Well, I don't see anything wrong with that.' But when I talk to the average middle-class white who is totally materialistic, he doesn't think of anything. He just, he don't even care, he just doesn't want to be bothered."

What does that white care about? I asked. What is his life about?

"Consuming," said Metzger. "He is the great product of economic determinism. The sort of the popular motion machine [he means perpetual motion machine]. You know, produce, consume, produce, consume. That's all he's kept alive for. If they can figure a way out to gain, hold power, and finance without having consumers, then they can get rid of us all.

"This world elite does not care anymore. They're callous, cynical. They know that they don't really need people at all. People are a necessary evil. Maybe unnecessary evil."

He returned later to the theme. I had asked him whether he would feel more identification with a white man who was sitting on his front porch looking at television or a Mexican sitting on the next-door porch looking at television.

"When I first started out in the racial movement I would [identify more with the white person]," he said, "but now I would have to know more about the white person. Because, like I say, there's so many whites that are brain-dead, there's nothing I can do to help them. I can preach to them until hell freezes over; in fact, they'd be the first that would want to kill me. And so, after becoming more educated about white people myself, I wouldn't make a snap judgment that, hey, he's my kinship. I would maybe give him a little bit of a break and say, 'Look, fellow, you know how it is.' But if he didn't respond, then I'd say, 'So long.' I wouldn't waste my time. But no, I wouldn't automatically see him as kinship, now. Not after my social evaluation of our race at the moment. It's at a low ebb."

He spoke of having respect for the gangs in the large cities in California, seeing them as a natural sign that people were establishing territorial claims. "As I said on the radio, I said, why are you shocked? With nothing else, people become tribalists, they turn the blocks into tribal zones, territories they carve out. And now the whites through the Skinheads will do the same thing. And maybe it's healthy, maybe it's a de-evolution of this plastic society back into a more barbarous sorting out of he who is strong and he who is weak. I call it the Mad Max World. Maybe we're moving toward that.

"Nature seems to, when things get screwed up too much, it balances things up again. When people become, you know, weak, passive, where anything is okay, then there emerges the barbarian again. And then trying to defend themselves against the barbarian, they get strong again and things seem to balance up again. It seems like that is somewhat the case. I saw a TV show a long time ago when I was just a teenager, I never will forget that one statement, one star to the other, he says, 'If there weren't so many sheep there wouldn't be so many lions.' "

Metzger grew up in northern Indiana. His stepfather and mother did factory work and some farming. His parents had separated when he was a baby; his father is an engineer on the West Coast.

Metzger's political wandering covers a long period of time and took him from conservative politics to the John Birch Society to the Klan (where he quickly became leader for California) and finally to his own group. Tax resistance played a role in this hegira. I was startled when he told me of his refusal, during the Vietnam War, to pay taxes—not because he was against the war, which, at least at first, he supported, but because he simply and very suddenly knew that he just wasn't going to pay. The story of this resistance is garbled in the telling and hard to follow, but I think it was a time of decision. "I told the auditor to 'go screw yourself.' She says, 'I guess you don't know who this is, you don't understand I'm with the IRS.' I said, 'I understand perfectly,' and that was the time that I just crossed the line. And I never went back.

"I understood then what my government really was: It was tyrannical. And the only thing they understand is force, because that's all they use against you. So let's quit bullshitting each other, don't give me civics, don't give me some church sermon, either I am strong enough to defeat you or you will smash me. It's simple."

The tax story goes on through many convolutions, ending with several agreements to try to pay back interest when Metzger was moving toward the Klan and wanted the IRS out of his hair. Most of the convolutions involve interesting stories of confrontation. The stories (and of course we are hearing only his version) reveal much about the way Metzger sees himself; they speak of a man who has stepped outside the conventional order, and about a man who has found a resolute core in himself. Here is how the first of them begins: "Well, I didn't pay for some time, and then they were trying to take my house. I remember they put signs up, my wife and I were going to go on a vacation up to Canada, see some friends. And somebody, the IRS came and put signs that they were seizing the house. And my wife says, 'What are we going to do?' I says, 'Hell, we're going to go on vacation, I ain't going to stop this vacation.' So we went on vacation, come back, and all the signs were gone; I don't know what happened, I didn't have anybody take them down.

"So they wrote me a letter, that the IRS man was coming over to see me. And I wrote him a letter and I said, 'Don't send any of my friends from the sheriff's department with them, because I don't want to kill any of my friends.' And I was very rhetoric oriented, more I think in those days than I am now. And so they come down, and they had six or seven treasury agents were with them, they surrounded the house. They were all in suits, but I know they had guns. Couple of them followed the IRS man down, came in here, and he handed me this paper. He was shaking like a leaf, he could hardly —I said, 'My God, man, calm down.' So I said, 'Well, I won't talk to you unless it's on a tape recorder.' He said, 'Well, I can't talk to you if it is.' I said, 'Well, that's the end of that.' So we finally come to an agreement, I made a deal with them, that I would pay them payments to pay off this thing."

The tax negotiations went on for over a decade, with occasional confrontations. Finally Metzger got rid of the debt with the aid of friends. He was very bitter about the government.

"I don't look upon these people like people who so-called keep their nose clean look at them. I look at them to be far more my enemy than any leader in Russia or Khmer Rouge or any place like that, people like that. These people are here. But these things are not isolated. It goes on against thousands of people every day across this country. For different reasons, different ideological positions. You don't have to be a white racialist to have to fight that kind of stuff."

We talked at length about conspiracy. We had been talking about who the enemy was and what the white racists meant when they spoke of the Zionist Occupation Government, or ZOG. I had suggested that ZOG meant the same mythical crew that were the protagonists in the Protocols of the Learned Elders of Zion, an infamous fabrication of the Czarist police that still haunts the minds of the credulous with its preposterous details of a conclave of rabbis meeting at midnight in a cemetery and laying out the steps by which to seize world power.

"See," he replied, "there is all kinds of conspiracy among all kinds of people." He went on to say that he felt that the Protocols had some basis in fact, that they were not a fabrication. The Jews were not the main problem, however; the main problem was white collusion. "Because if our leaders were doing right and were honest and running this thing right, they would not conspire with these interests, to sell out our country or race. Now obviously, because certain segments of Jewry have over the years for one reason or another become adept at this and that in certain business ways and all that, it has been the sort of thing where they automatically moved in to the bureaucrats and so forth, and finances, and like this. Essentially going with the powers that be. And that's what gets them in this trouble, because they do always go with the powers that be. And then where there's an upheaval, there they are."

The whites, he said, must face the issue of extinction. All groups must concern themselves with their own extinction. "And so whatever method you have to do to resist the extinction, has to be done." Sixty million white kids, he said, had been aborted since 1972. And a disproportionate number of abortionists, he went on, were Jews. I pointed out that a disproportionate number of doctors were Jews— a figure of which he claimed ignorance—and that if a majority of the aborted children were white, it was because a majority of the population was white. It was not, I countered, a war on whites.

"It *is* a war on whites," he said. "The psychology that has been promoted in the press and the books and the schools and so forth and the economic problem today that forces women into the workplace all together has caused this. And it was caused on purpose, it was not an accident. Because I have papers upstairs for back ten, fifteen years ago where certain political groups boasted that this is what they were going to do. Boasted to get the white, the terrible white man, to quit having kids and having abortions to get rid of kids, and then big shots wanting cheap labor flood the country and take their place with nonwhites. And it's happening."

These papers came from extreme left-wingers, he said, and radical women's movement people. I challenged him to identify the groups, but he could not recall. I said that radical left-wing groups hardly had that sort of power. Not directly, he admitted, but said that when the economically powerful took a look at such an idea, they would say, "Ha, that is a pretty good idea because it serves us. Bring in more cheap labor, eliminate people who would tend to strike."

I was scornful. Sure, I said, the heads of General Motors scan the Trotskyite press for their ideas.

His heated response was loud; to his mind conspiracy was a natural presumption. "Capitalism and Marxism work, as far as I'm concerned, behind the scenes, way behind the scenes, work hand in hand. The Communist party wants open borders, of course, for humanity to Mexicans; the rich capitalist says, 'Oh, yeah, I want open borders, too, for cheap labor.' So I mean, they come together. I don't think things happen by accident. I think things, most important things, are by design. They happen because somebody wants them to happen. And they're thinking twenty-year segments, at least, ahead.

"Most major things that happen, happen because somebody or some group or some people want it to happen. And then all of a sudden, it's in the schools, pretty soon it's in the churches, pretty soon it's in every newspaper. Then pretty soon the public: 'Oh, yeah, this is what we should do.' "

We argued about this. I raised a number of instances and challenged him to show me how they could be the result of design. He remained convinced of his position, finally saying, "Well, I think that in talking that way, the danger is of getting into the bag where people that think like I do supposedly are paranoid people."

I laughed and told him that I would print that sentence in my book in capital letters with arrows pointing to it.

He grinned and said, "But I think everybody should be paranoid, looking around at what's going on. They have no reason not to be paranoid."

I told him I thought the psychiatric label did not help communication, that we should speak instead of how much control people have.

"Most of the people," he said, "remind me of a fly trying to do the backstroke in the bottom of a Venus's-flytrap. And they just think they are in fat city."

I had been rereading our interviews, I told him, and I was struck by the contempt that he had for the average white person.

"I have contempt," he said, "for hypocrisy and the unwillingness to act to change things."

Metzger meant to have impact. We spoke, at several points, about the Skinheads. He was reaching out to them avidly; he was excited about them. "I think," he said, "they're a shot in the arm in a sense that it's the youthful vitality of young working kids. They're the first sign of the sort of disenfranchised type youth, post-Vietnam, sons of Vietnam vets. And that's what happened in Germany after the World War, it wasn't the vets so much as the sons of the vets that got really radical. That are coming on and they are saying, 'Look, I didn't do this to black people, I didn't do this, don't give me this shit, I'm in as bad a shape as they are and I ain't taking it no more.'

"That's good, because that helps the movement, and you need people around who, let's say, they walk down the street and somebody calls them a name, they're going to bust them in the nose just to get their attention. You have to have something to impress people that you are serious." You had to try to restrain them, he said, so they weren't just "people going to the streets and jumping on people."

Metzger saw in the rough street activity of Skinheads a force that could be a nucleus for his movement. We know from history the great power that organized street violence had in Weimar Germany —the ability of organized street violence to build an atmosphere that discredits the capability of the center to keep order, to protect the citizens. Street violence convinces the timid that they need strong hands to maintain order, and street thuggery draws to it similarly minded recruits from the pool of the vulnerable. Here, Metzger felt, was the surfacing at last of a form that could move events toward *Der Tag,* "The Day."

Metzger's involvement was never casual. Even as we spoke, his agents were at work among Skinheads in Oregon. Their coaching of the Portland Skinheads in street tactics and their incitement, later court proceedings demonstrated, played a significant role in the subsequent killing of a young Ethiopian college student by Skinheads.

Those court proceedings have reduced Metzger's effectiveness for the time being. His career, nevertheless, is far from over. He is determined, smart, and thoroughly dangerous.

SIX

Dave Holland:
Southern White Knights

Dave Holland had been recruited to the Ku Klux Klan at an early age by James Venable, the long-time head of a national Klan, now deceased. Holland had great energy and quickly became Venable's Georgia state leader, or Grand Dragon, but wanted more action than Venable liked and more recognition than Venable would grant. Holland split from Venable, though they remained friends. With other firebrands, Holland formed a new Klan, the Southern White Knights of the Ku Klux Klan. The Knights became one of the most active groups in Georgia, staging volatile demonstrations. Holland was quickly respected throughout the movement. He had taken on the work of organizing the annual Labor Day rally at Stone Mountain and he helped organize the provocative white opposition to the 1987 civil rights marches in neighboring Forsyth County. That large and raucous operation cemented his reputation, but also led to prolonged legal battles that forced him from active leadership by the end of our several years of interviews.

Holland was warm and affable during our interviews, direct and good-humored. Because he was not yet hardened, his words tended to deal with his real feelings, and not just be practiced rhetoric. I felt I was able to get a decent sense of the way his mind and his emotions really worked. I was reciprocally open with him; he liked hearing about the ways his operations were and were not like those of civil rights groups and peace groups to which I had belonged.

Dave Holland works out of the modest brick home he shares with his mother in a commuter town a little down the line from Atlanta. Dave is sturdy and a bit below average height, a "feisty bantam" according to one of his friends. He works outdoors in his own fence-building business; he is muscular and strong, with a bit of a beer gut. His hair is dark black. His twice-widowed mother, enfeebled by a dire lung ailment but who still smokes, dislikes his Klan work. ("It's a secret organization," she says. "So are the Masons. Secret. I don't see much good in it.") But she is very glad for his presence and his help.

Holland and I held our first interview a few weeks after the Stone Mountain rally. At his request, it was at Venable's home. We talked for a long time out in the yard, under a pecan tree. Our conversation centered on the issue of fanaticism, a word that he introduced.

"Hell," he said, "if I go to prison tomorrow, it'd all be well worth it. People you know, like Bob Miles, they're willing to lay their life down, and as a matter of fact they have by going to prison. He and Butler, who has put his life on the line many times. It's very few people who have the courage to speak out against what we call ZOG, or the system, because of . . . the Jewish money power. Hell, they control the media, that's well known, and in my opinion they control the government, lock, stock, and barrel. It's ridiculous the way the Jews control our politicians.

"It's just a shame and disgrace," he continued, "that white people are struggling who founded this country and built this country and now we're second-class citizens in our own country. They bring all those Haitians and Cubans over here, and bring all these exotic diseases with them, and as J. B. Stoner [a longtime white racist leader] says, *praise God for AIDS!*

"AIDS is wiping out the undesirables," he said. "And you know it's taking out blacks by the thousands; before long it'll completely depopulate Africa. You know they're over there, they're living like savages, and again, I go back to what Mr. Venable says, hell, Africa is one of the richest countries in the world—animals and timber and stones—and, hell, they're still living in trees and caves. But the government says they're equal to the white man. And I don't believe that, there's no way that that could be possible."

He brought up the name of Glenn Miller, the former North Carolina Klan leader. "I agree with Glenn Miller in a sense," he said, "that the Klan—I don't think the Klan can gain our country back, because of the name the Klan has, the type of people the Klan attracts.

"Whereas *our* organization," he said, "has been lucky enough to get good people, the Southern White Knights. Most Klan groups—I shouldn't say most, I should say some—they'll take in anything with the initiation fee. Our people have all neat haircuts; if they have a beard, it's well trimmed; they're well mannered. We don't put up with a bunch of cussing, and their uniforms are neat, pressed—most Klansmen, they wear robes that have never been even close to a washing machine, much less clean.

"Glenn Miller changed the name of his organization from the Ku Klux Klan to the White Patriot Party and had great success in doing it. Glenn would hold marches in North Carolina, five to six hundred people, where the rally you were at, the Klan had three hundred and twenty-eight in ours, which I think was great."

He was emphatic: "I don't think the Klan name will take us back to white control of our country. I think it'll have to be under another name similar to that of the White Patriot Party, or National Democratic Front, or the Southern National Front. That's why the Klan uses maybe front names for them, to get to where the Klan can't, such as the National Democratic Front, or Tom Metzger's White Aryan Resistance, or the Aryan Nations.

"It's going to take, in my opinion, a host of different organizations," he said. "I think the country can be regained by white people, but it's going to take dedicated white people and people who are willing to die and go to prison for their beliefs. And I think before it's over with a lot of us *will* die."

"Really?" I asked. "Do you really think so?"

"Certainly," he said. "Robert Mathews is a perfect example." He named also Gordon Kahl, another fugitive slain in a fight with the law. He was "another one who was fighting for what we believe, of Federal oppression, and you seen what happened to both of them.

Both of them were *murdered* by the FBI. The members of the Order are all in prison and will never see daylight again." He named members: "Of course, I don't condone what David Tate, Bruce Pierce, and the rest of them, you know, carrying out those armored car robberies. I think that was horrible. But I think that they were lucky in a sense to get to trial alive.

"As I say, I don't agree with the tactics of the Order, murder and robbery and such as that, but there *will* have to be *some* drastic measures taken. And I say a lot of people will die and a lot of people will go to prison."

He bore on: "But the members of the Order, they took an oath, and by God they've lived up to it as far as I know. I think one or two may have turned tail—" and he named a turncoat, and then went on. "But, I said before and I'll say it again, lawsuits and trials will weed out our weak people and that will only leave—which may be harsh to say—maybe the *fanatics,* the ones that are just *hard-core* dedicated, and we're going to weed out the tobacco-chewing, beer-drinking, truck-driving rednecks who are nothing but a burden on our backs.

"They're not the ones that'll help this country," he said. "They're what the media portrays as that's your typical Klansman: Put a ax handle in the back of his pickup truck, a Confederate flag in the window, and ride around and cuss niggers. That's not the way it's going to happen, that's not the way *we'll* win."

This distinction mattered to Holland: "As I said before, some people *will* have to die and go to prison. It's a bad thing to say, but when you have people like Bob Miles and Richard Butler, who they're willing to do that—and Bob Miles has proven his dedication and loyalty many times over—and J. B. Stoner and Glenn Miller, Louis Beam, Tom Metzger, and others—those are the, what I guess you might call, the *fanatics* who maybe are on that brink of going over the deep end."

I asked whether he would use that term for himself. "I would say so," he said. "If I didn't say so, I'm sure the FBI or the GBI would." (GBI is the Georgia Bureau of Investigation.)

"But that's sort of a term to put somebody down," I said. "What would you really call yourself? A fanatic is really like a put-down."

"I don't think so," he said. He laughed a moment. "I think maybe to say that we've reached the fanatical stage may be a pat on the back. Some others, I think some of the leaders call each other 'kinsmen' and such as that. I think it's gone past that stage now. Where we're really going to have to put our nose to the grindstones and don't look back."

Dave's attention turned now to basic forces: "It seems like the blacks have been well financed; I think they've been financed through the Communists. We know Stanley Levinson, a Jewish lawyer who is now deceased, thank God, he's the one that wrote the great speech "I Have a Dream," and everybody says it was Martin Luther King, well, it *wasn't* Martin Luther King. The *Jews* have financed communism from day one. As we all know, the founder of communism, Karl Marx, was a Jew. Stanley Levinson, legal adviser to King, was a Jew. Until Benjamin Hooks come down the pike, they were all Jews that were leaders of the NAACP. The so-called black civil rights leaders were either financed, advised, or led by the Jews."

I asked what he thought the Jews and the blacks were trying to do.

"Of course," he said, "our enemy—most people want to look and say, 'Let's go out and get a nigger, let's do this and let's do that.' That's foolish, you can't do that. I say leave the blacks alone. Without Jewish control and Jewish leadership, the blacks would go nowhere. And I'm not coming back to the old rhetoric, that they're stupid, they're illiterate, because they're not: Blacks have smart leaders, they have Andy Young, Julian Bond, Maynard Jackson—they're not stupid people, they're brilliant. But without the Jewish money power, the Jewish control, I don't think the black movement would go anywhere.

"The black civil rights movements of the sixties, it was basically controlled by Jews. Jews control, I would imagine, nine out of ten abortion clinics; while they urge white women to have abortions, they encourage black women to have children. Again, praise God for AIDS, that's destroying the enemies.

"Jews," he said, "they believe in segregation for their race, but not for our race. Their goal in my opinion is to destroy the white race and to destroy any resistance; if they can do that and then have a mulatto race, I think that they would then have the country.

"But as long as there's a good white man, such as Miles and Butler and the others, there will be a white resistance. But they're so few and far in between, as I'm talking about the *hard core,* the people that will get right out in the street and that might be what it takes, a street action, I think, like the Death's-Head Strike Groups, they take to the streets every chance they can get a permit, I believe. But I think the goals of our enemies today is to ruin, to ruin through interracial marriages our race and to brainwash kids into communism.

"If we would allow our enemies to take control, I think the white man would then be a slave to—hell, if they were blacks, I hate to keep using the word—to subhumans or undesirables. That's a word I use a lot at rallies to stir people up. And you know, without stirring them up, you get no response from them, so I do what I can *to* stir them up."

When he spoke of the bad situation of whites, I had pointed out that statistics showed whites doing much better in the country than blacks. He said this might hold for corporate executives—"but then again, when you're talking about the Klan you're not talking about corporate executives." He laughed. "The majority of white people," he said, "are the working-class people. Why should we—when I say *we,* I'm talking about the hardworking white people—be controlled? Why should we be bending over backwards for a minority? Let's be with the majority and not the minority. And there you come with things like these anti-Klan organizations. Why is this man working for the *minority* of the people, why doesn't he work for the *majority* of the people, which would be the white working-class people? That just *peculiar* to me; what would lead somebody to do such as that? Unless, of course, he's Jewish."

At our second interview, a few months later, held this time in his house, Dave began to talk about the issues of organizing. He talked about the ups and downs, how easy it was to waste time talking to people with no serious intentions. "Most people," he said, "want to sit back—'Well, I'll join next week, give me an application'—soon as they get home what they would do is they would show their neighbor: 'Look, I'm going to join the Klan. Niggers better not fool with me no more!'

"Which nothing could be further from the truth. Nothing. You know, I get letters quite often and phone calls, you know, 'My daughter's dating a nigger, I want you-all to come beat the hell out of him.' Well, goddamn, you know. They have more, a better chance, of getting me to jump over the moon! First off, I wouldn't even consider discussing anything like that, much less carrying it out. You'd be a damn fool to even talk about it.

"And, I've told, I've told umpteen people, I've said, 'Listen, man,' I said, 'evidently you've raised your daughter wrong or she wouldn't be doing this.' And of course they'll hang up and say, 'Well, I'm not joining you.' Well, good; she hadn't joined in fifty years, why in the hell would she want to join now?

"But," he continued, "I learned a long time ago, I don't even respond to mail that's foolish like that. I don't think there's anything to gain from it; the people never will join you or they wouldn't even ask you to violate the law. And I think some of that stuff may be instigated by the GBI or others. And I'm not about to take the chance."

Unlike most leaders, according to Dave, he did not wish to have units of his outfit in other states. Each state should take care of its own, he said. He had some scorn for the pretenses of others. "You know, why in the hell, all these people running around, 'Well, I'm an Imperial Wizard,' and hell, most of them can't spell their name. You know, that's foolish. And that's just crazy. If they, one state would mind his or her business, I think they would be better off financially, they would be more stable, instead of trying to run all over the country and saying 'I control all these people.' Bullshit. That's *crazy*. And you'll get nowhere, all you're going to get is problems."

I asked whether this had been his idea from the beginning. Yeah, he said, he'd had inquiries from the Carolinas, from Alabama, from Florida—"Here, recently, Wisconsin, a guy wrote me a letter and said he had thirteen members he wanted to join up with us. I wrote him a letter back and said thanks but no thanks.

"*Why should I?* The first time they'll have a rally, they'll want me to come to Wisconsin. Why, hell, I don't *own* nothing in Wisconsin,

I've *lost* nothing in Wisconsin, and I have no *desire* to go to Wisconsin."

He laughed. "It's just crazy. But most people will, I shouldn't say all of them, but a lot of them they'd say, 'Yeah, yeah.' You know, then they'd love to sit down and tell the news reporter, 'Well, I can't talk to you this week, I've got to go to Wisconsin to a Klan rally.' Why, I think it's crazy. And look what it would cost.

"Hell, let those people in Wisconsin worry about the problems there and we'll worry about them here in Georgia."

A multistate organization made sense if a truly qualified leader were to appear, he said, and this led to a discussion of Glenn Miller. This, he felt, was the man who was a leader if ever there had been one in his time. Miller "was charismatic, he talked on working-man's level and as you well know all Klansmen are, ninety-nine point nine percent of them are working people. He could really touch base, but now, look at Glenn Miller, he's under all these sentences, he's under these fines, twenty-five- or fifty-thousand-dollar fines."

Miller had been important—the Klan had been fading out in North Carolina and Georgia, and Miller had gotten things moving. "Glenn would have a march in North Carolina and he would consider it a flop if he only had three hundred people there. Why, hell, if I had three hundred people, I'd go crazy. And that's the kind of person he was, he could draw people to him, he was very likable, and he was a working man."

Now we came to the question of the uniforms, where Dave spoke with intensity: He cared about this. "And of course, Glenn, he was the first one—he wasn't the first to wear the army fatigues in our movement, but he was the one that made it popular.

"And when young people see that, I think that really attracts them. Now you go down, you see the Klan, I hate to say it, they'll be marching in robes—there won't be two people in step, there won't be two robes identical, the robes they do have will be *filthy!*

"I think that's *horrible.*" Dave looked hurt. "That's one of the reasons we don't wear robes. Don't need robes. First off, who you going to get to make them, how you going to get them to look neat? If you march, you'd want all your robes to be neat, in order, the way they should be. You march in fatigues, everybody likes them, they all look the same, you look like an organized unit.

"At our rally, if there were a hundred people in Klan robes, there were a hundred different robes. I mean I'll be honest, I hate to say it, it looks like a circus. Here's a bunch of people out here, fifty people, in fifty different-colored robes. That's stupid! And that's not what the Klan was designed for, to make fools out of each other. Some of the older people sitting down there and you know their robes hadn't been washed since two years prior. That's *horrible.*

"I don't care whether you like us or dislike us, I've told a million people that, you have to admit, though, when you get those people in fatigues, buddy, they look impressive. I've got an article right in there, the guy wrote an article about the Southern White Knights, he said all of the uniforms were neatly pressed. You know, when have you ever seen a reporter say that about Klan robes? You never have and you never will. And I think if we would have been wearing robes, we wouldn't have gotten that."

Deeper into this interview, after having talked about how only one in a hundred people who flirt with joining is worth a damn, Holland got into a long and conflicted diatribe about AIDS. He quoted J. B. Stoner, who has told his racist audiences that AIDS will lead the white racist movement to victory, that it is a racial disease among mostly blacks and Jews. "Whether it is or not, I don't know," Dave said, "but they said on TV the other week that AIDS was really wiping out Africa bad. Of course, as you well know, most of it's, in my opinion, that's Zimbabwe and the other countries, are still very uncivilized. They're savages."

Dave knew this kind of talk wasn't in fashion. He corrected himself: "I shouldn't say savages. But they're not clean, as you well know. Prostitutes in Africa, I think it's worse there than it is here. The women—I think, I think the whores or prostitutes or whatever you want to call them here, I think they try—to—to—prevent disease or whatever. But Dr. Fields recently published a article in his

Thunderbolt where the women down there said they didn't give a damn, they'll just have as many men as possible."

Fields is a racist propagandist; men like Dave soak up these bits of flotsam that float about in the movement. Dave, meanwhile, was having a hard time, flipping back and forth between sounding concerned and sounding cruel; he couldn't find a good place to meet his need to be a "nice" man and still be ideologically correct with the white racist movement.

"Have as many men as possible," he repeated. "Of course, I don't want to sound crude and no sympathy for people," he went on, "but the more, the merrier. It will wipe out the blacks."

But those words embarrassed him. "But I think that's a foolish statement for our people to make because, you know, that sounds just ungodly and un-Christian, where we're supposed to be espousing Christianity. You know, 'Good, let all the niggers die'—how crude and stupid can you get? And the news media expects that from a lot of Klansmen. 'Good, all the niggers are dead.' Damn, that will never happen, that's a foolish statement to make.

"But, on the other hand—there's always a *but* and an *if*. I *honestly feel*, I swear I *feel this* from the *bottom* of my heart, that, you know, of course there's a lot of innocent people affected by AIDS, but nine out of ten as you well know are either homosexuals or drug users, and I think that God is imposing this on them, and as you know, there's no cure in sight."

Dave now had himself almost in place, with a statement that he could live with. But not quite. "But, if it's true, you know, that God has sent this disease to wipe out our enemies—I don't see why, you know, babies are getting it bad. You know, this was on TV last night, I think.

"But that's just the way a Christian, I think, has to believe, that we have to trust in God. But I do think that queers, homosexuals, perverts, and drug users, if they're going to live that life, let them die."

You may notice the casualness of the assumption that God is in the business of sending endless misery and death to service racist white folk, but Holland by this point in his twisting and turning was just about home free. He could live with this: The plague is hitting perverted evil people.

"Let them die. I have no sympathy for drug users at all. I mean, if every one of them, honest to God, if they drop dead now, I wouldn't miss a minute's sleep. I have no use for drug dealers at all on any level. On any level. I don't care if it's pot or cocaine, it's all the same to me.

"And a queer, as you well know, is not, I don't care what he says, he can't live a Christian life. How could he? That would be like me saying I'm going to espouse Christianity and go out and kill every black or Jew. That's foolish and it's asinine. But I think that if they're going to live a perverted life, let them die. Because they're living contrary to the laws of God."

When we met some months later, Holland and I spoke further about the tactics of organizing. He had tried, not long before, to lead a demonstration in Atlanta at the site of the Democratic party's nominating convention. A large and hostile crowd forced Holland and his people back to their cars after a very brief standoff; the police had had to open a path by which the Klansmen could return to their cars. The event probably met many of the organization's needs: Massive media coverage took place; Klansmen experienced the adrenaline rush of confrontation and a sense of their own courage, since they held their place for a time in the face of a very large crowd; the Klansmen felt special, innocent, and potentially dangerous.

Meeting stiff opposition has mixed effects on white racist activists. They feel singled out and special, and they feel confirmed in their status as isolate warriors. At the same time, the repetition of such experiences does wear them down. The activists lose the greater part of their followers as dangerous confrontations multiply; the less intense followers decide after a few such experiences that there are better ways to spend time. That loss can take the momentum from the movement, despite Dave's claim that he does better with a small and fanatical following; the central core has no meaning unless it can build a following and a movement.

At the time of our interview, Dave was still energized by the experience itself, and a general discussion about strategies of organization led him to the subject. The old Klans, he said, were okay— but they just wanted to "put on the Klan robes and stand on the street corner. And *that's* not where it's going to happen. They're good about marching, rallying, and such, and again I don't ever want anybody to think I am criticizing, because I'm not. *But* I see that we have much more success in meeting people in the streets and having *confrontations.* When you get *confrontations,* you not only get larger crowds, you get *dedicated* people. Two weeks ago when we went to Atlanta, Lennie Raker and Arthur Prone were with us, and I told myself then, I said, every person that went to Atlanta, which was about eighty or ninety of us, they faced ten thousand mad savages, every one of these people deserve a medal of honor.

"Whereas most Klansmen," he said, "as soon as nothing but a little old lawsuit gets filed, most of them quit. I say, *good-bye, don't come back,* don't never bother to send me a stamp again, I don't need you, don't want you, and have no desire to see you."

It roused him, talking of it. "Something that Bob Miles said out there at Fort Smith, Arkansas," Dave recalled, "he was going on trial, he said, this is the hour we were born for. And I feel the same way about the Southern White Knights, this is what *we* were born for. We weren't born to sit in a Klavern, talk, drink coffee, and shoot the breeze, nor were we born to stand on the street corner like a bunch of gypsies. We—and when I'm talking, when I say *we,* I'm referring to all the Southern White Knights, I'm not referring to Dave Holland, Dave Holland is just a mere straw in the pile. Because without people like these we'd still be nothing but writing on the walls.

"I'm not afraid at all to go right down to nigger town with these people at all. At all. And no other Klan group would do it. Our group went down a couple of years ago to protest a faggot movie put on by the anti-Klan network. No other Klan group—they said, 'We're not going down there, hell, we'll get mugged.' Well, we went, I have the film of it. And it's not that we're looking for trouble, because we're not. But I say today, if we can have street confrontations, we'll get *dedicated* people, you get *more* people, you may end up going to *jail,* but that's the price the *niggers* have paid and look what progress they've made. So I think it's *worth it.*"

He talked of the confrontations in Forsyth County. "Street confrontations is the best way. I went to Forsyth for one reason only, because

I knew the world media would be there. I'm not saying I went up there to get my mug on TV, but I wanted people to know my feelings and the feelings of the Southern White Knights and the people of Georgia on integration in an all-white country, and I was very successful at what I done, very successful. We had several hundred people submit applications soon thereafter, about ten of which we accepted."

What was the benefit of confrontation?

"You can go either way. Down in Atlanta the confrontation went real good in our favor because, I think, after our march was canceled, we were then the underdogs. You know, the downtrodden, the oppressed, whatever words you want to use. And so when we went to Atlanta we were outnumbered probably five hundred to one. So naturally we're not going out then and look for a confrontation of 'Come on let's fight.' And so I think that in that instance it come out looking good, because we were the quiet—we weren't spitting, we weren't throwing rocks, we weren't cursing. And so I think it made us look like the knights in shining armor and made the opposers, you know, INCAR [International Committee Against Racism], Revolutionary Communist party and others, look like trash.

"And I'm not saying trash that they are, but they are trash. Anybody that will take an American flag and burn it on the streets of Atlanta—they did, I have the film—they're *trash*. It makes no difference who it is. And so I think that confrontation was good.

"I think if it would have been five hundred communists, three hundred Klansmen, then there would have been a riot. Because we're not going to back up—we didn't back up then, but we're not stupid. You know ninety of us go out and attack five thousand wild niggers— that's suicide."

He went on to describe the crowd they had confronted. "Just hordes! I have it on video. And I mean it was just hundreds and hundreds and hundreds, just surrounding us. You know hollering . . ."

His aide, who was sitting in with us, added, "Scum! People with —girls with mohawks, pink heads, blue hair—"

Holland added, "Rings through their nose. And I'm talking about children."

His friend continued, "Saying 'Fuck you!' "

"People who raise their children like that need to be horse-

whipped," Dave said. "Anybody that set up there and use vulgarity
like that—I'm talking about children. Spitting and just . . . undesirables.

"And of course I'm not for violence," he said, "but if there ever
should be anybody exterminated, I would say they should be exterminated, and they're allegedly white people. They would be the first
to go. They have every right to sit up there and cuss us and voice
their opinions, but spitting and things such as that, there's no call
for that."

Movement work could have an effect on you, he said at our next
meeting. "You know, over the years, the same BS, you do get *real
hard, cold.*" The people in his group, he said, had been through a
lot; "we are a organization of people who've been down the road.

"A lot of the things I may say and do *are* to get the attention of
people as propaganda," he allowed. "Such as George Rockwell
[founder of postwar American Nazism] used the swastika." Holland
criticized other leaders who would take the podium and start raving.
"Nobody wants to hear that shit. They want to hear something *interesting, emotional,* and *high-spirited.*

"I think maybe I use the things that are available to me to get my
point across. I'm not a media hound, but without the media we
couldn't get our point across. And so, you know, just like in one of
those pictures you seen a swastika in one of our demonstrations?
You know the camera is really going to turn out with it if you have
that swastika. And I think maybe, you know, I do use that as a tool
to get the attention."

This brought him again to the haunting problem of cleanliness.
"You know if you get people come up there in Klan robes, and I
hate to say it, you know these old men, with tobacco dripping
all, you know, it's horrible. But you go out there with neat, clean-
cut people, which all of our people aren't but most of them are.
Like maybe the SS, Storm Troopers, or what have you. That's an
attention-getter, people *respect* you whether they like it or not. They
respect you. If your boots are shined. And Arthur, you have to—I'm
telling you whether you like him, dislike him, or hate him, he's *neat,*
he's *polite,* he's *well mannered.* He always puts on a good presence."

I didn't entirely agree—Arthur, with whom I'd had a conversation detailed in an earlier chapter, had struck me as a tightly wound near-psychopath—but I thought it best to stay quiet. I did use the opportunity to get Dave to start talking about his family life, his personal history.

He told me about his hometown and growing up in the area near Atlanta. "My ma," he said, "was just like she is now, just worked all the time. You know, she never would stop. My dad, he was basically all the time drinking. Just not much of a father."

I was startled by this quiet and direct statement. He went on and described a brother and a deeply religious sister. Those siblings and his mother didn't care for the Klan. "My mama doesn't like it, but she's grown, I think, to tolerate it, seeing that I'm not going to quit." The Klan was never mentioned at Thanksgiving and Christmas gatherings of the family. " 'Cause they don't want to hear it and I don't want to talk to people who don't like it."

I asked whether his father had worked. "Yeah," he said, "he was a salesman, he was a good salesman. That was his problem, was he made a lot of money and made it fast. And he'd just drink and work. Just a bad weakness he had."

"Was he a hell-raiser at home?" I asked.

Holland's voice was flat: "All drunks are, in my opinion." This was a hard sentence for him.

All the family worked. Holland had a paper route in elementary school and worked at a gas station after school when he was in high school. "There was not any loafing around." The siblings and Dave's mother worked hard, too, the mother at two jobs for a long time. "I don't like lazy people, I don't like them at all.

"I—I—I used to drink a *lot*," he then said. "Yes, sir, all the time. And I spent thirty days in jail on a DUI charge and that stopped me from drinking, buddy!" That was about six years back. But he had drunk when he was in the habit. "Just hang out in bars all the time. I got sick of that. You know, just waking up *every day* feeling bad. But even then I'd get up if I was feeling bad and go to work. You know, I wouldn't lay around. I think I only missed one or two days ever, you know, because of out drinking and, you know, didn't get home until three or four in the morning.

"But I just, I've gotten, over the years," he continued, "to where I don't like *drinking, drugs*—has any place in our movement *at all*. People who are *drunk* have no *discipline*. They come in, you know, shirttails poking out, shoes not shined. And we have no place for that. And they're an embarrassment to the movement. I don't know of any leader today that's, in my opinion, in bad shape. You know what I'm talking about, drunks, or dope; I think all of them are *fairly* decent people. Even though I don't agree with all of them."

His father had died back in 1974 or 1975, he believed. His mother was now sixty-eight, still working. I asked whether she had remarried after his father's death. "Yeah, married a guy, Dan Parker [pseudonym], she worked with him, who I think is probably the nicest guy I've ever met. He was polite, he was mannered, he was real quiet, very generous. And he took to us—I'm talking about me, my brother, and sister—you know, just like we were his own kids. And we took to him because he was so polite to Mama.

"He was *very* well mannered. And he was fun to be around, even though he was quiet. He had a good sense of humor about him. He was just a *good* guy, a *damn good guy.*

"And everybody liked him. But he got cancer, then they operated on him and it just, you know, spread like that. You know, seems like when they try to fix it, that's when it really gets bad. And it spread and he was sick, I guess about six months. But soon as they operated on him it spread real fast. But he was a blessing to our family. I mean he was a good guy."

I asked how long Parker had been around. Dave said for about three years. He added, "You know, he was an Indian, full-blooded Indian. And, I'm not saying he was sympathetic with the Klan, but he didn't despise it. Because, being an Indian, he realized what it was like being a minority, to where I think it reflected to him that whites are now being a minority."

Dave's mother's remarriage had followed his father's death by a couple of years; the mother and Parker had worked together for many years. Again Dave said, "He was a real blessing. He was a good guy."

As best as I can piece together the time sequences from confusing accounts, Dave came under Venable's influence and entered the Klan rather soon after his father's death, and probably before Parker offered a better-integrated alternative.

The fifth meeting Dave Holland and I held began on a rather warm note. We had established some friendship in our two years of acquaintance, and now we each had been going through a bad period. I had had a coronary procedure, while Dave was being pressed hard by lawyers: He had lost a civil case that came out of the events in Forsyth; there had been heavy fines; attorneys hoped to get hold of any assets they could identify. Dave looked quite worn.

Shortly into the interview he suddenly left the subject at hand and said, "Of course you know I stepped down from Grand Dragon." I hadn't known.

He told me he had made the announcement at the annual Labor Day rally a month before our conversation. "I've been there, been in the same position for ten years, and that's enough, you know."

Then he told me he had turned the group over to Arthur. "I let your good friend and associate Arthur Prone take over," he said in a teasing voice.

"My buddy!" I exclaimed, and we both laughed.

We kidded around a moment about how welcome I would be at the next year's rally; I suggested that probably I would even get to be at the cross lighting, kind of hammered up on the cross.

Dave turned out to be rather bitter, about his comrades as well as his opponents. He felt unappreciated. "I tell you," he said, "it's just, you know, with this lawsuit, it's just a full-time job fighting them. And of course that's exactly what they want. And they have succeeded. You know, a lot of the members, they say, 'You're quitting, you're quitting because of the lawsuit.' Well, I've never quit. All I said was I'm stepping down. And I'll remain a member. They don't realize that something comes in the mail every day. This comes yesterday, just all these goddamn papers on tax-exempt status for the organization. I mean, that's just yesterday. Friday. Yesterday one of my friends had to go give a deposition in a case. Now I'm talking about just yesterday. Thursday we had to go down to my lawyer's office."

"And meanwhile you're trying to earn a living," I suggested.

"Right!" he agreed. "Wednesday we had to get some documents

together for my lawyer on discovery. Now that was last Wednesday, Thursday, and Friday. Do you know what I mean? And people think it's, think that, 'Well, he's lazy, don't want to do anything.' Well, let *them* fuck with it for a while! You know what I'm saying?"

This stuff hurt. "I tell you, man, it burns me up when anybody even *hints* that I'm quitting. I'm not quitting nothing. It's just that I'm tired and I just need a rest. Most people, as you well know, stay, as long as they ain't doing right, a year. Let *them* stick it out for ten years. You know what I'm saying? Let *them* cut it, buddy.

"I'm telling you, it's nothing but a financial headache. And fence building is not easy work.

"And I've let a lot of things slide," he continued. "You know, and you put the Klan first. And I'm tired of me suffering, my mother suffering, and because of that. And then what do I get out of it? 'Well, you quit.'

"You know what I mean? Fuck that, I don't need that shit. Let some of these other people run out and get sued once in a while and see what it's like to sit three weeks down in a federal courthouse when you ought to be out working, you know what I'm saying? And paying a lawyer for three weeks.

"Ha ha," he said in a very sardonic voice, meaning that things were not at all funny. "It's tough," he added.

I looked at him. "That's interesting," I said, "because five minutes ago when you were sitting there, I was thinking, 'Dave looks tired.'"

"I am tired," he said. "I'm beat! I'm beat mentally and physically."

He recovered himself: "But regardless, I believe in what I'm doing and I'm not going to alter because of a lawsuit. It's—things can't get worse. They have to get better."

I asked what was the worst that could happen.

"They can harass us from now on," he said. "You know, collection. We don't *own* nothing. We don't *have* nothing. And as you know, most Klan leaders, I'm talking about leaders, are self-employed or don't work at all, you know what I'm saying?

"I don't mind saying, I'm not going to pay it. But they're waiting for us to just come down to their office, billfold in hand, say, 'Here, we made two hundred dollars this week, here's your hundred, bye, see you next Friday.' That's insane!

"Ed [another defendant] doesn't own anything, I don't own anything. The organization, I don't need to tell you, has nothing! I reported income on the Klan last year, I think, of thirty-five hundred dollars. You know what postage costs, printing costs, legal fees? Why, shit, we had expenses of I'd guess five thousand dollars. I tell you, it's a son of a bitch."

There were other losses. Much later in the interview, I asked him in passing whether he was going to get married, now that he was thirty-four. "I don't know," he said. "You know, it takes a real . . . Girls that will put up with this are hard to come by. You know, I thought I had one, this girl here I dated for three years, she lived here with me for about two and a half. She was a good girl, but you know, when she'd want to do something on the weekend, I'd say, 'Well, we got a rally.' You know. And if leaders don't go to rallies, members aren't going to go. They say, 'Well, hell, if he don't care enough to come, why should I?' And you know people expect the leaders to go to everything.

"And it's hard. And you know prior to a rally you got to go out there and get the grass bush-hogged [cut], you got to get literature distributed. You got to mail letters, you got to possibly hold a press conference. And then work and make a living, you know. And hell, you can only do so much. It takes a special person to put up with it. So I just don't know."

"You want to quit?" I asked.

"Yeah," he said. "It's history. Go on to better things."

"It's been a rotten year," I suggested.

"Oh, God," he exclaimed, "it's been horrible." But one more time he pulled himself back up. Referring to the Southern Poverty Law Center, which had brought him to trial for the events in Forsyth County, he added: "But, as I said before and I'll say it again. Having Morris Dees sue you is, in a sense, in essence, a compliment. To know that you have to be effective or they wouldn't have fooled with you."

Dave Holland and I talked a while longer at this final interview, and we ended up on a strange note. I thought I had gotten to know him pretty well, and it seemed to me that, beneath his racist talk, there lay a decent idea: that white Americans who were poor had real problems and that no one really spoke up for them.

I respect that particular idea. Our misperceptions about people who are poor intensify many problems. If we ask the average American white person who the poor people are, he or she will say that the poor people are blacks. It *is* true that the *proportion* of African-Americans who are poor is much higher than the proportion of European-Americans. But in sheer *numbers,* the bulk of the poor are whites. This only makes sense: The bulk of the population is white.

The Census Bureau's tabulation tells how many people lived in poverty in 1990:

	Number in Poverty	Percentage in Poverty
All Americans	33.6 million	13.5%
White	22.3 million	10.7%
Black	9.8 million	31.9%
Hispanic	6.0 million	26.1%

The white poor, in their millions, experience much pain but have become strangely invisible. (We will meet some of them in my interviews with the neo-Nazi youths in Detroit.) The white poor were visible during the Depression; Steinbeck wrote about the displaced dust-bowl farmers; other novelists had spoken earlier of immigrant poverty on the Lower East Side; James T. Farrell described the working poor of Irish Chicago. Poverty became a nonissue during the postwar boom; sociologists spoke of a new era in which affluence had melted away class differences. Poverty again became an issue in the 1960 presidential election campaign, with its discussions of white Appalachia, and especially with the 1962 publication of Michael Harrington's book *The Other America.* A major result was alterations in Social Security, to the benefit of the elderly. (Between 1970 and 1990, the proportion of elderly in poverty fell from 25 percent to 12 percent.) However, the dramatic emergence of militancy in the black inner city during the sixties captured public attention, both fearful and sympathetic. The picture of poor people became a picture of people of color. For decades now it has been possible to mobilize white taxpayers behind reactionary politicians who wave before them the image of the "welfare queen," the "welfare class." Those catch-phrases now connote a person of color, not a white.

The intensity of the image of the poor black person—the image used by both friend and foe—has blinded most of us to the presence of white people who are poor. They are invisible and unrepresented. My growing picture of Dave Holland had been that he really cared about this. I thought I could tape-record a clear expression of that concern, and so I asked a number of questions in those closing minutes about the nature of the fundamental problem as he saw it. Those questions did not produce the material I expected and led us instead to a discussion of Jewish ritual murder, the "blood libel" of the Middle Ages.

I asked Dave to articulate his central concerns. He agreed soon enough that his movement wasn't really concerned about black peo-ple: "Now, you know niggers have really taken a backseat to any-thing," he said. "I mean they're no problem anymore, I don't think. You're very well educated, you spot the problems, I think, revolving around finances now. For all people.

"It's gotten far off the subject of black and white. Actually, the phone messages, our literature, most of it is derogatory towards blacks. But I think that's, I think we and others just use it as a vehicle to attract possible decent people."

"So," I said, "you and I just might happen to agree on what the issues are, the real issues."

He agreed. "Yeah, as I say, the black-white issue is an old issue. And you have to change with the times. And I just think that the white-black issue is a outdated issue, it's . . . doesn't even exist any-more. But you have to use it for a vehicle to attract people. When, you know, we have our groups such as the Institute for Historical Review, Aryan Nations, the *Spotlight*, and others, I would say pos-sibly attracts the more refined. But again use the Klan as a re-cruiting ground. And a vehicle for street activity." (The Institute is a quasi-intellectual center for Holocaust denial; *Spotlight* is a mass-circulation publication for the quarter-million racist sympathizers.)

Despite all this, he next presented quite a hostile picture of the black community. Whites, he asserted, were not at all welcome in black settings in Atlanta. Moreover, downtown Atlanta was a scene where "I was down there yesterday, nine out of ten blacks laying in the street, bottle of wine—you just don't see white people doing that often. Where the black race has a general feel that they are inferior to that of whites, because they see their people out pimping, and they see their people out drunk, they see . . . these shows on TV about crack, ninety-nine percent of the people that are arrested are blacks. They done a week-long special on crack and I think during the whole week out of hundreds they showed were arrested, one guy was white." Blacks committed 90 percent of crimes, he said. "I just don't believe, I sincerely don't believe, that white people are as prone to violence as blacks. I just don't believe it."

I pointed out that he had said the problems are not really black and white, yet that was what he was talking about. He laughed and said he guessed he was a Klansman. "The Klan issue never leaves. And, you know, again, it's the vehicle to promote the cause."

And so one more time I asked him what the real question was. Now he told me that, as one of the movement leaders had put it, you could just leave the blacks out of it, they were not the problem, "those Jews are the problem, with their money, financing the civil rights movement." He talked one more time about Stanley Levinson as the driving force behind Martin Luther King, he talked about most Jews being behind the civil rights movement, but staying in the background. Jews, he felt, were anti-black, because they were a proud group of people. "But at the same time I think they see that blacks are, again, inferior to the Jews and they're using them as a vehicle to promote their cause. What I'm saying is they're integrating schools, integrating neighborhoods. While the Jews live out where the elite live. Very seldom, I think, you'll see a Jew living in a poor neighborhood. I'm not saying it doesn't exist, I'm just saying I can't recall any. And you know most of us—and when I say 'most,' I'm talking our movement—we picture all Jews as living up on top of the hill, you know, with a Rolls-Royce or Mercedes-Benz, which I'm sure is not the case.

"But as a general rule," he continued, "I think most Jews are shrewd, they're good businessmen. Possibly some of our people are offended by that because they haven't made, you know, good business practice. But I'll always believe that the Jews have used the blacks to intermarry blacks and whites. And you know that Jews have told their own children in no uncertain terms don't marry out of your race of people.

"People will say," he went on, "well, they're God's chosen people. And there's nowhere in the Bible that says that. Nowhere. Just to the contrary. But people just won't believe it, they believe what they've heard, and heard on TV and read in the newspapers. And you know most publishing companies, printing companies are owned by Jews. So they control what's printed."

I pointed out that Jewish numbers in the entertainment industry and media were not matched by Jewish numbers in the oil companies, the auto companies.

Dave sneered. "How many people deal with an oil company every day and how many deal with entertainment every day? Everybody deals with entertainment every day of the week. Turning on TVs, reading the newspapers. Why should our own country be influenced by the population of three percent of the people?"

I explained the historical roots of Jewish skills in these endeavors and pointed out that for similar reasons Jews were heavily represented in medical research. Would he rather have polio still a threat, I asked, and have Jonas Salk playing with a yo-yo somewhere?

He listened to this and my further explanation of Jewish historical involvement with learning. But it meant nothing. "I agree," he said. "But, you know, I . . . I guess myself and others are offended at, you know, most Jews are, again in my opinion, sympathetic to the communist movement, pro-abortion. And you look at a lot of the un-American things; it's not a new issue.

"The ACLU, which has a great influence on our legal system, is controlled by Jews." (Dave was at that time using with gratitude the services of a Jewish ACLU lawyer.)

He pressed on: "I just think Jews are influencing our country. *Our* country."

"Well, I hope so," I said, "because they have got pretty good values."

"I disagree. Completely," Dave said. "They have no morals in their own."

I pointed at the lower divorce rate, the lower illegitimacy rate, the lower crime rate than either Protestants or Catholics. "How can you stand here and tell me they have no morals?"

He claimed Jews ran 99 percent of pornography—yet were only 3 percent of the population. I said I had no idea whether that was true, but it seemed trivial, and I asked again how he could sit there and say the Jews don't have morals. He assured me that he meant it. I asked how many Jews he knew, and he said, "I don't associate with Jews," and laughed.

Then began the astonishing discussion of Jewish murder of Christian infants. Dave told me at this point that Dr. Ed Fields, the publisher of *The Truth at Last*, a racist tabloid formerly known as *Thunderbolt*, has a lot of information on Jewish ritual murders and sacrifices. He brought me an article from the tabloid about a young woman named Rachel who had appeared on the Oprah Winfrey show several years ago and who had spoken there of "the secret rituals of a small number of religious fanatics who follow the Chassidic" and had spoken of "ritual murder of infants by Jews." (*The New York Times* of May 6, 1989, describes this bizarre incident, when the show recklessly included a severely disturbed young woman.)

Dave was proud of having this to show me. "She's your people, though, right? I'll say one thing about it, buddy, when you read it in Dr. Fields, you've got the whole lowdown. This is the news oppressed by the daily press. Tell your people now what the real truth is."

I was astonished, because Holland, a man whom I knew well, appeared to accept these claims as truth. Was he just agreeing to words, or would he still accept the idea if we converted it to concrete detail? I decided to try to be sure of his views.

"What proportion of Jews do you think kill infants?" I asked.

"Very few," he said.

"Well," I went on, "how many Jews are there in the country?"

"I would say a million," he said.

There might be more than that, I told him. "But anyway, let's say there's a million. Out of that million, how many do you suppose participate in killing—"

"Nine hundred and eighty thousand!" he jested. Then he went on, "No, I would say a very small portion. Probably out of that, maybe twenty thousand."

"Only about twenty thousand," I echoed.

He said he understood what I was thinking, that I was thinking he was condemning the whole race for the actions of the few. I told him that if I thought twenty thousand Jews killed babies, I would be in the front ranks crying out about it.

He backed up. "You may have misconstrued, I may not have made myself clear. I think a lot of them, I would say that many, in my opinion, are sympathetic to it, I'm not saying actually practice the murder."

"But they're sympathetic to it," I echoed. "Little Christian children, babies."

"Right," he said. "Right. God's chosen people. So you see how violent your people are now. You know," he continued, "Fields, when he does these articles, he goes right to the source. He puts out a good publication, I mean honest to God."

"Right," I said, "but I still want to get it straight what you are believing. It is important to me to understand what you honest-to-God are believing. So, like, twenty thousand approve of, go along with, this murder of Christian babies?"

"Poor babies," he said.

"How many would you imagine get murdered every year?" I asked.

He was conciliatory. "I would say a small, smaller number. Fifty."

"Fifty," I again echoed.

He pointed out that he was answering with no basis, and I repeated that I really needed to grasp what was in his head. He said that he did "think and assume that Fields did get more facts." I told him that I was not concerned about Fields, but rather with him, Dave Holland, a man I had known for some time.

Again he said, "As I stated before, a lot of the information I receive such as that is in *The Truth at Last*. I told you. Fields does good research work. And he has the facts. The facts as I see them."

"But you are living in . . . If I believed what you believed," I said, "I sure wouldn't like Jews."

He agreed.

"They would have to be weird fucking people," I said.

He agreed again. "They're strange people."

I asked what the scene would be like at these killings—would the twenty thousand who enjoyed baby killing sit in circles of a thousand each watching one baby get killed? He jested about it, but then said that "the girl on the show" had said that it was happening in people's neighborhoods—that it might be happening anywhere—in the fireplace or in the back or in a bedroom. But that the point was that it was not him saying it or Fields, but "the Jew girl" on *Oprah!*

We went in and out of these loops a few more times, but the basic point was clear. Dave was willing to believe this story, at least at the moment when he read it in the paper and at least at this moment as we talked about it. It did not feel strange to him, even when I forced him to talk about it in detail. It was entirely plausible to him that thousands of Jews colluded in, or at least applauded, widespread Jewish slaying of Christian infants. I told him that it was depressing that he could really entertain such concepts in his head.

He responded, "I'm telling you what would really be depressing is to have to be around them. That would be depressing. Nothing could be more depressing than waking up in the morning seeing Jews and niggers around me; that would make me want to go back to bed." He claimed that my shock that he could believe these things was simply parallel to his difficulty in understanding how people could believe in the reality of the Holocaust. He attacked that reality again, adding that everybody was sick and tired of hearing about it.

At the very end, I returned us to my starting point. I asked whether his basic feeling was that the issues confronting working-class whites had to do with Jewish domination. He reported that people frequently suggested to Fields that he was harping too much on the Jewish issue. It's true, Fields would say, but the movement can't ignore the issue. "I think," Dave ended, "most people don't realize how a small number, three percent, the Jew people in this country, influence our lives."

I closed the discussion soon thereafter.

So did Holland truly believe that Jews killed infants? Or was it fun for him to upset me—was it a relief for him, when he was at this point so bedeviled by legal matters? To what degree was he teasing me? To what degree, on the other hand, had he bothered to think about the reasonableness of that psychotic woman's story? What is the truth?

I called him the next morning from the airport. He stood his ground; he still claimed to believe the story. My words fell from him; he would not hear. He was in a hurry for me to be on my way. Shortly he was interrupting to say, "Bye, Brother Rafe. Bye, Brother Rafe." Dave had been tormented enough; he wanted to be rid of me.

What does it mean that Holland can believe this grotesque image?

Partly, it means nothing. I have been around a long time. I know by now that most of us can believe any number of contradictory things at the same time. We are able to believe anything. A large literature in social psychology grew up a few decades ago suggesting that people need to have their beliefs be consistent. That literature, based on laboratory experiments, failed to distinguish between central beliefs and peripheral beliefs. It is most likely the case that we do need a few absolutely central beliefs and sentiments to have some unity; this unity may be the best test of the centrality of a belief. At the same time, however, we have no such difficulty with peripheral beliefs. They don't matter; the evidence surrounds us in every direction that people by and large give less than a damn about contradiction. People care about handling the demands of daily life and they care about taking care of their families. Period. They will believe whatever makes those things work well; the human mind is careless, lazy, and pragmatic; it cares about what works. Does Dave really believe that Jews slaughter babies? He readily can believe it at ten o'clock and doubt it at eleven; this is the nature of most of us.

But something is dreadfully wrong with your sense of who humans are if you can believe this of the people in the next town on so little evidence.

I began my study of white racists hoping to grasp their human character without losing sight of the evil consequences that flow from their actions. What do I make of Holland's mix of good and evil, honesty and evasion?

Dave's youth leaves him rather open. We get a sense of his center. Later, he will be hard, more callous, allow less closeness and thereby less understanding. The core that comes through is the *political* man who *acts*.

In our own mythology, we in the literate middle class want to see a white racist leader as a gibbering hate-demon, driven beyond his own control by inner spite and bile, driven by a hatred centered on race. Dave clearly is *not* driven beyond his own control, is not filled with vile hatred and bile, and is not driven by hatred centered on race.

Holland is a *political man*. He finds his core by *action*. He is good at organizing. He thrives on the hard work and complexity of devoted organizing. He thrives on being busy. It is critical to him that that activity is attached to a political end—that is, that he is mobilizing men, he is organizing a force that can find an opposition to confront.

It is extremely important to him that he has demonstrated that he can recruit men and can keep them. It is extremely important to him that he can move men's emotions as he speaks.

Holland has been a national leader in the making. He may or may not return to the fray. But this is the raw material from whom the long-term leaders are forged.

The core is *leading,* not race hatred. Dave Holland does not like blacks or Jews, but his dislike is pretty ordinary; he would not stand out in most white American circles.

Dave is fuzzy about the nature of his enemy when we are sitting back and talking. Whenever I try to point to the identity of the enemy and get straight Dave's enmity and the grounds for it, he slides off into trivia or repeats barely relevant scraps of movement pseudo-history.

When he is at rest, Dave has no intellectual focus regarding the enemy; lots of interchangeable images can be put in the slot; the category *enemy* lacks substance. In action, on the other hand, his mind instantly generates the necessary, full-bodied image. He can rant; he can flexibly, stingingly, direct barbs; he sees and can make his listeners see and take arms against The Enemy—the Establishment; the upper world; the world of the smug, fat, power-holding Them; those who run the world. Who are *they?* They are the same for all the leaders of the movement and probably for most white racist followers: They are those who rule and those who collude in that rule—the heads of corporations, the heads of government, the heads of churches, the heads of schools, those who run the media. Is that a racial image? Not really. That enemy is an amalgam of collaborating whites and Jews. Blacks are their pawns. The fundamental *racial* content lies in the identity of those *ruled*. The rulers aim their war at the whites, those whites who are outside the circle.

The racial content lies more in Holland's *We* than in his *They*. *We* are decent, hardworking, God-fearing, plain-spoken, honest white men and women. *They* are the smug rulers who take from us, have taken from us, will take from us. Who look down upon us. Who assume that they can take from us forever.

The cry must be one of the oldest in the world: *We are the dispossessed. Our rightful inheritance is taken. Damn those who have taken it.*

In a competitive society in which each day some must lose, bitterness will live always. And talented men will find careers—emotional careers based on concepts of identity—shaping and mobilizing bitterness.

All this is *reaction*. Holland cannot plan a *program;* there is no program, there is no strategy, for the same reason that there is no intellectual content. The movement is powerful because it contains all that bitterness; it is powerless because it has nowhere to go.

The deepest characteristic of Germany's Nazism was that it was dynamic. It was about nothing but itself. It lived only for its own action. Its goal was everything. And thus it killed itself, choosing the suicidal war with Russia when much of Europe lay already at its feet. Just so the American white racist movement is about nothing but its own dynamism, is only about conjuring up the image of the enemy, is only about feeling if only for a moment that one is fighting the enemy, fighting to regain one's inheritance.

All this is the material with which a talented man can work. And also the limits of what a talented man can do.

What brought this particular talented man, Dave Holland, to this particular engagement? Accident probably played a role, as in most careers. He seems to have bumped into the avuncular Mr. Venable at about the point that his own difficult, alcoholic father had died, a death that must have posed problems for the son.

Once in the white racist movement, Dave found quick success. That he was effective at rallying men must have meant a great deal for the child of an alcoholic father, and the brotherhood of men must have meant even more. There is the echo of the alcoholic's child in Dave's repeated references to people who are clean and decent, to uniforms that are well kept, and to his disgust with the disorderly and the unkempt.

I remember interviewing members of the first American team to climb Mount Everest, just prior to that assault. No one in our team of psychologists heard a word about the lure of extreme risk or other exotic motivation. What I heard in most stories was that a youngster had started going for walks and hikes, found them good, and kept extending them. The activity felt right; the hikes got longer and higher.

Just so, I think, the potential leader falls into the first encounter and finds it good; extends the involvement and keeps finding it good; and more and more finds his own worth *in the activity*.

Dave Holland is good-humored, energetic, and likable. He has built an organization that fosters contempt and violence.

SEVEN

Richard Butler:
Aryan Nations

Richard Butler, like Tom Metzger, has been organizing for decades, but Butler did not begin until he was in his forties; Metzger is harsh and militant, while Butler is worn out. Butler met me at a compound in Idaho. He took me to his office, grabbed some papers, and led me to a corner of his wooden church building.

I set the tape recorder down on a folding table filled with literature, we unfolded two metal chairs, and we began work. I looked at his wrinkles; his voice was reluctant and hesitant; but soon he got into the story.

Butler wore a sport coat, sweater, and tie. He might have been an aging, somewhat complacent minister anywhere. His voice was smooth but distant. He was talking directly with me, but I could feel his fairly deep disinterest. He was old and recovering from a heart bypass operation. More than that, however, the man I was meeting —when I talked with him in interviews, when I sat in the church and heard his Sunday morning sermons, and when I watched him conducting a regional conclave—was cold. Absorbed in himself.

I certainly understand his coldness to me. What use would he have for yet one more interviewer, especially a self-identified leftist Jew? And I understand better today than I did at the time how debilitating heart surgery can be. All the same, the extreme narrowness of his vision and the coldness of his tone when he was preaching and otherwise onstage for his followers—the self-absorption—always has made me wonder how he had become one of the most revered leaders in this movement.

The church building could have seated a hundred. In times past, the compound had swarmed. Now few people were around and on Sundays only fifteen or twenty came to listen. The organization was in shock and still reeling. The Order had had some of its origins here; Butler's group had not recovered from the violence and the trials with which that murderous cell was put down.

Although the church was almost empty, Butler preached every Sabbath and audiocassettes were mailed around the country. I asked for one after hearing Butler preach; there was much embarrassment and I was asked to wait a few hours till the tape was "finished." All became clear when I finally played the tape at home. On it, the sermon began after a rousing chorus of some lusty hundreds who were singing "Stouthearted Men"; at the actual event, twelve of us were present, and we preceded the pastor's words with a thin and trembly chorus of "Onward Christian Soldiers"—in my own recording of our real chorus, we sound to be the flimsy audience that we were.

Butler traveled extensively. He was a featured speaker at every important white racist conclave. Several other leaders have admitted to me that they found his actual speeches soporific, but all honored him for his long service and his devotion.

Some professionals among the anti-racist organizations credit Butler with a critical role in the late seventies and early eighties in bringing the Nazi and Klan elements together and in renewing the militance of the movement. They say he had a gift for work behind the scenes.

My interviews, taking place when he and his organization were at a low ebb, served to make clear the critical role of Christian Identity in the movement and the dangerous character of that doctrine. The interviews also shed light on Butler's personality.

Butler impressed me as representing a kind of old-fashioned, unthinking, smug racism that rests in total unsophistication. He seemed certain that life centered on himself and his kind, the sort who sees nothing except through the filters of his own parochialism. He seemed stubborn and self-righteous, obsessed by a strange doctrine.

The doctrine, of course, was Christian Identity. As I discussed earlier, Christian Identity is a doctrine, born in England, that claimed the "Aryan" peoples—the peoples of Northern Europe—were the lost tribes of Israel. All the stories in the Old Testament, the doctrine asserts, were stories about the Aryans, who had left Ur under their leader Abraham, gone to Egypt, and then had conquered Canaan. Expelled from there, they had settled Northern Europe. Also present in Palestine had been a thin rabble who were the real Jews; they lurked on the fringes; they built the golden calf. But none of the other people called Hebrews or Jews in the Bible were related to the people now known as Jews. The history of the white race thus is old and illustrious, and Jesus was an Aryan, not a Jew.

God, Identity tells us, is white. The white race, the Aryans, are His chosen people. The white God has now called his chosen people and drawn them together in America. Here they are to do His bidding, to fulfill His plan for them, which is the domination of the earth.

That domination is to include domination of the nonwhite people. The nonwhites are not the creations of God, the White Being. They are otherwise created. The dark races, the "mud people," result from the mating of people (whites) with animals. The other living group, the Jews, result from the mating of Eve with the Serpent, or Satan.

God's chosen Aryans are to rule forever over the mud people; God's chosen Aryans are to struggle to death against the spawn of Satan.

This odd doctrine ends up as a dangerous one. It preaches—and it is preached from hundreds of pulpits in the country—that whites and nonwhites are different in their essence. We are not the creations of one loving Father (or Mother); we are not possessed of souls that are made of the same stuff. We are different from one another at the very core. And, centrally, the core, the essence, the souls of the nonwhites are dumb, animal, and brute. The nonwhites should be ruled and should be tended, like cattle. And the core, the essence, the souls of the Jews are evil. The Jew should be destroyed.

This is lethal doctrine.

Butler began our first interview with a set piece that he obviously has told many times, a story of his political awakening—how the words of a simple black man, a Hindu, brought Butler to understand the destiny of the Aryans. Butler, stationed in India during World War II, was pulled into conversation by his bearer, an Indian named Jerum. Jerum told Butler about the independence movement among Indians and then brought Butler the *Rig-Veda* and several other books to read. Soon Jerum said to Butler, "Sahib, *you* represent the great Aryan race. You're a representative." Moreover, Jerum told him, Jerum also had Aryan blood.

"Now, wait a minute, Jerum," Butler cried, "you're as black as the ace of spades. You can't tell me that you've got Aryan in you."

"Oh, yes," Jerum said. "I've got mine traced back. I'm sure, back in the days when the Aryans ruled India, that I had some of it.

"The reason," Jerum went on, "we are where we are today—as you go through the districts, you see black people living among white and whatnot—is because we've mongreled our race."

This made a great impression on Butler. "You know," Jerum elaborated, "you're fighting your own race. You're committing suicide, your racial suicide."

Butler continues: "And here he was, I would say, probably twenty-one or twenty-two; he had been educated pretty well in the British school; he spoke the King's English and very accurately; but he understood and knew something that I hadn't even thought of. And he was very caught up in the fact, and tried to explain to me that Hinduism actually was part of the ancient Aryan religion, that they had modified it a lot and so forth, so he had done elaborate studying on this. Maybe he had at one time, I never really asked him. But he was going to become one of the gurus or whatever they have over there.

"And of course I was young myself, but later on I began to think about some of the things that he had told me. So sometimes I believe that he as much as anything else awakened my instinct. And it seems kind of funny that it would be one of these Indians. Now, his features were Aryan, the nose and the mouth, the lips and everything else, but he was just *black*. Blacker than the ace of spades.

"So he showed me, of course, the various classes, and we'd get into the caste system and he told me why it was, in order to preserve the racial integrity from the top on down, and they had all these various levels. But I think more than anything else, he made me understand that I better study. Show myself a proof, so to speak. And there was a lot of questions that I hadn't thought of asking or hadn't even thought of being asked."

This was a remarkable story, and Butler told it to me several times at interviews. It suited his clerical mode—words of salvation from an unlikely source. I recognized the smug white condescension—words of wisdom from the sleeping-car porter, from an unthreatening and powerless source who is not individuated at all. The white man can take the words of wisdom from the third-world personage—and simultaneously push the third-world person and that person's culture even more firmly downward; neither the person nor the culture is *seen*, nor is there any feeling that an effort to see should be made.

The story works as an allegory, and it fits Butler's taste for the exotic—strange, strange, he is telling us, that the words that brought this major figure to the struggle for white supremacy (or "white survival") come from the lips of a man "as black as the ace of spades."

Yet the roots of his conversion may have been developed even earlier, Butler tells us. As a child he had watched repeatedly a movie in which a German ace was downed, hoping each time that this once the German ace would win. More than this, he tells us, there was a matter of "The Red Napoleon," a story that was serialized in *Liberty* magazine when Butler was a boy.

"In my youth I used to carry [deliver] magazines," he said. "I'd carry the *Ladies Home Journal*, the *Saturday Evening Post*, and *Liberty* magazine, and so forth. I had a little route. This was back in Denver. And there was a fellow by the name of Floyd Gibbons, he was a great World War I reporter. He wrote this story called 'The Red Napoleon.' He had a great influence on me, I couldn't wait for the next issue of *Liberty* magazine to come out for 'The Red Napoleon.'

" 'The Red Napoleon' was about the Soviet Union coming in and conquering the United States. They come over the pole, they conquered the Canadian provinces, part of the Canadian provinces, and drove down in the Midwest, as I remember it now, through the plains and so forth. And the Americans were fighting in the Rocky Mountains and back in the Alleghenies, and it was really a mess, you know. He conceived of these diesel-powered airplanes that were really fast and the hero of the book was a pilot who was shooting down all the Russian airplanes and he was also a special mission man who was carrying secret orders here and there.

"The politically active part, as I say, probably had its beginnings in India where my thought process started to take shape. And yet it was back then, I could look back and see reading 'Red Napoleon' and a few things like that, and going to the movie, where perhaps maybe it was my genetic instincts that were there but they had never been awakened."

The other early influences on Butler may have included his parents. He spoke of a mother who took enormous pride in her heritage from Germany, tracing her lineage back to the 1600s. While his mother did not like Butler's political involvements, feeling that he would do better to keep on as an engineer in the family's aeronautical engineering business, the German heritage made an impression on Butler, whose sermons referred again and again to both Germany and the German-American community. Butler spoke little of his father—"He never had much of a political opinion, one way or another"—but Butler is fairly sure that his father was a member of the Klan in the 1920s. On the other hand, he pointed out, lots of people were Klan members then.

There were some fifteen or twenty years between Butler's pivotal encounters with Jerum the bearer and his conversion by Dr. Wesley Swift, the American father of Christian Identity. Returning to southern California from wartime service, Butler went to work in the family's machine shop but also became very active in a series of right-wing endeavors centering on anticommunism, especially the Christian Anti-Communist Crusade. These activities led ultimately, when Butler was about forty, to an encounter with certain American Legionnaires who told him that he "needed to go to church." Not so, Butler told them: "Ministers are nothing but mealymouthed lying windbags." The Legionnaires told him that Dr. Wesley Swift was different, but Butler did not yet hear the message.

The Legionnaires pressed the contact. At a critical meeting, they asked Butler, "Now, is communism a faith or is communism just a political party?"

It was political, Butler replied.

The Legionnaires disagreed. They told him that communism was a religious faith. They told him that communism was Jewish, plain and simple. "You really don't know your own faith, do you?" they said to him. And now he had to agree. Therefore, they told him, he really did have to go to church. Finally he went to hear Dr. Swift; he had agreed to go to the church just one time. Swift's impact was sudden and total. Butler had found his moment.

Butler even today is illuminated when he recalls Swift: "I finally agreed to go there one time. And I must say, when Dr. Swift spoke, he spoke in Technicolor. The words came out and you could just see in living color what he was talking about. You could—he was a master orator, just a master orator."

Dr. Swift, he said, "was a unique man. He had the photographic memory, total recall, the ability to speak and to put together a story form, as I said, in Technicolor. He was just absolutely fantastic.

"Now, he died when he was about sixty-one or sixty-two, he was on a circuit that, honest to gosh, I don't see how any man could have stood up under it. The speeches that he made all up and down California and into Arizona. And he had this circuit that was big all the time, constantly. And he would put a hundred thousand miles a year on a automobile. He had drivers driving it for him.

"I think all of us have a unique purpose, a singular purpose each of our lives. But his was a kind of a special one, he had a certain purpose, and that was to get out a story, to get out a message. And to make Identity live in the minds of people. Now, his tapes went all over the United States to the little groups, and I think right now the fact that what is called Identity, there's all kinds of brands of it—you find people in Arizona, in Florida, Arkansas . . . So it is this kind of spread, we're not numerically very big, I would say that perhaps a million people have heard of the Identity. How many of them are totally convinced I don't know, probably a tenth, a hundred thousand, I'm just saying, would be my guess.

"But there was never a man that could speak, that I ever heard, like Dr. Swift. Now again, Hitler was a great speaker; of course, I can't speak or understand German. Or Goebbels. [They] were supposedly both great speakers. Dr. Swift was not political, he was always theo-political, he always tied the movement of men, government, and so forth as part of God's eternal word and scripture. Of course, he went more into scriptures than most did, I mean he went beyond just the sixty-six books of the Bible, he went to some of the lost books of the Bible, and so forth."

What was it like, what was the experience, I asked, when Butler first started to hear Dr. Swift?

"Well, I tell you," he responded, "it was like . . . sitting there was like somebody turned on the lights. Just one after another. I'd anticipate a question I would like to ask, pretty soon he'd answer that question, pretty soon another one, he'd answer that in his speech. And you just—you know, just was a great thrill, just a great thrill."

I asked Butler whether he had gone to a conventional seminary.

"No," he said, "just with Dr. Swift."

"And he ordained you in his church?" I asked.

"Yes. I studied with him for about ten years. He had a magnificent library. Probably one of the greatest private libraries I've ever seen."

I asked what Swift had been like as a person. Butler replied vigorously, "He was jovial! He was the original pun man, he could make a pun out of anything you said. He laughed, he liked to laugh. He liked to go fishing. We always went out, we had a lot of fun with him. And he was very, very interesting to be around, very, very interesting. He had went and studied so much, and of course he had done that ever since he went to college. And he was a very brilliant conversationalist."

The involvement with Swift was a great change for Butler. "As my wife will tell you, I was very anti-church." He and his wife had been raised nominally in the Presbyterian church, he said, but had had little to do with it later. His wife got him to go to church a few times after their marriage, but he found the minister there a new young fellow who preached progressive doctrines. What he preached, Butler said, was communism. The man was what Butler called "a liberal one-worlder" and had adopted a child who was "an Oriental and black mixture." The minister one Sunday began a sermon about the

United Nations and Butler simply walked out; the couple didn't return to church.

With this background, Swift was a revelation. "That was my religious background, it was just the fact, up until Dr. Swift. And then I became a believer. I became one who understood who I was, where I came from, and why I was here. I became one who read diligently, started reading the Bible, started searching for myself in the Concordances for the meaning of words, and then started reading secular history—*really* reading secular history, to see if the things Dr. Swift was telling me were true, and I found out, hey, it came through. We have a race of people who by their tribes and various divisions of the family had gone over and done these things, you know."

Halfway through our first interview, I finally realized the function that Identity theory played for Butler and his followers. I had told him that I found the belief system strange, but could see that it was important to his movement. It was, he said; it was "the *heart* of it.

"See," he continued, "what we never had, say in the old Klan, which was the white man's organization, and they claimed to be Christian, but they didn't know why. Now, what I seen," he said, "I used to travel with this old Army fellow, a colonel, back in '62, '63, and '64, and we went all through the South, and he was giving Identity messages and so was I, to the limit of my understanding. Various Klan members through the South.

"And of course at that time the Klan was pretty big, comparatively. But my observation," he said, "was the Klan would go, and they would fight for the life that their race—in other words the constitutional issues, the political issues that they seen was being forced upon them. And then on Sunday—the South was a deep religious group, the Bible Belt . . .

"So what would you have? You'd have the Klansmen putting forth their rhetoric, putting forth their understanding that the Constitution of the United States, and what they felt their national state was, was being destroyed—and then on Sunday they'd all go to church, they'd hear a minister like the ones I heard, telling them that they were going against God, that they were contrary to the godly order.

"And it was tearing them *apart*. Six days they were one thing and then the seventh day, why, here would be another side, whatever this character's name was, he called himself a preacher in the Presbyterian church, and tear them apart. So the Klan was being tore apart.

"Ideologically, they didn't have the foundation to stand on, the way it was set up. So, what the colonel did, and of course Dr. Swift did, was give them the foundation that they could believe and know within themselves, yes, this is right, this is true."

I listened intently. I had puzzled for some time over the utility of this belief. "You're giving me some understanding which I have been looking for," I said, "because I have not understood. Who cares? my feeling has been," I went on. "What difference does it make, what difference does it make whether the lost ten tribes disappeared in Assyria or whether they became Eskimos, or Danes—what possible difference does it make today, why would anyone bother? I don't mean to offend you, but I've been looking for someone to explain to me why it matters."

"The matter is the preservation of the race and the culture," he said.

If I was hearing him right, I said, the colonel and Swift and he had been able to *give an identity* to the white racist movement.

He agreed. "That's what they haven't had, they didn't have any identity, they didn't have any *reason* why they should be separate, segregated. The word of God gives you that reason. From beginning to end you are a separated people."

But even so, I asked, what does it matter? If you were a white racist and you did believe that the races were separate, why would one need this background, what does the ancient history matter? His answer added little, but I was content with the story of the travels through the South. The legend and myth had served a clear purpose. An action-oriented movement that expressed itself in divisive acts deeply at variance with Christian concepts of brotherhood and sisterhood had been given a strong justification for its schismatic behavior. God had created this people, this white race, as His special children, set in His image, with a particular mission: that of dominating the earth (curiously enough, the goal they attribute to the

Jews). His people, the whites, were called upon by God to preserve their dominion over the lesser races.

I was very interested in Butler's story of organizing in the South, and I tried to picture how it worked and to figure how it meshed with Butler's workday life as an aeronautical engineer. I asked how he had found time to design airplanes and to go on the road. "Well, I had my own machine shop," he said. "You know, my father had a machine shop during the war, then he passed away and then I inherited the machine shop. So I could take off whenever I wanted to. And the other fellow, he was on a pension from the Army and he could go. And he had worked also for a mutual fund, he made some money doing that."

Butler had been about forty years old then and had gone out proselytizing very soon after meeting Swift. "Within a year," he said, "I was full force. After the war I had been, during the time I was running the machine shop, I had been studying communism and anticommunism, I was constantly trying to awaken our people, to say something's really wrong out there. And the '54 decision [*Brown v. Board of Education,* on desegregating the nation's public schools], I started saying, hey, there's something wrong, we're losing, you can't have two people be citizens of the same country at the same time, you know, two races."

I asked him to paint a picture for me: "If I try to imagine a day when you're out on the road there, what happens? What's it look like, sound like?"

"This Army fellow knew a lot of people," he said. "It was a lot of fun, we enjoyed it, I enjoyed it, going down through the South. We'd go, we'd stop and see people along the way who had been on Dr. Swift's tape list. And we'd meet them, and they'd say, 'Well, look, stay over, and we'll have a bunch of friends come in.' So we'd talk to them."

"So somebody would gather people in the living room and the two of you would explain to them the Identity message?" I asked.

"Right. That was how we did it. We went to Klan meetings. We had a big Klan meeting in Alabama and we spoke there."

"Had folks heard anything like it before?"

"No," he said. "They hadn't heard much of it at all."

"They must have been very surprised when you started," I said.

"They were. They're in the Bible Belt, they have been taught, you know, the so-called orthodox traditional way, and yet when they started reading the Bible from the point of view that we had given to them, why, there it was, it made sense, you know."

Butler, like most of the racist right, bases himself in a crude social biology. He takes for granted that races exist, that one meaningfully divides people by that label, and that races have distinctive characteristics (in his case, divinely ordained) that express their natures, and that the law of nature is struggle to the bitter end. He spoke repeatedly of a concept he called "Life Law" and was proud of having helped develop that idea. I had asked at the beginning for him to describe the central mission of his organization; it was, he said, to carry "the law word of our Father and God to my people, my race."

What was that word? I asked, and he replied that it was the Life Law.

The American founding fathers, he pointed out, had spoken of equality before the law. They meant by this the white race, he said, the free white race. They had not considered blacks or Orientals or others. There was no *hatred*, he pointed out; even today there was no hatred of them.

"When you really think of it, yes, *I can't hate the cattle down in that field there,* I can't hate anything that exists on the face of this earth. I just can't; they are what they are. And that's part of my Father's creation.

"He created them, fine. And we use them, not to abuse them. We're supposed to protect them, give them their chance, their staff of life.

"Of course, we know the jungle, that the lion will eat the rabbit, and the rabbit doesn't have any right. He doesn't have any right to life, he has a right to use the endowments that nature and the genetic program have, to save his life. In other words, to run down the hole when he sees something coming after him, a coyote or something."

He told me then he and his group had produced several booklets on Life Law, one of them authored by a principal member of the Order. He rummaged about to find one, from which he read me a paragraph:

There exists no such thing as rights or privileges under the laws of nature and nature's god. The deer which is stalked by a hungry lion has no right to life. However, he may purchase life by obedience to his nature-ordained instincts for vigilance and flight. So today men have no rights to life, liberty, or happiness. These circumstances may be purchased by oneself, by one's family, by one's tribe, or by one's ancestors, but they are nevertheless purchased and are not rights. Furthermore, the value of these purchases can only be maintained through vigilance and obedience to natural law.

Pastor Butler found this pretty significant as he read it. It does challenge things one may have believed when in first or second grade. In any case, it led him down the racial path.

"Now, this probably may be a little unusual from the standpoints that you've been used to. But as we look at the laws of nature, the laws of the universe, more and more we've become certain that this must be. We are flesh and blood, we live on this earth as a species, and each species lives its own culture.

"And as I've said many times in my sermons, robins are programmed to be robins and they have been for what, sixty million years or how many ever. And when you think about it, the genetic instincts or the genetic programming, like a computer program, is a program from the egg into the robin back to the egg and so forth. He builds his nest the same way—he's never seen the nest built, he was never instructed to build nests, but as he grows up, he selects another robin and they come, build a nest, lay the eggs, and go through the life cycle. And they never have any thought of—you know, a male robin doesn't look over at the meadowlark and say, "Hey, I'd like to marry her." No, he automatically goes to the robin. So he has no thought power, only *we* have the will to disobey or to break nature's laws.

"So I think that was what the garden scene was all about in the first chapter of Genesis. 'Of all these trees you may eat, freely eat, but of the tree of knowledge of good and evil, you may not eat.' And when Eve and Adam disobeyed this, this is where we've got our problems here today. [Later we will find that the disobedience he refers to is miscegenation.] And until we learn to understand that we must, we are—our very existence, the only thing that keeps us living here is—we must obey certain ironclad rules in the laws of nature.

"And if we disobey them, we will be like lemmings, we'll all run off into the sea and destroy ourselves. But of course there's always the lemmings come back in a few years' time and they do the same thing over again. And, of course, we see like the book of the Judges, the Israelites would get free and would sink down with the same depravity and come to the point where there's no swords left in Israel and they're really under the Philistines and they are having a real heck of a time, and then there comes along a man and he raises them.

"The root of the problem," he explained, "is that we as a race have been led away from our natural ordained Life Law position and we're now the seed of our own destruction.

"The natural Life Law position is that we should—to have our community, to have our territorial imperative—we must have our race as the center of all things, we must know our history, we must no longer be deceived by people saying, 'Well, mongrelization is fine.' We must come back to the original Life Law that all of our ancestors had, because we wouldn't be here if our ancestors hadn't practiced it.

"So, biologically, we know, you have to have a territorial imperative for a species to live. This doesn't mean that robins don't exist in the same forest with the blackbirds and whatnot, but it means that their territorial imperative of their food chain and everything has to be, so that they can operate. The wolf has the same thing, the eagle has the same thing, and so forth.

"Each race, each part of our species, has a cultural inheritance that is passed on to them that is their ultimate being. In other words, in Africa, in Haiti, or any place else they have their natural priesthood order that evolves and they have their cultural attainments—*to me it doesn't seem too much culture, but they do* [Butler's emphasis]— they have their own cultural attainments, their own lifestyle. And I think this was exemplified when the Congo was returned back to them, the Belgians were taken out and the troops were taken out and so forth. And immediately they dispense with the Catholic church where they had it there for a couple hundred years. And the former bishops and that, they took over as priestcraft, the witchcraft priests, and they even ate some of the nuns and priests that were left there, the white nuns and priests. But actually, it isn't to blame them, they were returning back to what they inherently know, are inherently born.

"So I think we have to recognize things as they are. So looking at them inside, you see each one is programmed and they each have these value systems that is inherent from when they were created. In my view. That is why they are Japanese, this is why they are Chinese, this is why they are blacks, and there is different levels of attainment.

"Now, Hitler put it his way; he said there are the culture creators, the culture maintainers, and the culture destroyers."

He spoke finally here of the role of the white race: "The white race was to be light bearers of the world." Or, again, "The issue is that we must live up to our first responsibility, which is that we're to subdue the earth and have dominion, which is the first chapter of Genesis. And in righteousness. And we haven't even begun to accomplish that, and I think that was the purpose we were put here for. In the image of the most high God to have dominion. So, we can have dominion if we follow His righteous law. But if we don't, why, of course, we are in danger of extinction or something."

This struggle for survival was the theme of the discourse. Again and again, the alternatives were posed. The whites—progressively undermined by corrupters, progressively weakened—must gird themselves, the whites must struggle with the enemy, the whites must conquer or be destroyed. We stood at an End Age and were dealing in an issue of natural selection.

There was an ultimate split between the races in nature and in destiny, he said, and there was a purpose to this—a testing. And so "we have two sides. The ultimate split. The object between the two of them is domination, world domination."

What were the two sides? I asked.

"The two sides," he replied, "the ultimate split between communism—what is called communism—Marxism and Judaism is the ultimate split."

On the one hand, I said, you have Marxism, Judaism. And on the other hand you have what?

"Well, you could call it Identity or white racialism."

Where was everybody else in that picture? I asked.

"Well, I think everybody else is the pawns in the game. In other words, the Japanese, the Chinese, the African, the Indian, and so forth are all being affected by this titanic battle. But nevertheless they are just the victims of the indiscretions of either side as we go along.

"Now, if I'm right," he went on, "or if all of us are right we have said this thing, we are the chosen, or the sons and daughters of God.

"Now, today, of course, we are very much in the minority, very much put down; the media and the academics, your schools here, is all opposed to this tiny segment. Which is true. Now, when Hitler took over Germany, he took over the news media, over the educational system and everything else, and run it the way to benefit, as he saw fit. When the Jews take over, they are going to do it for them, as is natural.

"Why shouldn't they? It's natural. Obviously when you're in a battle you're going to use whatever you can use and get the position that you want to get, you know.

"And I don't think that there should be hatred. You know, in the war you really don't hate the guy out there, the other side that wears a different uniform. It's just the fact that he's a threat, it's either you or him."

But then, I said, if I heard him right, either the Jews or Identity would attain power.

"Yes," he said. "World power. And that's the end of the story of the battle.

"Now, what I've tried to portray here," he said, "is the true thought pattern. The great majority of the world, the great majority of Christians, believes that the Jews are God's chosen people and that at the ultimate end they convert to Christians. Which is an insane position.

"It now practically dominates the world, the Soviet Union practically dominates two thirds of the land surface of the earth. England is no longer a factor, no longer a power. France is disunited, Germany is a conquered nation.

"So there is only left the North American continent, where there still exists the fighting will of a few of the white race. Now, if we are conquered completely, then it means that the world will be run on the Marxist-Zionist principle. It would be the end of the story.

"If we do hold true, and there's a lot of biblical support for this, that, for instance, George Washington's vision, that we will be at a point where we will be almost conquered, almost through, and then the brilliance of a thousand suns will come on and we'll get some help and have a victory."

I said to Butler that I didn't hear God in this story anywhere.

"Oh, yes," he said. "He is, God is there. He is the controller. And, of course, it's inconceivable to me that we could lose.

"We are engaged in this great tremendous battle," he said. "The battle has several purposes, one the natural selection to weed out the weak, the ones who are susceptible to the bribe, susceptible to the things of this world. That get caught up in—today, whether they are called the Yuppie generation or so forth. You know, they would sell their own mother for a quarter.

"The ending of the war in May of 1945 was the defeat for the white race," he continued. "The white race lost the war."

Hope lay, he said, in trying to get the message across. "I don't think, you see, two thirds of our people are never going to hear the message. They hear words, a dog could hear words, it could hear sounds, they can hear a lot better than I do. But you see there's a difference between hearing and comprehending.

"Some writer, I forget, some writer, he said that our people are practically to the point where they cannot carry a thought through to a logical conclusion. I think television has mesmerized them up to the point that they can't hold a thought, take that thought, and then think it through to a logical conclusion. And I think a lot of our people are that way. I think a lot of them are totally lost. *Drugs, alcohol, and women* have destroyed the *manhood* of two thirds of the white race, really. Two thirds of the white race is mentally castrated."

Butler dealt in the end with the question of the Jews—their identity and their nature. He began with a historical note. The Jews, he said, "are our adversaries." He pointed out that throughout history, "for good or evil, back in the Middle Ages and on, every once in a while, whether they were in Poland or in Germany or in England or something, the people would rise up and they'd say: 'All Jews out! Go!' "

(Like most racists, Butler takes the centuries of attack on Jews as proof that something must be wrong with the Jews. What is wrong with Jews that excites these endless attacks? the racists ask.)

The Jews, he went on, never had a place of their own. This held, he said, if one accepted Identity's position that Israel, Jerusalem, "was of the white race. That those who came out of Egypt were the white race and not Jews.

"Now, Jews came with them, if I read the Scriptures right, because it said that many of the strangers also came with the children of Israel."

Do you think that those strangers were the Jews? I asked.

"I feel that some of them were the Jews, right," he said. "I think that the strangers could be anybody, but *my* view is that yes, they were the Jews. I think we've had the Jews with us ever since the garden scene, ever since Cain and Abel we've had Jews."

This confused me. Where were they in the garden scene? I asked. I did not realize the Pandora's box this question was to open.

"Well, in that scene," he said, "I think that Cain was the product of Eve and of the Devil or whoever Lucifer was. The Devil is actually a God. The Devil is a God, in other words.

"I *believe that their God is our Devil. And our God is their Devil.*"

This was astonishing. "We have," he continued, "two different perceptions of God."

I asked what was meant by "Devil"—did he mean the absence of God, or was Devil an entity?

"Well, the Devil is an entity," he avowed, "inasmuch that he has children and God has children.

"It is there: *the ultimate split.* So we have two opposites, we have the opposite of which, we, which gives us the enmity between the Jews and between the—what do you call us, we are the *goyim,* or the *goy,* which just means nations—the ultimate split."

I tried to put this together, hoping that I wasn't understanding. In the garden we have, then, the Devil, I prompted him, and he picked it up: "Okay, in the garden we have what—we had Adam and Eve, and the voice of God coming to them, stating that of all the trees of this garden you may eat, but of the tree of the knowledge of good and evil you may not eat, for in the day that you do you shall surely die. So then next we find Eve being taken in and eating of the fruit of the garden."

I asked whether the Serpent appeared in the words of Genesis. He said yes, "In Genesis it appears as a Serpent, right."

"And is the Serpent the Devil?" I asked.

"Yes," he said, "right, that's just a form. That was a seduction of Eve where she said the Serpent did deceive me."

"And the Jews are the children of the Serpent and Eve?" I asked.

"The serpent and Eve, right."

In a later interview, Butler made quite clear that he meant what he was saying. Eve had made love with the Serpent, to produce the Jews. "In my understanding, in my understanding of 'beguiled,' I believe the seduction was a physical seduction. She was seduced as, you know, a woman of today could be seduced. And it was the first law-breaking, the first major law-breaking."

In the current interview, I needed still to check again. "This concept still startles me," I said. "I've heard many things said about Jews, but I haven't before had it suggested that we were the children of snakes."

That phrasing rattled Butler. "No," he said, "the Serpent, no, the Serpent is also—if you look it up, they are not children of snakes literally, but they are the ones who are the *opposite* of what the children of God are. So the Devil is the one who is Judas, in other words they deviate from the norm, we're taught.

"And I don't look at it, see, as—in other words, the meaning— when I was a kid, I used to box, in amateur boxing, and I boxed with Mexican fellows, with a black and so forth, in California as a young man, years ago, growing up. And I didn't look on him with hatred or anything else, it was adversary and I was in the ring and I was trying to do my best to fight him, and he was trying to do his best to knock me out. But I don't know how I can explain it but in this war, I look at it as this, there is the *purification* of my race."

"The struggle is for purification?" I asked.

"The struggle, right," he said. "And I believe that all of life is a struggle." Butler was comfortable again by now; he had gotten to familiar ground. "Without struggle, why, there wouldn't be anything. In other words, we are set forth upon this earth, everything has to struggle to live.

"But I think this," he said, "that there's only a small amount of my race that's going to live through the final conclusion. The ones that do are going to be the ones who have been the purest of heart.

"I think that in a Resurrection, yes, you will see Rudolf Hess. You will see a lot of the SS. A lot of the people. That's my perception of it. Now whether we'll recognize them as SS or as Rudolf Hess I don't know. But what I'm saying is the entity that will go to their death believing and in every essence of their being that they were right and true in what they tried to do and to live was something that they couldn't go back on. In other words, they were strong enough in their character, strong enough in their will, that they were actually obedient to what Jesus said, was fear not that which could destroy the body, but fear that which could destroy the body and the soul or the spirit."

As this talk wore on, my heart had grown increasingly heavy. The set of concepts was unusually dangerous—as I said to him, he was positing the Jew as *opposite,* as in positive/negative, or as in electron/proton, and it made acts like those of the Order take on a sense of necessity. This is a doctrine that says the Other is not human; the Other is Enemy; the nonhuman must be killed before it kills.

Sitting in this funny little church building, hearing this propagandist comfortable with his truly dangerous concepts, depressed me suddenly and sharply. "You have to give me a second to let this sink in," I said. "It makes me very sad to hear you say this whole set of things."

He was not fazed. "It *is* sad," he said, "it is sad in a lot of ways. But this is the *struggle,* we're in a struggle. We have been losing for seventy-five or eighty years or probably more. My race has been losing, we've been losing, no question about it.

"If I am right," he said, "and I believe with every fiber of my being in it, that ultimately a small part of our race is going to come through. And be the sons and daughters of most high God."

I closed the interview and drove away. My mood was grim. Butler has worked in the white supremacist movement for decades, bringing the Nazi wing into alliance with the Klan, spreading his doctrine, planting his seed. The stupidity and the ignorance appalled me. I was driving through incredible countryside, a high plain among the hills, and its beauty mocked me. How many people had been killed over the centuries in the name of such ignorant claptrap! How easy and careless this old man was, spinning his self-indulgent fairy tale, investing his life into gathering together the bitter and disappointed and teaching that we who were not white heterosexual Christian men were subhumans or snakes to be crushed with the heel of the boot.

There will always be an audience. There will always be a following. Humans need to feel dignity, and this fairy tale is as easy to believe as any. Humans will believe anything that makes them feel good.

As I thought of Butler, I kept thinking: *Self-indulgence.* His ease sickened me.

EIGHT

Reflections

Here are three leaders, then. First, Metzger, who is tough and knows himself, a man with considerable imagination, a man relatively free of conventionality, an effective and dangerous man. He is intelligent, flexible, and determined. He will adapt to new conditions and probably create new forces for decades to come.

Second, Holland, a young man who likes people—at least, familiar types of people—and wants people to like him. Like Metzger, he has no boss and depends on his own energy to earn a living. His way with people, his unassuming confidence, his enormous energy, and his taste for action quickly won him lieutenants, followers, and a reputation.

Holland is much less cynical—so far—than Metzger. He grew up in a more recent time and knows that racist statements don't sound right; more than that, he has real respect for the skills of black American organizers. At the same time, he is a Southern boy and really doesn't think highly of black people. Holland has genuine class loyalty that Metzger pretends to have; Metzger in fact cares only for himself but wants to use class loyalties; Holland likes people and could have been a good union organizer. Holland knows people and how they work. He has not read much, on the other hand, nor had much education, and he is not likely to come up with original ideas nor to move beyond run-of-the-mill movement thoughts.

Holland lacks the fanaticism of most longtime major leaders and

probably will not reach their first rank—he simply will not persevere.
If he sticks it out, hard times probably will sour him. More likely,
however, he will remain slightly involved and find a new vehicle in
time for companionship and for advancement. I have presented him
in detail because his present openness lets us see the mental processes
of a potential leader at an early stage. He lives in an absurd mental
world but receives enough friendship and adulation in that world
that he does not notice its absurdity.

Third, we have the aging, shallow Pastor Richard Butler. Butler's
success is attributable partly to his skill as a negotiator and concili-
ator among leadership factions, according to several observers. It also
is attributable to the kinds of people who are ready to be followers.
Among the great variety of people to be found in the movement,
quite a few are earnest, a bit simple, a bit lost in the contemporary
world, and lonely. Many grew up in families and towns where fundamentalist Protestant axioms were taken for granted. The idea that
there is a God—male, muscular, and white—who cares intimately
about the acts of each of His creatures; the idea of a death struggle
between Good and Evil; the idea that every act of a man's life (and
possibly an occasional act in the life of a woman) has consequence
in that awesome march to the End Days—these conceptions, central
in the emotional atmosphere of the movement, are familiar and comfortable to many who have grown up in a fundamentalist culture;
the call to join the Lord's struggle resonates with their souls.

Pastor Butler himself seems to have grown up in a fairly nonde-
script culture, but he believes what he is saying. He is very tired,
however, and at times in interviews it seemed he was on automatic
pilot. I could hear him more genuinely in his sermons, and they were
the sad claptrap of a third-rate mind. The intricacies of Christian
Identity doctrines had given him an inviting garden of weeds in which
to wander and become absorbed; he had not been pushed into any
hard thinking and seemed rather atrophied.

What distinguishes a major leader from a minor one—why do some
men rise? Why does one man remain a follower in the movement,
another become a lieutenant, another a local leader, and another a
major leader? At every level you have to be comfortable with racist

ideas. Intelligence—or at least cunning—is needed in greater quantity at each successive role. Sheer perseverance is highly important. You must be able to inspire some trust. Most important, you must have audacity.

The appearance of courage is critical; followers must be able to believe that they are enrolled in a combat organization. The reality of courage also matters. You can't rise by being deferential or thoughtful. A man must thrust himself forward. He must seize positions, stake claims, stick out his chin. High positions are dangerously visible. Police units, from local to federal, keep close tabs these days on racist groups. (Publicized actions against dramatic groups help police units win funding.) A prominent leader can expect to serve prison time at some point.

Most important of all, a leader must have a personality that allows followers to believe. He has confidence. If he has doubts, they are brought out only in privacy. But probably the appearance is the reality: He *is* at ease. At some point in his life he has committed himself to the role. He has understood that life is risk. He has decided to *act*. His courage originates in that decision. He has put everything on the table. Nothing is held back.

The bulk of men are unsure, know their doubts, know their fears. They are glad to give the leader their allegiance—to share his certainty. Men want to be able to believe.

All this would apply, I think, to any political or religious leader. Religion and politics are spheres where most action has to do with faith, not with data, and leaders will always be those whose bearing permits followers to believe.

The white supremacist leader has additional characteristics. He works inside a movement that basically is secret, that is an alternative form of society. His life is a direct challenge to conformity and convention; he is not a likely candidate for corporate middle management. By instinct he is led to the life of the lone wolf. He draws to himself somewhat similar men with somewhat less courage.

If I were on my way to a first meeting with a white supremacist leader whom I had not previously seen, I would expect the interview to gradually reveal that this man—and, again, significantly, it is always a man—sees himself at core as a very special person with a special destiny. He would let the charismatic power of that conviction draw men to him, but would also half veil it lest it offend them.

I remember from childhood that sense of special destiny, and I think it is a common fantasy of childhood. The white supremacist leader may be a man whose conviction as a boy was deeper or more firm, or who avoided those disillusioning encounters that teach the rest of us that we are not magic. The white supremacist leader has proven successfully to himself that he *doesn't* have to make it in the ordinary world. He has taken risks while acting out the strange role he has created for himself, one in which he plays out a declaration of war on mainstream society. Successful actions while taking risks convince him that he is right. He has tried out his style on a small world he creates, and on the sector of the mainstream world with which he interacts.

He avoids distracting entanglements; he builds a small world, mostly of followers, that confirms him; he avoids entanglements that would cause doubt.

What kinds of people are drawn into the movement as followers? We shall now look at the lower ranks of the movement, meeting the members of a Detroit neo-Nazi group and their small-time leader.

Part Three

DETROIT

NINE

Introduction

The leaders draw their following from many kinds of settings, among which are isolated pockets of whites remaining in the inner cities. A block or two, or even a house or two, in the midst of an African-American neighborhood will hold several white families that were too poor to join the general white flight to the edge of town or the suburbs. The adolescent males in these houses have been especially vulnerable to white racist organizing. White racist ideas and the comradeship of the organizations give them desperately needed reassurance.

The following chapters present a series of portraits from the Death's-Head Strike Group, a neo-Nazi group built from such young men in Detroit. The portraits arise from my interviews with and observation of the members. You can see here the kinds of lives and thinking that lead a contemporary young white kid in an industrial city into a militant white racist group. We need additional studies from similar and contrasting settings, but my experience tells me that the lives and mental patterns displayed in the Detroit group are frequent throughout the white supremacist movement.

These chapters will sound different from the earlier ones, however. The fear of black people is squarely at the center of the lives we are about to explore. These recruits live in a world in which African-Americans are the majority. (Some of them estimated to me that black people made up 60 or 70 percent of the American population.)

The extreme economic vulnerability of their single-parent families underlines their terror. The white supremacist movement—for a while, at least—is a lifeline for these kids. Their involvement, focused on the fear of blacks, is distinct from the national white racist leadership's central thesis that "the Jew" is the real problem. Hatred and fear of black people has been part of these Detroit kids' upbringing; Jews haven't been relevant to their lives. The white racist movement has to educate these urban poor recruits into anti-Semitism; by and large they have little idea who the Jews are or were and why they should be feared.

The Death's-Head Strike Group arose in the late 1970s when a young man named Paul Madden led a few friends away from an earlier neo-Nazi group active in Detroit. Paul and his friends were restless under the earlier group's leadership; they felt that the commander didn't appreciate their ideas, wanted too much discipline and subordination, and was uncomfortable with their conduct and shabby clothing. They were convinced, moreover, that he was siphoning dues and profits from book sales for his personal use. Paul and his friends had originally seen themselves as a protective security force for this older fellow; they now separated and created their own group, with insignia taken from the German SS.

Paul was the oldest of the people involved, but at the time of the split had around him several people close to his age, then about twenty-five. These older members had fallen in the five years before I met Paul, but the group had grown nevertheless, pulling in clusters of very young recruits from three separate neighborhoods. The group was at the height of its activity, holding frequent public demonstrations, often once a month. Paul usually made sure that the media were alerted to a forthcoming demonstration, so that counterdemonstration was guaranteed. Paul took great pride in successfully taunting counterdemonstrators into crashing through police lines to attack, so that the counterdemonstrators would be arrested. The group also performed literature drops, fanning out into neighborhoods to put leaflets with white racist pictures and slogans under windshield wipers or on porches. There does not seem to have been much vandalism in the years of our interviewing and only a little graffiti-spraying. While the group took great pride in calling itself "street-active," there seems to have been little violence.

Every year several members of the group went with Paul to the south Michigan farm of Robert Miles for his autumn or spring gathering. These were gatherings similar to the Aryan Nations congress in Idaho—leaders from the Midwest and farther afield gathered for two days, sitting on metal folding chairs in a large Quonset hut Miles called the "Hall of Giants" to hear speeches, and gathering in Klan robes, brown- or black-shirted Nazi uniforms, or Levi's during the evening for a cross-lighting in his back acres. The gatherings gave Paul and other members heavy doses of education in the white racist movement's party line, and the ideas and slogans they picked up would be taught to those who hadn't made it to the farm. You would hear identical ideas from everyone in the group, and quite frequently with identical wording; I heard again and again that homosexuality was wrong, that "if God had intended homosexuality, he would not have created Adam and Eve, but Adam and Steve."

My active research with the Strike Group went on for three years at a time just before I began meeting national leaders. The picture here is of the group a few years ago, but there is no reason to think interviews today would be particularly different. Some of the interviews of members were held in their homes or in a community center; others were at the leader's house. Several other members might be in the leader's kitchen while I spoke with the interviewee, or even in the same room reading movement literature, but I found no signs of self-censorship in those interviews. At its peak, the Strike Group had a nucleus of seven to ten members, with ten or fifteen others in looser connection. I held repeated interviews with almost all of these people. Still another ten or fifteen friends could sometimes be mobilized for a specific action, but the steady membership was the seventeen to twenty-five of the center and its first outer ring.

The group did not have regular meetings, but the members spent the bulk of their time with one another. The group was made up of three or four friendship circles, representing neighborhoods and periods of joining. People in those clusters saw each other almost every day. And almost everyone in the core made his way to Paul's house, which was the center of the group, every other day or so. There was constant checking in with each other in person and by phone. They spent a lot of time at night going to bars together, to rock concerts, or to house parties where one could find liquor and music.

There was a tension generated around getting things ready for a rally, and around taking part in it, providing a rhythm of anxiety, fear, and catharsis. After the rally had taken place, a lot of time was spent in succeeding weeks talking about what had happened—the group members' versions usually differing markedly from reality, and constantly being shaped to reflect greater and greater heroism and victimization. During their conversations with each other, group members spent a lot of time looking at photographs of the most recent rally. They had many pictures of everything they had done, and could look at them again and again.

At the demonstrations, the Strike Group members were in uniform. The uniforms, modeled on those of the German SS, were impressive from a distance. Close up, they turned out to be Army surplus material dyed black, decorated with purchased insignia and with silk-screened swastika armbands.

The group was at its peak during the early years of my research and was the object of media attention. Toward the end of my study, it had fallen into decline and could scarcely mount a rally. Paul himself, as we shall see, was eventually silenced for some time by court action.

The members lived with a fair amount of fear and suspicion. They had some fear that black people or members of Jewish groups might shoot weapons into Paul's house in the evening. Several times they had gone out in the morning to find that a truck they had rented to take them to a rally had had its tires deflated during the evening; they assumed that this was done by far-left groups that appeared often as counterdemonstrators.

There was a lot of suspicion among the membership. Periodically a member ran afoul of the others—they would decide that he was a thief. At their economic level, this meant stealing a cigarette lighter or a pair of jeans. In any case, the scapegoated member would be isolated and pressured out of the group.

Most of the members came from sections of Detroit in which whites were a very small minority, and the members were afraid of black strength. While they demonstrated and rallied in the outlying white suburbs and in white towns some distance away, such as Ann Arbor, they did not rally at all in the black core of Detroit and were careful not to appear in uniform in any areas with a significant black population.

The decline, when it took place, had its humorous aspects. I recall a spring during which I learned from Paul that he and several others had gone to North Carolina for a Klan get-together, riding in a bus rented by an allied Chicago group. The bus broke down in North Carolina; no one had enough money to pay for its repair; and ultimately Paul had to raise money from relatives for his air fare home so that he could tend to the group's maintenance, while waiting for his followers to make their way north by hitchhiking. This fiasco prevented that year's installment of the annual Ann Arbor rally; at the usual rally date, Paul's followers were strung out (in more ways than one) along the highways of the South. The media at Ann Arbor did not know this, and Paul, in typical movement fashion, dropped several hints that the group was probably coming.

The Strike Group was almost entirely male. The leader's young live-in lover was heavily involved when the research began, but she left him and the group soon after. Several other women appeared at one time or another after this, usually as girlfriends of the leader, but with these rare exceptions it was a gathering of young men.

The median age of interviewed members, when research began, was nineteen, with ages ranging from sixteen to thirty. (Four members were nineteen; eight were sixteen through eighteen; eight were twenty through thirty.) Recruits to the Skinheads have been similarly young, and the emerging neo-Nazi violence in reunited Germany seems equally to be coming from young men with older ideological leaders. Young men have high energy, few restraining obligations, and little caution. (The median age of terrorists worldwide is thought to be only twenty-two.)

Almost every Strike Group member (eighteen of twenty who were interviewed) had lost a parent when young; usually the loss was of the father (sixteen of eighteen losses). This rate of loss is unusually high, even for a poverty population.

Most of the losses (fifteen of eighteen) were due to divorce or separation. The other three losses were due to deaths or to causes not revealed to the child.

The median age at which the parent was lost was seven. (Four members lost the parent when age three or younger; seven when six through eight; five when nine through thirteen; one at twenty-one; and one at an unknown age.)

In the following chapters, where an individual member speaks, we will hear his ambivalence about the missing parent. A sense of abandonment and uncertainty can flow from the early loss of a parent if it is not counterbalanced by strong work to buttress the child's understanding and the child's sense of himself. These particular young people were isolated and grew up, I believe, with a deep sense of vulnerability.

Poverty and loss of a parent can affect character; much depends upon the context in which the family is living. Our conversations revealed an unusually barren context. The absent parent typically had no contact at all with the spouse or child; once out, he quickly vanished. Stepfathers typically were cold, rough, and abusive, as were transient boyfriends. Connections with grandparents, uncles, aunts, and other relatives outside the nuclear family were frail; there was little sign of parenting-in-depth through an extended family. Connections to external community institutions were fragile. Church typically played no role in the family's life. Social agencies other than the police were conspicuously absent. Workplace chums of the mother had no place in the child's life. Ties between the child and his brothers and sisters were minimal. Those in the same house spent little time with one another; ties to siblings who lived out of the house were almost absent.

School was only a place to meet friends. No memories suggested that school had had any role in helping the child to build a sturdy sense of self. Usually the recruit had dropped out of school early. We know the school history of sixteen members. Six had quit school in the ninth grade, three in the tenth, and four in the eleventh. The three who had graduated from high school had each taken a semester or two at a community college or a junior college.

No member ever mentioned a teacher who had been important for him, nor a class. School was remembered with resentment as a place where teachers forced you to listen to lectures on Black History Month and where black students in the hallway hassled you.

A few members spoke spontaneously of parental alcoholism or violence; a few others were responsive when I asked questions. I think that a lot was held back from me. Seven members reported alcoholism, six reported family violence. Seven members spontaneously mentioned serving time at detention centers, jails, or prisons. I am fairly sure from the stories involving street fights and the hints about drug use and pilfering that there was a good deal more penal time than this. Several had been farmed out to foster homes during childhood.

The members came to the group in batches based on friendship clusters. The great majority had come from one or another of three distinct neighborhoods. Two of those neighborhoods were extremely poor; in those neighborhoods, there were only two or three white families to a block. The third neighborhood was a half white, half black neighborhood, with families ranging from working class downward—a struggling but not destitute neighborhood.

The fathers had been working men. None of them left any child support money behind. Most of the mothers worked as cooks or waitresses or were on disability payments.

The members had grown up in neighborhoods where they had to fight a lot. This would not have been entirely easy, since most of them were rather thin, rather slight. They depended on fighting real hard once something broke out, and on their experience. They were wiry and tough, but preoccupied with their thinness.

They were not good physical specimens. A surprising number had been born with a childhood disease or deficiency—such as being born a blue baby or born with half a liver. There are a lot of hospital stories in the interviews.

Most lived a desperate teenage life, getting work when they could, scrambling hard for spending money, partying hard when the chance came, drinking hard, smoking a lot of weed, doing cocaine if somebody gave them some, sleeping late and lying around till it was time to hitchhike over to another part of town and find a buddy.

Most had no work and no prospects of work. Several had steady work at low wages; others found an occasional few days of casual labor, tearing down old houses and the like, and hoping that the person who had hired them would really pay them at the end of the day. In another era, they might have expected to end up with jobs in one of the small shops supplying the auto industry. When I met them, those prospects were drying up rapidly. The members looked to me like people with a very limited future, the vanguard of a new white underclass. If the American industrial sector can transform itself back into a competitive position and begins rehiring, there will still be no place for these undisciplined, inexperienced, and uneducated dropouts. They are not fit.

The motivations for involvement in the Strike Group are implicit in the patterns I've described so far, the long list of absences—the absence of the father, the absence of involvement at school, the absence of work or the hope of work, the absence of wider family or community involvement. These people are isolates. Their daily lives do not generate involvements that give them a future to imagine.

But there are other motivations for membership in such a group. One fundamental push, I believe, is terror.

I made careful field notes after each encounter with the group, looking first at the primary emotions I felt during the encounter and the emotions I believed my respondent felt. By the time I had been meeting with the Strike Group members for a couple of months, the field notes spoke more and more about fear. These were people who at a deep level felt terror that they were about to be extinguished. They felt that their lives might disappear at any moment. They felt that they might be blown away by the next wind. The cues to this were not obvious; they had to do with the way the voice was used, the body was used, the things that were left unsaid.

Joining a tough group made sense on the face of it if you were afraid for your survival. It made even more sense as I came to know the members' mental associations with Nazism. I would ask how they had come to hear of Nazism, and all told me the same thing: They had learned what they knew from late-night movies on television. Their associations with Nazism, in other words, were the same as yours and mine. They had seen movies in which tough soldiers in field-gray fought desperately, they had seen jackbooted columns

marching implacably down cobblestoned streets, they had seen the
massed and unstoppable tanks rolling over all opposition through
the French countryside, they had seen the fierce Stukas strafing the
fleeing civilians, they had seen the hawk-faced officers with high
cheekbones giving pitiless orders. They had seen a force without compassion that overcame all odds, that did not fear even to murder.
And in placing a swastika armband on the sleeve, they declared their
identity with that force. And, moreover, in standing shoulder to
shoulder with comrades at demonstrations, and in withstanding the
hostility of the counterdemonstrators, they found fresh evidence *that
they were alive* and would not be extinguished. The very ferocity of
the counterdemonstrators—the vigor of the response that the Strike
Group members had caused—was a sharp declaration that they were
alive. Surviving the hostility next to comrades was further assurance.

The Holocaust has particular importance in terms of this need to
overcome a personal fear of extinction. Truly dreading that you can
be liquidated at any moment, it may be terribly important that the
force with which you are identifying is a force so very ruthless, so
very determined, so very cold, that it *could* murder in cold blood,
could murder in astonishing numbers. White racists pay incessant
attention to the Holocaust. Even denying, they *must* speak of it, perhaps because the appeal of the Nazi example is exactly that the Holocaust *did* happen, that the force one has joined is exactly a force
that *could* do this and *did* do this.

The haunting terror of extinction is probably a portion of the
motivation of many other sets of white racist group members. I certainly think it must play a role among the Skinheads, who also are
young and also come often from disrupted personal settings. It may
extend through other wings of the movement as a part of the moti-
vational mix.

The Strike Group members feel many of the other motivations that
I have noticed among older groups. They feel strongly the urge to be
shocking and to scandalize the Establishment, and nothing serves the
purpose easier than the swastika. They see the white supremacist
movement as a way to deal with a sense of orphanhood. And there
are doubtless times when members of the Strike Group experience
the urge to macho brutality, the need to feel strong, masculine, to
have your interactions with comrades reassure you that all of you

are tough guys. However, this particular outfit is not a group committed to doing violence nearly so much as it is one committed to provoking it.

Shortly I will present portraits of individual Strike Group members, and you can form your own conceptions of motivation. Motivation, of course, is only part of an explanation of a group's behavior. Motivation and circumstances can account for a person giving energy to a group, but the nature of the group's behavior may have more to do with the group's history and its organizational ties than with the motivations of the members. Members can ignite action, but may very well not really determine the nature of the action.

This does not at all mean that character and motivation are irrelevant. There is a match between a group's nature and the people who are drawn to it. And the third element in that mix is the objective social context. The objective peril in which the Detroit youths lived—their lack of future—activated the elements of character that made the Nazi group appealing; less stressful circumstances might have activated other parts of character and led those young people elsewhere.

In this light, today's profound changes in the American economy are particularly disturbing. We are widening the gap between the technically sophisticated *haves* and the unskilled *have-nots*. We are creating at the bottom of the economic ladder a stratum that will never be fully employed, along with a just-barely-higher stratum of working poor who will never earn enough to do more than survive. To see those two strata will always frighten the layers just above them, those still employed; they know that little protects them from falling into the despair they see among their neighbors and former neighbors. All three of these strata would be ripe for racist and reactionary and jingoistic appeals, as were comparable slices of the German public in the 1930s.

One final word: Look at what is *not* here. When the young people in Detroit happened to become involved with the Nazi group and found it compatible, nothing from family or environment got in the way. Nothing had led them to internalize revulsion about the swastika. My stomach ties in knots when I see one; these youths could slide one on their arms without a thought. Equally, when I was in New Orleans looking into the support of David Duke, I found sophisticated middle-class people who did not care that the man was a racist—who were aware of his organizational ties, but simply didn't find them relevant. I think that a lot of our educational efforts about racism and Nazism may have drifted in recent years into fairly shallow rote exercises with passive audiences. We are teaching children what to say to sound respectable, but shirking the more scary task of interactions that respect their real fears and their circumstances. As we restudy our efforts, we might heed the thoughts and emotions we hear in the interviews with these young racists. Their presentation of racism without filters or pretense can tell us about a part of what we and our contemporaries feel and think but do not acknowledge.

These young people—or at least many of them—could have been saved. They did not have to be Nazis. Most were members in this extreme racist group because the membership served a function, not because they had to enact their racism. Given another format in which they could have relieved their fears, given an alternative group that offered comradeship, reassuring activities, glamour, and excitement, they could easily have switched their allegiances. They would have remained racist—like their neighbors who hadn't joined a group—but they would not have needed to carry out racist actions in a group setting. Within four months of beginning my meetings with them, I knew that I could have led the bulk of the membership away if I had had an alternative to lead them to. No one for many years had treated them with the serious attention I was giving them, asking about their lives and listening carefully; they quickly built ties to me, despite my clear status as a Jew and a progressive.

We are accustomed to thinking of members of these groups as people who are driven by extreme hatred and so must remain isolated in their extremist groups. These young people showed powerfully the impact of their class position: They were poor and their lives had been deeply affected by social disorganization. They experienced great fear. They harbored deeply racist sentiments, but they did not need an organizational setting in which to act on those sentiments. They did need some setting or some involvement that would let them find some relief from their fear. The racist group had been an effective setting thus far; other involvements could have done the job just as well.

Much more to the point: What about prevention? Each young person who happened to bump into this group and join it represents hundreds who never came across it. Thousands of young people in the city are equally vulnerable to the group's appeal. Poor kids find a number of ways to deal with want and with the lack of status; many of the pathways are harmful to them and to the rest of society. Accident may determine who joins a racist gang and who moves to one of the other ways to hurt oneself or others.

The critical issue seems to be the sense of belonging somewhere and having a continuing source of care; the critical period when racist involvement begins seems to be the middle school years. We need programs beginning in the later years of elementary school that offer a sense of membership and a role that affords dignity and meaning. Alternative activities can compete with racism if the alternative activities offer glamour, excitement, a moderate level of risk, a sense that one has some value to the society, and a sense of comradeship. The Strike Group members might readily have identified with the most radical environmental groups, for example, where direct actions were mounted against the corporate establishment.

In the next chapter I detail the steps by which I made contact with the Death's-Head Strike Group, and the chapters that follow are the stories of representative members.

T E N

Contact

This book had its beginning some years ago with a visit to a bookstore briefly operated by the Death's-Head Strike Group. I had seen excited newspaper stories saying that a band of Nazis had opened a bookstore on Detroit's west side, and I had phoned reporters to get the address. It turned out to be close to the route I took when I taught a weekly extension class, and the fellow who rode with me didn't mind if we took a brief detour.

I'd never seen anyone who called himself a Nazi. As a social psychologist deeply interested in political movements, I had observed meetings of a local cell of the John Birch Society in the sixties; the Birchers, if ultraconservative, sought respectability and were not overtly racist. More recently I had held a number of interviews with a pair of strangely isolated right-wing loners who were trying to build a political group based on the old George Wallace party. Their religious intensity took them far past the anti-communism of the John Birch Society; I strongly suspected a Klan connection. I was fascinated, in their case, by the way the struggle against a pervasive social enemy was associated with an intense struggle against sexual impulse. That interesting corroboration of psychoanalytic theory whetted my appetite for meeting the overtly racist core.

I did not expect the visit to the bookstore to have much impact. I had just completed a long period of collecting life stories in a very poor black neighborhood in Detroit; I had seen and heard about so many traumatic events, I had watched lives of such great difficulty, I did not expect to be particularly disturbed by a simple bookstore, despite its sponsorship.

The street we drove down that dark, cold February evening was a heavy industrial feeder, connecting Ford's River Rouge manufacturing complex to the commercial downtown. The bookstore lay in a tough neighborhood. The adjoining stores sold green or khaki factory shirts, steel-toed boots, heavy wool socks, olive-drab Army surplus sweaters. A recruiting station displayed the flag; its posters invited kids from this working-class district to advance themselves by enlisting. I parked by the recruiting station and walked forty yards down to the bookstore.

My rider waited in the car. He had been still a boy in 1938 when his family escaped from Germany at the last moment, scant weeks before *Kristallnacht*. He remembers the bloodlust and the uniforms; he remembers the voices singing the "Horst Wessel Lied." "When you heard that, you knew to bar the door. That was what they sang when they were out to murder." My friend is a fine teacher and a social activist, but he did not need to see more Nazis this night.

A large display window took up the front of the space the bookstore was renting, but you could not see inside the store—large sheets of plywood filled the window. The plywood, painted black, bore posters about getting rid of the blacks and the Jews. The American flag hung from a short staff jutting out over the doorway.

Walking inside, I found a narrow room. Long tables lined three walls. Stacks of literature covered the tables; more posters were pasted on the walls. A group of young men stood together talking at the back of the store. I moved slowly and without speaking along the tables.

Heavy black headlines screamed from the stacks of newspapers and pamphlets: JEW MURDERERS STEAL CHRISTIAN BABIES; THE LIE OF THE SIX MILLION; THE JEWS ARE OUR MISFORTUNE. The tables were entirely covered by these piles of paper; everything I could see attacked Jews. There were even little stickers to be bought, palm-sized bits of hatred to carry concealed in your hand and to slap on a store window—a swastika and the words THIS STORE OWNED BY JEWS. The proprietor could come later and see this anonymous attack, chilling in its replication of the slogans with which Hitler's Nazis began the process of isolation and dehumanization.

Hundreds of separate items lay on the tables. I had spent years interviewing poverty-stricken black people and connecting myself emphatically to their stories; at my evening extension course I worked with my largely black class on the issues they faced as public school teachers and that their black students faced; I was accustomed to dealing understandingly with someone else's grim encounters. But now these piles of pamphlets, newspapers, and stickers told me that *my* people were hated, that *I* was a target. The back of my neck tingled: fear.

Finally I had worked my way almost to the back of the room. Pretending to look at the pamphlets, I stood near the young men, listening to their conversation. The five of them looked to be nineteen or twenty years old. One fellow had a large stomach and a sloppy brown sweater; a second wore blue jeans and a synthetic leather jacket; a third sat on a beat-up couch in an imitation motorcyclist's jacket with a Nazi armband. They were pale, with long hair, two with mustaches, all undernourished. The clothing, the pallor, the general shabbiness were the stigmata of social class that you saw on kids at a detention center. I was listening hard; they asked each other what they ought to wear to a gathering in Ohio. "We could wear our uniforms," one said, "but then if the guys from Chicago don't wear theirs, they'll laugh at us."

"Yeah," another said, "but if we don't wear ours and the Chicago guys do, they'll think we are punks."

It sounded like a locker-room conversation in a junior high school. The foolishness of the exchange, the sadness of the clothing and of the pasty complexions, contrasted sharply with the gravity of the printed material with its lethal intentions.

The Nazi kids now began to complain about the names other people called them. Why were people saying these things about them? they asked, and then began to roll the words off their tongues, teasing each other: "sadomasochistic," "psychosexual deviate." The terms had come up in a newspaper article; I assumed that a reporter had gotten some quotable remarks from a psychiatrist.

I listened and looked. It was easy to see that these were adolescent children from poor white families, young people from a distressed sector of the world, kids who had found a gig that lifted them for the moment from anonymity. They seemed insignificant. But at the same time, the material they were peddling made me feel weak. That incongruity needed to be explored. In addition, the pitifulness of the young people rested in their isolation; the same kids would be dangerous if they had power, and would certainly not be kind users of that power.

As I made careful field notes that night, I was still shaken by the encounter with the youths and with their wares. I was sure that I wanted to find a way to speak with them, to find out what was taking place in their minds, what they feared and what they hungered for. I wanted to confront the incongruity between the pitiful practitioners and the poisonous materials. What brought this shabby crew to this dance? I asked myself. What could their lives be? Could these people be led elsewhere?

The Nazi group came to my town, Ann Arbor, a few years later. I had not been able to find them after the bookstore folded, despite pursuing leads from monitoring agencies, and I had been too committed to other research to put more energy toward this project. (That relieved the man who then headed our department at the University of Michigan; he felt that study of such an organization would be "scientifically unprofitable.") One spring, however, the group posted fliers in town announcing they were coming to Ann Arbor to hold a rally on the third weekend of March.

The city sprang into agonized reaction. A coalition of militants mobilized for strong counterdemonstration while an Establishment coalition asked people to ignore the Nazi gathering and meet later in the day in a thoughtful program to celebrate democracy. Despite that plea, large clusters of older students and townspeople congregated on the appointed morning at several possible downtown sites that might be chosen by the Nazis. After hours of rumor, word spread that the group had arrived; hundreds who were waiting at other sites now ran down the streets to the Federal Building—a post office, courthouse, and field office for federal agencies. Terraced steps led from the sidewalk to the plaza at the front of the building. Up on the plaza, seventeen figures in black uniforms stood braced, feet apart, holding up shields made from stop signs. The shields had giant swastikas as well as KICK ASS stickers from a Detroit rock station. The Nazis wore red, black, and white swastika armbands. They had a large swastika flag. A few wore motorcycle helmets with dark face-plates; others were bareheaded, and we could see that most looked about seventeen or eighteen years old, and one was a young woman. Their leader was trying to talk through a megaphone. The crowd was furious. Few of us had ever seen a brazen display of the hooked cross, the swastika. It was staggering.

Like most Jews of my generation, I had spent years trying to come to terms with the mass killing of Jews in Europe. I run scenarios in my head, to try to grasp what the last moments must have felt like. Now these young people stood up on that plaza, *displaying themselves in Nazi dress.* They looked scared, but they also looked pleased. They had dared to come and stand in this liberal town, the birthplace of SDS, the town where the plan for the Peace Corps was first announced, this town with a radical history—they had dared to come to this place and now stood displaying the symbol that commanded the deaths, the symbol that flew over those Nazi camps and killing installations. They stood, scared but grinning. That display said that the killing of Jews had been only one more thing—*nothing special*—that people could debate about. It defiled the memory of the deaths. Those who died helplessly must at least have hoped that the deaths would be remembered. The deaths could not become just one more item in political discourse. That arrogant display of this group, that implication that we could *talk over* the question of murder, *discuss* the killing of infants, *discuss* the killing of children—all that was obscene to me.

(One can rewrite the paragraph above, substituting the word "blacks" for "Jews," "Klan" for "Nazi," and "America" for "Europe." It remains an obscenity.)

Others had similar thoughts, and the crowd grew noisy. People deep in the crowd began to break chunks of ice from nearby mounds of snow and fling them across the police lines at the Nazis. Others, less innocently, flung flashlight batteries or glass bottles. The crowd chanted, louder and louder, *"Go home! Go home! Go home! Go home!"* A window and a glass door broke behind the Nazis. The young men tried to protect themselves behind their clumsy shields. The police began to herd them away from the glass front of the building and along its side, down an alley to a waiting sheriff's bus. We ran after them, some still flinging objects, all crying out, *"Run home! Run home, bastards! Eat shit!"* We ran madly, chasing, screaming. *"Eat shit! Run home!"*

I ran with the rest, wildly excited. Yelling.

A picture, abruptly, flashed into my mind: a mob of Southern whites screaming, running at a group of civil rights activists.

I stopped running.

The bus pulled out; the crowd jeered.

I mumbled my own curse. I was glad we had driven them off; they shouldn't be allowed to think that the world would permit their obscene insult. But we had been one more self-righteous pack inflamed with our own virtue.

The liberal core of the town had its counterrally later in the day. It was a pretty event, and it should have made someone like me feel better. It didn't. I was still upset by our own behavior, and this counterrally offered the chance to be civilized, mournful, and restrained. But that left me cold as well. It was too damn civilized. The fact was that the group had been here, had wrapped itself in the name of a terrible evil. The liberals' rally felt like the sort of funeral that is so *positive* and *affirming* that the fact of death gets overlooked. The bitter, hideous evil that was celebrated under the swastika was real: deaths without number, strangulation by gas, starvation, torture. The damnable violence of our morning's swinishness at least said *no.*

Almost all of the Nazi group members discussed in this book took part in that demonstration.

A year later, accident presented the opportunity to make a research contact with the group. I had won a seat on Ann Arbor's City Council, where our caucus struggled to overcome local effects of the Republican cutbacks. Council members regularly received large sets of documents from city departments. Leafing through these one week, I found copies of a letter to the police department from the Nazi group. The Nazis said they wanted to put on a demonstration, as they had the year before, and asked for cooperation; their letter had symbols—swastikas, eagles, skulls—and slogans—"HONOR, LOYALTY"—and a phone number.

I called that number and asked for either of the two men who had signed the letter. "They don't live here," a woman told me. I called again the next day and asked whether I could leave a message. She called a man, who got on the phone.

"Who the hell are you?" he demanded in a rough, angry voice.

I laughed and gave him my name. I told him that I wanted to get together to talk, to see whether we could do some work together. I explained that my research as a professor was to visit with people who were doing something that seems different to most others. That I had found that almost everyone leads a life that makes good sense to himself or herself, and that I liked talking with the person and letting the person explain to me the way that the life makes good sense. I told him that I would like it if we could get together and talk with each other, to see whether that kind of research would feel reasonable to both of us.

"Were you at the demo last year, there in Ann Arbor?" he asked.

"Yeah," I told him. "Probably you were, too, but probably we weren't next to each other."

He told me to write to them, to explain what I was doing, and gave me an address.

"Who's your boss?" he asked. "Let me have his address. No, his telephone. Let me have his number. That way we can call and check you're who you say you are, not some hood from the ADL trying to set us up."

He had to break the call abruptly at that point, for unexplained reasons.

I wrote to the Strike Group on university stationery, repeating the message of the phone call and indicating ways to reach me.

A week later I reached the woman again on the phone; she gave me a new telephone number to use. After several tries on several days, I reached Paul Madden, the group leader, the man with whom I had spoken. He agreed to a meeting the following Sunday. He told me to come to a McDonald's on a corner that he named in the western suburbs of Detroit. We were to meet at two in the afternoon. That Sunday, he phoned my house at one o'clock, just as I was about to leave. He changed our meeting place to a different McDonald's, a few miles farther from Detroit than the first one, and moved our meeting time to three. I had some more coffee; I wondered whether Paul was trying to foil any dangerous plans he might think I had set up by switching locations at the last moment.

It was a chill, nasty, gray afternoon as I drove out to meet Paul. For some years I had driven through the bleak terrain along that same freeway, week after week, going into Detroit to talk with poor black men and women who were trying to build lives in the city. Now I was driving that road to meet the leader of a deeply racist group. I was apprehensive that the new location Paul had indicated might be a phony one—what if there was no such intersection? What if there were no McDonald's there? What if, most simply, the guy just didn't show up? What if the chemistry of the meeting turned out to be bad, no connection could be made, no work would make sense? But along with these questions rose excitement at the possibility of doing a new exploration: What is this part of the world *really* like?

The McDonald's was there, a few miles north of the freeway, a long, flat block of red and orange, brick and plastic, a slab in the midst of grey asphalt. I was a little early and walked toward it, scanning the tables I could see along the glassed walls, trying to figure out whether one of the people was Paul.

"Hey! Over here!" It was a brusque voice from the side. A sallow face leaned out of the window of a van. "Here, Professor." His long black hair was tied in a ponytail.

It had been easy for him to spot *me*; I had told him that I wore glasses, that I had gray hair and a gray beard.

I walked over to the van, studying his face. The van had no windows except in the front—it must once have been a delivery vehicle. It was black, but all the sheen was gone from the paint; it was old and worn. "Climb on in," he called. I was surprised; I had assumed that we were going to work inside the McDonald's. I tried the passenger door. "That door don't work," he said. "Come on in on the side; just slide it open." I hesitated, looking at the blank side of the van; I had no way to know what was waiting inside.

I opened the door carefully. Nothing waited there. I climbed in and swung up into the front, settling in the passenger seat. We looked each other over. He slouched in an Army surplus woolen coat. I saw fatigue pants and work boots. He was medium height and seemed chunky.

We talked for several hours in the van. I explained the philosophy of the work again, and he asked a few questions. He talked at great length, laying out the group's basic rap—that it was a group devoted to helping white unity, that whites had to learn to stick together. He answered questions about his life: He was thirty, single and childless, unemployed, didn't know what sort of work he would like—maybe hooking up cable television in people's homes, or installing telephones, or running mail from the post office to an airport, or working in the shipping and receiving department at a plant—something not too demanding, he said.

He was cooperative and it looked as if we could do the work, but the inner world I could hear was barren: when he talked, I didn't hear about individuals in ways that suggested life, I heard about stock figures and heard his intense but badly throttled emotion. Everything about him seemed choked. My head soon hurt.

Paul was tape-recording our conversation. He said that was so he could play it for members of the group if they had questions. When we were winding down, he suddenly interrupted his own discourse. "Now, one thing," he said abruptly, "another thing, while this tape's going, that I got to put on it. This makes no difference to me. But people are going to want to know a little bit about some of your, ah, personal life. By any chance, ah, what is your religion?"

Good, I thought. *Here we are.* I looked at him. "I'm a Jew."

"All right," he said. "I had to clear that up."

"Sure," I said. "I was wondering when we were going to get to it."

"No," he said, "because, see, I myself don't care. You're doing a study. If you are, ah, for real, you'll print the truth of what I see."

I was going to tape-record what he was saying, and that was going to be what was in the book, I told him.

He said he just had to know, because he didn't want one of his members to say, Hey, didn't you know the guy's Jewish, he's going to set us up and turn everything over to the Jewish Defense League. Therefore he was telling the other members that he would use his place as the spot for interviews, they could leave their own homes. "If something happens that you turned out as bad as can be," he told me, "and turned over the information to the JDL, all you'll really get is myself and where I live. So this way, people that are paranoid would get out of it."

I told Paul that I appreciated his taking the risk. He said that they didn't really go after somebody for their religion. "We go after people in the Jewish religion that have the control of things like the media, or support for Israel, stuff like that. We feel we need the money here."

On that note he switched off his tape recorder and we rechecked our arrangement for the next meeting and said good-bye. The work had begun.

ELEVEN

Paul

Paul was a small-time local leader, playing little role nationally. But without him, his group would not have existed.

I left our first meeting, the conversation in his van, with a vicious headache. I drove home, thinking of the words and the feelings of the encounter. I felt pity, surprise, faint warmth, and distance. Paul wanted to be a nice guy; almost automatically, he was interested in helping me. Equally he sort of took it for granted that if people understood what he was trying to do, they would think well of it and appreciate him. He wanted to be appreciated. I picked up a sense of hungry loneliness.

Paul's life and his way of speaking of his life seemed wretched. He seemed miserable, and there was nothing going on that was likely to make him feel better. The phrase that kept sounding in my mind was: *hollow man*.

I thought of the contrast with my friend Joe Volk, a peace activist with the American Friends Service Committee. It was not just that their axioms about the world were so different. Joe talked about a world with *people* in it—distinct individuals—and he cared about the people, and his stories were full of life. Paul's world didn't have people in it; there were blanket stereotypes; there were no actual individuals.

Paul, in contrast to Joe, was caught up entirely with defense. It took all his energy to maintain a constant militant stance.

The world Paul spoke of was not a world of possibilities. He lived in gloom. There was little humor or life or imagination in his talk.

My head ached this first time from the strain of staying open, encouraging continuous interaction, with a man who felt so discouraged, finished, depressed, and yet hungry, as well as from the strain of exploring the images, encouraging the elaboration of images, that all began with axioms I rejected.

Our continued meetings only reinforced these first impressions. The man was sullen and constricted. He had a sweet side; he definitely wanted to help people when he could, and cared about what was happening with the kids who came to his group, but life felt sour to him most of the time. And he had no hope.

He was drawn into himself. His body seemed drawn in. His strangely flat voice grated against itself, trying to get out. And each sentence ended with a downturn of inflection.

He limited himself. He had no belief in himself. His discussion of political actions was peppered with the phrase "keep a low profile."

He had involved himself in the white racist movement when he was fourteen or fifteen, a year or two after his parents separated. He had had a couple of semesters of college, had done some factory work, but was currently unemployed and drawing welfare.

Paul could fall into dejection and passivity. Movement work would energize him. He could start a conversation in fairly abject depression and become excited and lively as he began to retell stories of injustices done to him and the group, invigorated as he talked of having to fight with "Red scum." He was definitely thrilled by the excitement of confrontation at demonstrations. But after confrontation came letdown. And even in the conversations, after talking about the struggles with the Reds, there would come the reminder that the authorities would step in, that one would not be allowed to do much after all, that one would need to "keep a low profile."

I tried repeatedly over the years to arrive at a satisfactory sense of Paul's deeper feelings. Late in the work I decided that *shame* was the great theme of his character: that he was haunted by a pervasive sense of shame, and that one could assume that much of what he did showed that shame while also representing ways of fighting it.

Paul, as we shall see, had a lot to say about physical mutilation and rather tangled relations to aggression. He had surrounded himself with young boys—teenagers. His father was a drunk who abused Paul's mother. Paul created a central drama of group activity in which he provoked an aggressive response from others, whereupon he and the other were restrained by authority. I suspect that this pattern of provocation, counteraggression, and impotence replays early incidents involving the abusive father, the mother, and the child, incidents that were the background for the persistence of his shame.

Paul told me one evening, when I was asking about good and bad memories, how awful it had been when neighborhood parents stopped letting their kids come over to his house because of the rotten fights his parents had. The recollections upset him.

"A bad time?" he said that evening. "I can name one, it wasn't really bad affecting me, but it got me in a bad mood. Of seeing the old man drunk, whipping beer bottles at my ma. And he said she was going out on him, and I knew she wasn't, because she was home cleaning the house and I think I didn't even have school that day or something, I knew that there was no suspicion. That was the first time I seen them fighting. And he said that she had been sneaking out on him with another man, and I know it wasn't true because she was the peaceful type that didn't really have any spirit to go out and meet men and try to get out in the world. She was just kind of the home-type person.

"And when the old man would get drunk, he would try and accuse her of stuff so he'd have an excuse to throw a few punches at her, something. And she never give him any, so a couple of times I guess he whipped a couple beer bottles at her, and I didn't like it all, but there was nothing I could do. I was just like about ten years old. And me and my sister, she was like six years old, we just took off out of the house. And we went down the street and looked for our friends for something to do. Because the neighbors were all out in the yard, they could hear the shouting and stuff. Houses were pretty close together.

"And we wound up getting, me and my sister, like, oh, iced out of the neighborhood, no one could hang around with us, because they said, 'There's fighting down there, don't go near their house, don't bring them kids down here.' And before that, we always had everything going in the neighborhood. We had played baseball there so much on the front lawn, we had worn a diamond in the grass and stuff from playing. We had a sandbox and all the stuff in the backyard for kids to play on, and everybody used to come down there. But then after my folks were fighting, all of a sudden everybody stayed away from us like we were lepers or something.

"So that was a sad time, that first year when they were fighting. Because I got used to it after that. I seen them argue every time the old man come in drunk. I'd see him pull up real slow outside, and I'd just take off until he passed out. So that was sort of a bad time there."

Paul, disappointed and sour, often spoke harshly. Early in our contact I noticed the brutal way he spoke with his seventeen-year-old lover, Terri, about the death of a young Arab man who had been the lover of Terri's best friend, Alison. Paul was callous and scorned Terri's good impulses.

The young man, Yakoub, father of Alison's baby, Jonathan, had been dead for two months, leaving Alison with the child and no money. Terri went over to Alison's to help her periodically. Paul growled that the baby should be put up for adoption. "From the white viewpoint, where the whites stay with the whites and the blacks with the blacks, seeing this white girl who was bad enough to mix with the Arabs, now she's got a baby by one, that's what we call the ultimate sin."

Terri pointed out that it was not so simple. "After you have a baby, you carry it for nine months and then have it for another thirteen months, Paul, it's not that easy. You can't just give it away." Terri brought up other families they knew who had children of mixed race.

Paul became angrier. "Well, that's up to them. I myself, I just don't care for it. And I'm not going to mix it and I think you guys who are preaching white power and having anything to do with these mulattoes and mixed families are just looking like fools! You're in the wrong business."

Terri wouldn't give up. She pointed out that Paul hung around with a black guy called Painter.

That was not the same, Paul said; that was just a person on the street; he could talk to blacks on the street, he could go to a movie with a black man, and those examples were not "the extent of race mixing I'm talking about. I don't like the mulatto baby and the girl having it," he snapped.

He was angry. "They preach no race-mixing. But yeah, it's okay for this girl and everything. They seem to have an attitude about it that it's okay for her. While for the rest of the white crowd it's not, for us it's not, but for this one girl, her circumstances, it's okay."

Paul's voice had become mean: "*No one gave her a hard time when she was going around with this pack rat, this drug-dealing scum before.* No one gave her a hard time, blackened her eyes, and said stay away from the camel. Her girlfriends didn't shun her, they encouraged her. They're all responsible for it. They're all guilty, everybody in the neighborhood.

"All her girlfriends are just as guilty of her having this baby, because none of them tried to talk her out of it. And set her up with a decent young white man to raise a family. No one tried to persuade their friends—"

"Yes, we did try," Terri interrupted.

"You tried very, very poor," Paul scolded. "You didn't try hard enough. When you try to get good grades in school, the result is your grades—"

Terri interrupted the moral lecture again to say Alison had started going out with Yakoub when she was only thirteen years old.

Paul steamed on. "No one gave her a hard time. You guys should have been blackening her eyes every day you caught her on the street. You would've saved her in the long run. Instead now she has an albatross around her neck, a curse!"

"It's just a baby," Terri said.

Paul said he knew, "but it's a symbol of everything that's wrong and evil."

It wasn't the baby's fault, Terri said.

Paul agreed, but went on. "He'll be another clerk in another party store. Screwing the white man out of every hard-earned penny and dollar that we come by. But it's just a bad situation that turned worse, because no one ever tried to teach her a lesson and make her stay away. So we got this bad problem now. And because she's a friend of a lot of people, they don't actually want to say anything that might sound a little bit harsh or critical."

Terri defended herself. "Myself, I happen to love Jonathan. It's not his fault he's mulatto. He didn't ask to be mulatto."

Paul said there was just no excuse for it ever happening. "It should have never happened. She should've got birth control pills, she could've made sure the camel had some type of protection to ensure that he wouldn't get her pregnant, she could've done a million things. Or just plain said, 'No, I'm not going to go to bed with the man at this time, I might get pregnant.' There was no care. There was no consideration. No responsibility.

"Maybe I'm just too old-fashioned, but that's why I'm involved in white power, to keep people white. And when they start mixing like that, it's everything that I been preaching."

Terri said Alison began going with Yakoub when she was thirteen and knew no better. She had made a mistake and fallen in love with him.

Paul snorted. "Well, nonetheless, I'll beat the love out of any family of mine that gets involved in that. That's not trying to sound mean or cruel, but I'm not going to allow it—I'd throw them out of the family, I'll do something. I'll tell them, if they're eighteen, drop them out of the family. If they're under eighteen, beat the hell out of them."

Paul's relationship with Terri lasted a few months more, until her accidental pregnancy. Terri panicked and returned to her mother, then gradually broke her ties with Paul. He saw the baby only once. Within the year Terri and the baby had left the state for good.

Paul's mother had moved to the Southwest some years earlier, along with his younger sister. Paul had little to say about the mother and seemed to have little connection to her; I heard no emotion in his voice. The sister was pursuing a respectable career and avoided him. I think he felt the two of them thought ill of him. The father had moved to West Virginia a few years before our talks and was in poor health; Paul visited him periodically and spoke of trying to take care of him.

Paul had served six months for possession of a controlled substance when he was twenty-one. "We were at a [rock] concert," he said. "They raided the men's room, everybody was in there smoking joints and partying. I got six months for a couple of pills." He served his time at a prison farm.

His parents had not helped him fight the case. His mother was already out West and was frightened. Paul was living with his father at the time and took a court-appointed lawyer rather than have the father put out the money. "My dad said, 'Well, you'll learn! I told you. You'll learn. You had to find out the hard way. I'm not going to put up with you kids messing around.' "

Paul had little to say about the bust, the trial, or the six months —passed it off as no big thing. But I noticed how unsupported he had been.

Images and thoughts of bodily mutilation came spontaneously to Paul's mind and seized his attention. I heard this first at our initial meeting, in the midst of a long discourse on black life as he imagined it.

"Soon we [whites] won't even be the majority, because the blacks and Hispanics are breeding like flies and they're going to outnumber us. The whites are on a downslide. Because every white family wants to stay with, you know, maybe one baby or two, something they can afford to take care of right. Where the black woman, some of them say, 'The more I got, the bigger ADC [AFDC] check I got.' Others just say, 'Well, another baby in the family.' " (Paul himself was living on welfare.)

"And they have no supervision, they don't care. They roam the streets. You drive down through Detroit nine or ten o'clock at night, see kids seven, eight years old running the streets. I was never allowed that when I was little. If I wasn't in by dark, I got beaten, I got beat bad. Nothing that could be child abuse, I'm just saying, for my experience, at the time, a good whipping was a good whipping. But, yeah, was probably, oh, good for me. I might have been killed out after dark. Maybe one of these child molesters could have picked me up and killed me. So my folks, oh, actually did me good. But you don't see the black concerned with their kids. They let them roam and do as they please.

"It's like they don't care. 'Well, they're outside somewhere, I don't care what they're doing.'

"Some do, some don't. I believe the majority doesn't. There's just too much crime, too much trouble. You've got ten-year-old kids murdering people with guns, knives, and anything they can get their hands on. They'll strangle an old woman for a social security check —nine-year-old. It's in all the papers. I'm not just talking of Detroit, I'm talking of the whole United States."

Most whites, including his sister, had no views, he said. "I feel sorry for her, she's into believing that everything's going fine and good. She's not exposed to what goes on. And if she hears about it, she says, 'Oh, wow, that's too bad.' But that's the extent of it.

"It's like all these whites," he said, "they hear somebody who's mutilated and killed, they go, 'Oh, well, that's bad, man, what next?' 'Hmmm, don't surprise me; you hear about that all the time.'

"They've got this attitude that it's no big deal. They should be shocked. They should want to go out there and do something about it. Take a mob of vigilantes to tear down the jail door and drag the, ah, butcher out and hang him, that's what it deserves, that's what he deserves. Because they're sure not getting the right punishment in court."

What is he talking about? I wondered. But not for long.

"There's a lot of evil stuff that isn't even what you could call somebody, oh, robbing a bank and shooting a policeman when he's trying to get away. Or somebody, oh, getting mad at their wife or something and they'll start wrestling and she hits her head and dies.

"That's not what I'm talking about. I'm talking about the mutilations and, ah . . . all this *sadistic, degenerate, evil* things that happen.

"And it's like Jack the Ripper–type stuff."

He needed me to hear this.

"And that goes on. You can, you can hear about it all the time. We have a few friends that work in police departments and they see the, ah, behind the scenes of a murder that's not put in the paper. You know, they say, 'A body is found so and so.' They won't actually all the time put in there to the extent of it. Or someone was stabbed. People don't get the picture when a body's stabbed eighty-seven times: what they look like, what it would look like.

"Maybe if they put those pictures in the paper, we could shake some people up to get out and help vote for the death penalty. At least for these butchers. If not, get 'em mad enough to change the people we have in office right now and mad enough to go and drag the rat out of behind the bars and string him up.

"We've got these mutilating murderers and these real sick people, if they plead insanity, they beat the case that way. Then in a couple of months, they prove they're okay, and they're out on the street.

"Either way—sitting in jail, they've got it made; sitting in the nuthouse, they've got it made. They've got three meals a day, a shower, at least once a week, if not more. Some people in prison have televisions, radios, they've got all the latest magazines, newspapers, it's almost . . . sure, they don't have the freedom of the streets, but they've got it made in there. As far as the person they butchered and slaughtered who died a *painful,* very painful, agonizing death . . . they just weren't shot once and died instantly, they were cut up slowly or tortured and all this stuff. And maybe it took them hours to die of, ah, pain."

When Paul spoke about mutilation, his voice was intense. His normal speech had an air of disengagement. But when speaking of mutilation, he needed you to hear, you were to take it seriously, and something had to be done about it.

There are many images that can stick in your mind. Paul's life left him needing periodically to revisit an image of slow, sadistic torture. I have to guess that this need derived from fearful relationships in his early years, and that the fear had stimulated his bogeyman costume and the careful acts of defiance at the rallies.

These images recurred as the work went on. In a later conversation, for example, he had been talking about circumstances in which normal people might become violent.

"It's like if someone had me on the firing squad for somebody like Charles Manson. All they'd have to do is read me the details of the court case, and then put a rifle in my hands and take the man out to the firing squad line, and I'd fire without batting an eye.

"All I got to hear," he said, "is the sadistic murder and torture that someone did to another person that didn't deserve it. To feel sorry for that person and to take his side and say, 'Hey, you shouldn't have done [that] to that man. It's sick, this is not right, you shouldn't have done it. You pay with your life.' Shoot him or pull the rope that drops the trapdoor, and hang him, something perfectly legal. I would not be against that because I feel this man has done wrong where there's not excuses.

"I'm not talking somebody who the cops are firing at him after he robs a bank and he fires back and gets the cops. All right, technically that's still a guilty offense. I would not have the same feelings towards getting rid of a person like that as I would somebody where they got the report where they knifed him up, and then they slowly killed them here, they burned them with cigarettes, there's so much mutilation going on with people, die so slowly and so painfully by other people. That somehow this stuff has to be avenged.

"People are getting worse and worse and worse. And when you take a stand against crime like our party does, you say, hey, we're not going to tolerate it. It's not necessary. We're all trying to get ahead in this world, trying to keep a family, keep people together. We don't need somebody taking advantage of others, and then on top of that, mutilation and murder and torture and all this. Just for the sake of laughing and enjoying it."

I decided to dig. "Have you ever seen anyone who was mutilated?"

"No," he said, "but I've heard all about it. Don't believe that Sharon Tate was not mutilated. That happens. I've talked to people in police departments that have seen the bodies. And have gone to houses where people have been slowly killed. And it shocks them every time."

Was it not strange, I suggested to Paul, that he had named the group the Death's-Head Strike Group? The name and the insignia consciously referred to the German SS—a group, I pointed out, that most of the world believes practiced sadistic murders for a decade. Almost all the world believes that, I said. Wasn't that a strange choice for a name, from somebody who really hates sadism?

Paul found nothing odd in this. The SS skull and crossbones were "only to strike fear in the heart of the enemy." The SS at root, he said, was a protective organization, Hitler's bodyguard. And perhaps he is accurate in saying that his main motivation in choosing the name was a connotation he found of protection—if protection from the very sadism that the symbol suggests.

I should add, for accuracy, that quite terrible things *were* happening on the streets. Not long after this, Alison was stabbed a number of times and her second Arab lover was slain during a brutal assault on her flat by a couple who were looking for drugs and cash. The issue is not whether torture and murder happened, but why they were so important to Paul. He had no sympathy for Alison even after this assault, nor did it catch his attention that her assailants were white.

Paul's relationship to aggression was tangled. He specialized in creating provocative situations but was ill-at-ease in his mix of fascination and fear. He inched up to violence and drew back from it.

"I'm what you would call a nonviolent person," he said. "We go to this Ann Arbor rally. I don't care if people that don't like what we stand for show up. And hold up signs saying we don't like you here, you guys are telling lies, it's not this way at all. Fine. Let them just stand there and remain silent and we'll tell the message to people who are interested. But instead all these rats come down trying to kill us.

"We don't need that. It was in the paper that the Nazis need the counterdemonstrators, they need all this trouble. That's a lie. That's the biggest lie, that's as bad as the lie on the six million gassed.

"But we don't want no trouble. We don't need this hassle. We have to go out carrying shields and motorcycle helmets with face shields on and all this type of riot gear, clubs that are big enough to split a man's skull in one swipe."

That caught my ear.

"We don't want to carry heavy sticks out, heavy shields, helmets that make your face sweat and cover you. But we have to because these rats have tried to kill us. Hit us with bricks, batteries, rocks, ice chunks, tomatoes, eggs, all kinds of vegetables, bleach, ammonia, red paint—a thousand eggs, if I didn't mention that, a thousand eggs.

"And they think it's some kind of a joke. They think it's some kind of joke."

Resentment then led him to lash out—and as quickly to retract his attack.

"They think it's some kind of a joke. I tell you, if I had my way, I'd consider a thrown object, like a rock, attempted murder. And if I had my way I would carry, well, a pistol. I own pistols and rifles, all legally registered. I'd carry a pistol on my side and a rifle slung over my shoulder. And if someone threw a rock and I blocked it, I would pull out a pistol and shoot him dead: See, he attempted murder on me, now I fire back in self-defense.

"But there's always innocent people in the crowd. Reporters, people who come to hear what you got to say. Friends of yours that support what you're into but cannot put the uniform on and get up there with you. So the chances of using our right of self-defense was wiped out because of it being an open crowd.

"We don't need these attempted murderers. Let them stay home. They come down and try and injure us and then make a big deal about it, trying to say how they scared us out and everything like that. It's going to come down to it, when the police start running out of money and can't afford to enforce the law, if we have some type of civil breakdown, and communists attack, it'll be like in Greensboro [a tragic incident in 1979]. When the communists pulled their guns on the Klansmen, the Klansmen pulled their guns out of the trunk and laid into them. They [the leftists] started shooting with .25s and .22s. And the Klansmen opened up their trunks and were shooting .38, .357, .44 Magnum, thirty-ought-six and double—and shotguns, twenty-gauge pump shotguns. The communists were shown in various pictures, holding pistols, laying over their dead comrades. They fired those pistols first. That's why the Greensboro comrades were found not guilty."

As in every white supremacist conversation, the Klan is nonaggressive, despite appearances; the movement is at all times a victim involved in self-defense. Paul nevertheless could not recite the Klan's version of this incident without being seized by the detail of the Klan weaponry.

These statements grossly misrepresent the events at Greensboro. Later court proceedings made it clear that heavily armed Klansmen methodically shot down unarmed leftists. The attacking Klansmen knew that the leftists did not have weapons readily available. The leftists belatedly pulled several light weapons from a car trunk and responded, much too late.

Paul showed me his own Magnum one day, a great brute of a pistol. We always sat with a drum-shaped little table between us, on top of which I rested my tape recorder. He showed me finally that a door on his side of the table covered a compartment from which he took the Magnum; he had been keeping it there all this time.

Paul's head was jammed with ugly thoughts about black people. In his view, random violence—assaults, killings, rape—came mostly from blacks and blacks didn't care about the consequences. "They catch the man, the kid, and they'll say, 'Why did you do it? You're facing twenty years now.' He'll shrug his shoulders like it's no big deal. They don't care if they lose twenty years of their life."

The worst part, Paul continued, was that blacks stuck together, while whites didn't. "You fight one nigger, you fight 'em all. The niggers jump one white man, they know they've got him because the rest will keep walking. I've seen that happen."

In every conversation, Paul spoke of "the niggers." They were violent, savage. "You can't trust a nigger." "What would you expect from a nigger?" It was in essence a street viewpoint—"niggers" were no damn good, "niggers" were the other team, a rival gang.

I watched him at a rally the group held in Dearborn, a white suburb at the edge of Detroit. It was a pretty day in June. Eight people from the group had gathered, along with an older fellow, a hospital attendant who was trying to start a local branch of one of the Klans. The members had with them two U.S. flags and one Confederate flag. Paul and Terri and one other member were in black Strike Group uniforms, the rest in camouflage fatigues. They wore swastika armbands. They had signs reading: WHITE POWER; GOD IS WHITE; WE WANT JOBS, NOT COMMUNISM; and KILL! ALL REDS.

The members posed along the street, flanked by the several flags. Paul marched about yelling, and recording his yelling in a tape recorder. The group chanted together:

"What do we want?"

"White power!"

"When do we want it?"

"Now!"

This plagiarism from the left was followed by chants of "White people/ United/ Can never be defeated."

Paul paced about, chanting, yelling. He arched himself and gave Hitler heils to passing cars. Dearborn paid little mind to any of this.

All this time, the Klan organizer had been crying out into a bull-horn. He didn't have the knack. Paul now took the bullhorn and worked with it. He understood how to get volume from a bullhorn, and led a long series of chants. Over and over his chant came: *"No more niggers! No more niggers! Run the niggers out! No more niggers! Keep Dearborn white! Smash communism! Run the apes back to Detroit! No more niggers! Join us! Join us! White power! No more niggers! No more niggers!"*

I was close and watching carefully. He got great pleasure from this. He loved the music of it: *"No more niggers!"*

A car drove by slowly; a black man mooned them from the car window.

From the beginning Paul had spoken of his concern about white unity, his anxiety that whites unite. I had taken this as a smokescreen until finally, one night in the second year, when he was very upset, he spoke with such passion on this issue that I finally believed that it meant something to him. My field notes that night read: "Paul describes a vicious fistfight. Things fall into place! Paul has meant all along what Paul has been saying. Paul is the catcher in the rye. Paul is in truth desperately trying to hold the world together. The world that matters to him must not fragment! He must be accepted!"

The conversation that stimulated those notes had begun with my questions about Paul's loss of contact with Terri and the baby he had fathered, then had gone on to questions of struggles between racial groups. Conflicts arose, Paul said, because nonwhite groups wouldn't leave whites alone.

"If they would leave us alone, we would not even be discussing them, there would be no problem with us. We'd be just concentrating on getting whites to drop their differences.

"You don't need another race to have a Nazi party," he said. "You don't need any enemies. You have to get the whites to drop their differences and have like a folks spirit. That's what they did in Germany. They stopped all their differences, in economics, in family background, and everybody became one.

"If we had no problems with niggers and other races here in this country, we still would be far from having a white racial pride. If we had no enemies, we would still fight among ourselves. That's what we're trying to get stopped is like people breaking off into little groups and different class of people. We're trying to make everybody the same, but only of the white race.

"So if we went even to Australia, we still would not fit in because the rich Australians would not want to associate with the poor, and the ones that like this sporting event would not want to mix with the ones who like that one, and you can find things. People don't like the looks of your clothes, they want to be against you. They don't like the music you listen to, they want to be against you."

"Hold it, Paul," I protested. "That's so silly, I can't believe—"

He was adamant. "It goes on, *it goes on! You* don't *see* it! *You're* not in touch with reality. *I see* the fighting going on."

"You're fighting about what kind of music people want to listen to?" I said incredulously.

"That's right."

I stared at him. "How many people have been killed on this block in the last year because of—"

"You don't have to be killed," he answered. "You can have your ass beat and you can be shunned. And you can be refused friendship and just somebody to speak to.

"If I were to go to one of these bars with all short-hairs, no one would talk to me and if I tried to talk to them, they would shun me or somebody would say 'get the hell out of here, you don't fit in.'

"My old man's bar where he used to go a lot—everybody in there was the short-haired-type construction people, and I'd go in there and tell him come on home, I had some dinner ready, I'd walk in, they'd stop talking and look at me and I could just tell they were giving me dirty looks while I was over there talking to my dad. They didn't say anything, but they sure would've liked to."

"The way you look, back in the sixties, they would've said you're a hippie," I said. "What would they say now, you're a biker, or what?"

"No, they just don't like it. I don't think there's a name for it. You'll hear that term again, 'Hey, you goddamn hippie.' To try and start a fight. 'Hey, you goddamn longhair son of a bitch, you a faggot, or what?' Nobody's ever said that to me in the last few years because I'll fight to the death on a bogue [insulting] remark from anybody. A fight-starting remark like that. But you can see it in their eyes, you can just feel the hostility in the air.

"If I go to the [bar] where it's mostly people that are twenty to thirty-five, office-working men and women with their shirts and ties, even if I wear a shirt and tie with my long hair and that, people aren't going to hassle me like the rednecks at the old fogey bar. They're just going to snicker and talk down about me in the fucking bar. There is too much goddamn division being made. Like games, where people root for one team and somebody roots for the other, and they want to beat the hell out of them for it.

"*This stuff goes on!* I've seen parties where people, I've been jumped and beaten at a party of seven or eight people jumping on one over nothing. Somebody says oh, I didn't like the way the guy was looking. He didn't know anybody here.

"There's a lot of hostility. People are looking and taking out on somebody. So it has nothing to do with racial. Everywhere I go, it's all white. And yet I see whites fighting each other. And I'm always standing in the thick of it, trying to break it up. And if they want to try and jump on me then, I say I was just trying to break it up. You want to swing on me, I'll hook 'em. And I'll go down beaten to the ground before I give up."

"What's the last time you had a fistfight with somebody?" I asked.

"Oh, I was at a party about a year and a half ago and two guys were fighting and just some guy was drunk and had bumped into a couple people and spilt their beer. And another drunk wanted to beat the hell out of him for it. And he was knocking him around pretty good and a crowd was gathering around, and I says, 'Hey, you guys, you should break it up. This is a party, man, you're bringing everybody down, you're going to get the cops here.'

"They was fighting it out on the ground, and I had a crowd in front of me, and all I did was mention something like that, this level of voice, a little louder than I'm talking to you now. 'Hey, break this up, it's a party, not a fight!' And like a crowd of these six dudes in the back turned around and all started throwing punches on me, saying, 'Oh, yeah? We're going to fuck *you* up, motherfucker! We're going to fuck *you* up.'

"And I managed to grab the first one in front of me and get him by the face. I pulled him to the ground and they're all trying to kick me and everything while I was huddled with him on the ground, and I gripped him under the eye sockets and I says, 'I don't know about you, bitch, but you're being blinded.' And I tried to blind that son of a bitch while his friends were all kicking and throwing punches at me, but they couldn't get me because we were down and I was rolling, but I had a hold of that punk's face.

"And finally a chick that I knew at the party came over. She was going like this to the guy, 'Leave him alone, hey, leave him alone!' And she was kind of like straddling over where me and the guy were. And a Mexican pulled out his knife and came running over to stick me in the side just as she reached across to break it up and it split her knee open. And she had to get like thirty stitches across her kneecap, was in the hospital for about a month because of the position of the knife. And no one could prove that the Mexican did it. No one caught him with the knife, but it was just rumored.

"And that was all just because I made a comment, 'Hey, this fighting shit's for the birds, man. Let's break this up before the cops get here.' That wasn't hostile. And here these six, seven, eight white dudes that I had never seen before, that were a few years younger than me, and to beat the hell out of me just because—and I wasn't drunk, I was peaceful.

"This was at a party, out at Seven Mile and Telegraph. After that, him and his buddies took off because the girl's leg was cut open. I think they knew the Mexican or something. The guy, I heard later, his eyes were all swollen up and bloodshot for a week after that. Because I knew some people that knew that crew. They were from like the other side of Telegraph, neighborhood over there. And they called him B.J. He said, 'Yeah, you almost blinded B.J., he's been seeing double all week and his eyes are all swollen up and bloodshot.' And I just laughed, and I says, 'I would've blinded the son of a bitch.' "

"Paul," I asked, "were you in a bad mood already tonight, before I brought that up about Terri?"

"No, not at all. I'm not in a bad mood now."

"You sound kind of angry when you're talking about that fight," I said.

"Because it wasn't, it was unnecessary. I've seen a few since then that I haven't been able to put a stop to.

"And at some house party, eight or nine motorcycle punks from one of these scum gangs were beating the hell out of one guy and trying to chase him down. And I was just too wasted to do anything about it, but I thought to myself, before I was going to the party, I was going to think of carrying a pistol with me, just for the hell of it, under my jacket, but after that I was glad I didn't. 'Cause I knew I hated them motorcycle rats so bad and jumping that one guy that I would've pulled it out and shot two or three of them, laid them out, get revenge."

"You talking about that Magnum of yours?" I asked.

"Yeah, because they were jumping on some guy, beating the hell out of him, and no one was doing anything."

I looked at him. "If you'd shot someone with that Magnum, you would've torn him into pieces."

"I know, but I was so drunk and seeing this guy hassled by these motorcycle rats all wearing their—"

"What have you got against motorcycle people?"

"Not people who ride motorcycles—these gangs. They're gangs out to break the law and take advantage of what they are. They use the group, an organized group, like Hell's Angels.

"We've got so many white women we know around the neighborhood that have been raped by these gangs. We've got people we know who have been beaten and jumped and had their money or their car or something stolen by these gangs. When you fight one, you fight them all. And they always jump a person with three or four of them, they don't care what happens. A lot of them are in prison, in and out of prison all the time. They don't care. They'll go to jail for attempted murder. Or for killing somebody.

"And they're all white, and you'll see them wearing a swastika and white power symbols only because they consider it a threatening thing and something evil. It's something to intimidate people. That's why they band in these gangs. It's not out of brotherhood or to be friends with people."

These were the most unguarded words, the most direct words Paul ever spoke to me. I believed his concern. I saw it as a concern about himself, that he be accepted in the only community that was real for him, the world of whites. The white world is the world that the white racists care about—the one that feels real to them—and the primary meaning of the white racist movement is a struggle for a competitive place in the white world. This is a struggle for acceptance by the only community (or imagined community) that matters to them.

The Strike Group was Paul. He cared day after day; he was at the phone when members called; he told them to come on over; he listened, he talked with them, he fixed them food. He told them about things he had read, told them about things he had seen on television. He handled the correspondence and the phone calls from the curious. He helped put together the newsletter; he received newsletters from other groups and studied them—what ideas had other people had that the Strike Group could copy? He studied the papers and television, looking for ideas—what would be a place to have a rally that would bother people, what was happening that ought to be protested? He went to Miles's farm and learned the white racist movement's viewpoints and analyses; he brought back to the group the catchwords and the ideas. He pushed the activities, hectored people to make sure they would come to a demonstration, make sure they were at the house the night before to sleep over and to leave together as a bunch. With Terri and a few others he got the uniforms together, stored them at his place. His was the energy that kept the thing going. At a demonstration, the members typically formed a line facing the enemy; he paced behind them in his officer's hat, moving from side to side, talking constantly and nervously, keeping up their spirits; then he placed himself in the center of the line and began to call out slogans on the megaphone. He spoke when reporters came.

He was the one who thought, between actions. He sat in his old stuffed chair in the dark flat and got depressed; he sat and chewed on his disappointment; he sat and after some hours would remember something—would think of something the group could do that would drive people nuts: "It's building, Rafe, it's building! We're celebrating Hitler's birthday at Belle Isle [a Detroit park], and they can't stop us! They're going crazy!"

He carried the members about the city in his ancient van; he spent a lot of time working on it to keep it running. He scraped up money from the people who had work or could get it from their mothers, then called the truck rental company. They rode to the demonstration site, packed in the back of the Ryder Rental. Paul drove, sitting in the cab with one or two friends. Paul was the leader, Paul was the older person, Paul was permanent.

Paul had put a lot of years into this. He had traces of a life outside: He really cared about the rock scene, music meant a lot, partying meant a lot. He had had factory jobs; after several years of unemployment and welfare, he finally found a new one; he hated driving way out to the job on cold mornings. He didn't want to take on any training that would let him get better work; he got discouraged if he thought about it. He was flat broke when I met him and never did much better.

He was less and less available for a regular life. At the same time he was involved in a strange life as the older presence, the older brother or uncle, for these terribly young, terribly naive, terribly unformed teenagers. I looked at him one summer evening in the park. It had been a broiling hot day. A long road looped through the park; vans and motorcycles and beat-up cars were parked along the road; guys in their teens and their twenties stood around the vans, sat on the curb of the road, sat on the hoods of cars, everyone with one or two beers in their hands. Paul stood in the road next to his van, a beer in each hand, barefoot and shirtless in cutoffs. He stood with his chest and his stomach bare to the slight breeze that periodically came. I stared at him and thought about him surrounding himself with the thin young men. What function did all this play for him? He seemed at that moment Peter Pan—"I won't grow up." He seemed presexual, the youngest of all, naked and hungry.

Paul, five years after my interviews with him began, was arrested with several other people (none from the group) on charges having to do with drugs and guns. The Strike Group had declined to near inactivity.

He was refused bail because police had seized in his flat a videotape about the group that included scenes in which they were learning guerrilla tactics with carbines. The judge felt that the tape showed the man was too dangerous to be on the street before trial. The weapons on the tape, as it happens, were not weapons that belonged to the group. Group members did have a ragtag bunch of weapons, but the frightening-looking carbines had been supplied by someone else for filming. Thus, once again, the focus on image had boomeranged and hurt the image-caster.

I tried, unsuccessfully, to visit Paul while he was in jail awaiting trial. At his request, I wrote a letter attesting that I knew of no violent acts that he had committed. The arrest apparently had to do with his role three or four years before, helping a narcotics agent make connections to buy pills. Paul pleaded guilty to a version of the possession charges and drew several years in prison. He served his time in a bitterly cold prison camp near Duluth. His parole, after an early release, forbade him contact with organized white racists and he put in several bored and dissatisfied years with his father in Appalachia. He returned after his parole to resume his leadership of the group.

We will look next at Paul's followers, beginning with his lover.

T W E L V E

Terri

"**D**o you mind if Rafe drops me over at Alison's?" Terri asked Paul at the end of our second conversation. "It will beat walking a mile in the snow." When she had asked, I had told her it was not out of my way. "Alison may call while we're on the way. Be nice to her on the phone," she begged.

"Alison is my good friend," she told me in the car. "The reason I said to Paul to be nice is that Alison had a baby by an Arabian guy. Well, she was young and she didn't know anything. And I think he is a beautiful baby. I don't care what Paul says. Jonathan is a beautiful baby."

Terri talked quietly with me about her life as we rode. It was a strong contrast to the brittle ideological things she had been saying in the interview. That duality recurred through the half year of our acquaintance.

Terri was seventeen. She and Paul had been living together for almost two years. Where she was youthful, he was surly. He treated her brusquely and spoke with grudging or contemptuous tones. She wasn't earning money, and he treated her as though with badly strained tolerance. He acted the big guy who is putting up with a flighty and irresponsible young woman. You had to guess what was in it for her; he was older, he had money—or, when he was still employed, had had money. She was anchored if she was with him.

192

Most of her friends had by now been caught by unwanted pregnancies and had responsibility for an infant. Terri was genuinely tender toward Alison's baby but terrified of being similarly enmeshed. She couldn't fail to see what was happening to her friends; unlike the male teenagers in the group, she knew her life could turn around radically at any moment. It scared her.

For now, however, Terri was making her way through the world, adventuring along. She was brighter and more spirited than most other members of the Strike Group. Her racism was standard for her neighborhood: an ignorant contempt for and deep fear of black people. Her enrollment in the organized racist group reflected her adventurousness, which responded to the idea of confrontation and involvement, and reflected the happenstance of her involvement with people who were leaders in the group. The group, for her, was a form of activity, as against settling in.

Let me add, as I recall a video that a film team had made of her and the others a year or two before, that the group gave her a setting in which to be provocative, saying confrontational things in a nasty way; she could be a conspicuous rebel with a sharp edge, while standing next to the protective form of the larger, older leader. She could say rotten things to the interviewer with the camera, then look over at Paul to be sure he was there, and then lash out again.

Terri was thin, with a quick mind and an expressive face. She enjoyed using her good looks, dressing herself tough and sexy. It was fun to be around her. She was lively; she could be bitter, she sometimes fell into sullenness, but I mostly sensed her openness and her youth.

Early in our contact, I suggested to Terri that people's parents must be surprised to find their children involved in a Nazi group. Her mother didn't really care, she said, except that she worried about Terri "going on rallies and getting hurt." Her mother didn't agree with the things the group believed, she said, "but, as far as it comes to blacks and everything, like I was going to public school here, and as soon as she heard they were going to bus—I was in the third grade—as soon as she heard they were going to bus the next year, she put me in a Catholic school." (The family was not Catholic.)

"And then after the Catholic school," she said, "I had to go to public high school, because there wasn't any Catholic schools in our district. And I only went there for a week. And I couldn't go no more."

She paused. Actually, she said, she never even made it all the way into the school the very first day. The first day, she said, there was "kind of a black and white riot going on."

According to Terri, an undercover policeman, for no reason, broke the nose of one of her friends with the butt of a gun during this riot.

"So I didn't go back," she said. "I just turned around and went home and stayed there. I refused to go back.

"That's why, like all my girlfriends and I, we haven't made it through high school. Just because of that fact. And we're all trying to pick up different trades and things like that, because it's just too bad to try and go to no school."

Dropout stories in the group often feature racial fights at school. There's no way to know how much this story has been dramatized over the years.

I asked whether this meant that she had not gotten through ninth grade. "No," she said, "I made it through ninth grade, because I was into Casa Magdalena, which was a girls' home. Because I had a truancy from school, and a girl shot me with a BB gun, and that's kind of a long story, we got into a big argument. So I went in there, and I was in there, and I finished ninth grade in there.

"But I had to get out of there, too," she said, "because the blacks ran that, and if you said anything wrong to one black person, all of them were on top of you. And the whites were so scared, because it was like twenty-eighty percentagewise, twenty, you know, for whites, so that they didn't want to stick up for you.

"And I was so young, all the rest of them were like up to my age now, and I was only thirteen, fourteen in there. So I didn't stay in there too long, either."

I was by then confused and tried to straighten the story out. "Let me understand, Terri. You didn't go back to the high school after the first day because of your friend being hurt?"

"Yeah," she said, "and it was this big riot going on and I was scared to go back."

"And then," I asked, "you were staying at home and they picked

you up for truancy and they delivered you to this institution, or
what?"

"Well, I was staying home from school," she answered, "and my
mother worked. And my father hasn't been around for a long time.

"My mother worked and she was gone all day and everything.
And she kept telling me I had to go to school. I had to go to school.
So it was part of her putting me in there, too.

"I wasn't a state ward." That was important to her. "It was my
mother *and* the state. They sat down and they talked about it and
she said, 'Well, I guess she's going to have to go in there if she won't
go to school.'

"And I wouldn't. I would not go back to that school, I was scared
to death."

"Terri," I said, "you sound like you've been without your dad for a
while."

She told me about it.

"Yeah, my mother and father filed for divorce two days after I
was born. And the divorce was final when I was three and I haven't
seen him since I was three. Haven't seen him since.

"He got remarried to a girl he was going out with before he went
out with my mom. And they have two kids. He's living in Canada
now, so he wouldn't have to pay child support."

"Does it hurt?" I asked.

"No," she said. "I've never really lived with him to know—it's
not like I lived with him till I was fifteen or something years old and
then they got divorced and he left. So I never really—only he was
coming around before he got remarried, I was so little at the time
and it would only be like every two weekends or something, so I
didn't—"

She sounded confused. I asked whether her mother was bitter.

"No," Terri said, "she has a good job, she had a good job the
whole time, you know, so it wasn't like we were broke or anything.

"She's a little bitter that she doesn't—she's mad at him not because
he doesn't get in touch with her, but because he doesn't talk to me
or anything. And then she feels he may have two other children, but
he has to take care of, he's forgetting about the one that he had

before. You know. That's the only thing she's mad at him about.

"But otherwise she's glad that they did separate when they did because he was—she was supporting him, he was a semi-pro football player, and he wasn't making any money. So.

"We lived with my grandparents till I was six. So really, my grandfather is my main father, really. Did all the necessary, like when it came to spanking and things, he did it, and I'm his little girl."

There was a silence. "So," she said. "It doesn't really bother me at all that he's gone," she added.

I asked how she would see to it that the marriage worked out if she got married.

"I wouldn't get married. No, I would live with the guy or whatever. And you might as well say that you're married then, just without the legal paper and the diamond ring or whatever. And then that way, if you got to leave, you don't have to go settle a divorce and this and that.

"And try not to have a kid, either. Because that's who it hurts the most, if you got a—unless she, unless it's like a fairy tale and you have a beautiful marriage. Which really doesn't happen too often. No.

"All my girlfriends are, you know, having kids and getting married and everything, and they regret it. So I'm going to wait until I'm at least thirty before I even think about having a kid."

"You've got friends who are married and having kids, and you're seventeen?" I asked.

"Yeah. Five of my best friends that all of us hung around in our clique, as you may call it—all of them have kids. One's not married, her boyfriend died. One's married. The three other ones are living with guys. They're not married, but they might as well be. And they're all miserable.

"I'm the last one that doesn't have any kids or whatever. They're miserable."

One of our conversations took place a couple of days after the Strike Group had held the third of its annual demonstrations in Ann Arbor. That demonstration had ended almost as soon as it began; counter-demonstrators had rushed at the Strike Group members as soon as they had appeared, and the police had whisked the Strike Group members away at once. I asked Terri whether she had been rushed by the crowd.

"Yeah," she said. "I didn't get hurt. They kind of all just rushed around me.

"I had my hands full. One of our friends from Chicago was carrying something that went with the sound system, and I had my shield, his picket signs, my picket signs both. Everything happened and then by the time I got him his picket signs and I was ready to go out and do some damage, it was all over.

"And the cops were pushing me, in fact they practically knocked me down three or four times. They kept saying 'Go here' and I thought he meant like underneath the ropes they had, so I went over there, he goes 'No, no, no!' grabs me by my shirt, practically swung me over the rope. Instead of bringing me under, he practically threw me over the rope. He says, 'No, no, no, this way, this way!' So I just kind of walked away.

"If you compare, we had too many people. Like last year, the cops didn't do nothing. They let two thousand of them rush us, smash us into the back of the wall, and they didn't do nothing, until their building's windows started getting busted. That's when they decided to come in.

"This time, I don't know, this time they just didn't want any of us to speak, because they're scared that we're going to get more members. Because last year we were only there with fifteen. We doubled it with thirty this year.

"The Reds are always telling us to go home, but they're the ones that will burn an American flag. Last year that's what they did, they took our American flag and burned it.

"When we carry a swastika, that's not a German symbol, that's a white power symbol. And you can be carrying an American flag and a swastika flag. Where they just carry a red flag with the sickle and the hammer. They just carry that and don't believe in—you know, they're always putting down America.

"Well, if they feel that way about it, why don't they go to Russia and see how it is over there? Live under, you know, their laws.

"Especially the blacks, because Russia is so against blacks, you know. Blacks, if they only knew they were fighting for someone that would just as soon see them die, they wouldn't be doing it. But they're just so stupid or something, I don't know what it is.

"After they kicked us out, they let the communists have their rally down there," she added. "They let them stay and have a rally. And it wasn't even in the papers. You know, the Reds are not going to say, 'Yeah, we were throwing ammonia bottles.' Because, well, ammonia and bleach mixed, if you do that, that's a poisonous gas, you mix ammonia and bleach."

"How many women were in the group last year and this year, who came down?" I asked.

"Me, just, last year," she answered, "and the lady from the Klan and another lady from Chicago came this year."

Terri's heavily mixed neighborhood had once been all white. Here she was, she would say, in the area she was born and raised in, and here were blacks "coming in from God knows where and hassling me. They hassle all the older people, too, that are stuck here, that don't have any money to get out. They're all standing in front of the drugstore up here where everybody goes to buy your bread and milk or whatever. And you walk up there and they're all standing out in front and hassle everybody—everybody that's white. If you're black, that's a different story, that's 'Hey, Brother, what's happening.' "

She spoke resentfully of earlier years, of which she had heard from friends, when "little black kids would walk around school with these black fists, black power T-shirts." Whereas now, if a white kid were to come to school in a shirt that said WHITE POWER, he'd be made to go home and change, "because that's discrimination against those poor, poor black people." But the black kids got to wear what they wanted. And the blacks had the NAACP. "And if you try to tell me that the leaders of the NAACP aren't racist, you're crazy.

"And the mayor, Coleman Young," she went on, "is the most racist black I've ever seen. He is so racist, you would not believe. All of his council members are black. And if they're not black, they should be, because they all act like him."

Terri had absorbed the movement's pseudo-histories. "I think we did them [the blacks] a favor when we brought them over here," she said. "Because in Africa, at the time, the strongest—oh, savages or whatever you want to call them, the strongest gangs or groups down there, they'd go and kidnap and kill all the other ones, and keep them in a pen, and feed them and feed them and feed them, until it was time for them to have a great big feast, and then they'd eat them. So now, you know, when we brought them over here, we did them a favor. Because maybe they did have to work and be slaves, but they were over here and they got fed. It was just like, oh, working for your room and board.

"And now, myself, I would never even have brought them over here, I would have let them kill all their selves over in Africa, you know. Never brought them over here. But in those days, this country was just being built up and the whites needed help. You had your revolution between the whites over in England and the whites over here that wanted to start a new thing and they needed, you know, help to build it up."

It was not unusual to hear this sort of disclaimer in the movement. Life would have been simpler had there been no slave trade in the first place, they felt. But never did I hear a word of compassion for the African captives who died in the Middle Passage or lived in travail on the land. Terri, an exception in many ways, felt love for Alison's half-Arab baby. But the bulk of these young people had no empathy to spare for anyone, probably because they had no love to spare for themselves.

Terri's venom about blacks, who filled much of her everyday world, was not matched by her feelings about Jews. She said she did not know much about Jews "because I never was around them or anything, but from what like I've heard and stuff—which it may not be true because I just heard it, I don't have any facts on it. But like Jews are always saying, the thing makes me mad is like, especially the Jews that are in the communist party, and you can tell the Jews because their last names are Goldberg and whatever, they're saying, 'Mix, mix, mix, mix, mix! You have to love your brother!' But if they were to marry a black person or white person or even a Christian, no matter what color, their parents would disown them.

"They think that the Jews should stay pure because they're God's chosen people. Well, now, who says they're God's chosen people?

The Jews say they're God's chosen people. I'm white. If I go up and I say I'm God's chosen people, because I say I'm God's chosen people, that doesn't make me God's chosen people. You know what I'm saying? And that's just what gets me about them.

"I don't really know," she said, "like, how they run all the businesses and stuff. And they do run most of the media, you can tell by the names on the things afterwards, and what TV programs go on and what ones don't. And things like that.

"And mainly the thing that bums me out about them is they say 'Mix, mix, mix,' but then they won't mix, either."

It was clever of the Jews, she felt, to push the propaganda of mixing, to get all the races to mix except themselves.

To explain the flaw in mixing, she introduced a familiar image from the movement. "That's just like, okay, I'm not putting us down on the level of dogs or any kind of animal, but say you've got a two-hundred-dollar Doberman or two-hundred-dollar Great Dane, okay? You mate it with some two-hundred-dollar German shepherd, you're not going to get two hundred for those puppies. You're not going to get nothing for those puppies. Where if you mate a two-hundred-dollar Great Dane with another two-hundred-dollar Great Dane, you can get two hundred for the puppies. See what I'm saying?"

Then Terri, being Terri, introduced some qualifications. "I'm not saying all whites are perfect," she said. "Because there are a lot of white trash. Just like there's a lot of Jewish trash or black trash or whatever, but there's all these good people, too. We're not out to kill all the races. We're just out to separate them, because we can't live together, no matter what anybody says. We haven't been able to do it for the last two hundred years."

Terri spoke to me of bad days, when I asked, and I heard again the capacity to express tender feelings that distinguished her from the young men.

"Two days I can tell you about that were bad," she said. "One day was bad when one of our friends, Ernie, died. And I felt he was one of our white power comrades and that was really, really bad. Because I still miss him a lot.

"And another day was bad, it wasn't so much bad for me, it was more or less bad for my girlfriend, but she's my really, really good friend, so it made it bad for me, when her boyfriend died. That is the father of her son, too. So it was kind of a bummer."

I asked why these two, who must have been young, died.

"Ernie just, he just died in his sleep. He had a heart attack because, before, he had cancer, and what is that they do? To cancer people? Chemotherapy, yeah. He had all that done and everything and after a while it just got too hard on his heart. So he died, he was only twenty-six, I think, twenty-five, twenty-six.

"And my girlfriend's boyfriend who died, Yakoub, he was thirty-five. And he had a heart attack, too. Died in his sleep."

Why would he have a heart attack at thirty-five? Terri replied that it was kind of his own fault. Paul, who was with us during this conversation, added that Yakoub had been "a dope addict." I asked whether he had been on something heavy.

"Freebaser," Terri said. "He did like eight grams in eight hours.

"He went through, how much was it, three ounces in the time of like two weeks. And it was just getting to him. After doing it and doing it and doing it. He was becoming a freebase junkie, if that's—"

I asked what freebasing was.

"Like you get coke, and it's been stepped on so many times, you boil it down so you just get rocks, solid, from coke rocks, and then you smoke it."

"It's more powerful then?" I asked.

"Yeah. You get more of like a head rush or whatever."

Paul added, "He burned his heart out from the speed effects of the cocaine."

"I kind of like it myself," Terri said, "but I tried freebasing once, and my lungs couldn't handle it. My lungs felt like they were going to explode."

Paul needed to explain. "We do the cocaine when it's free, that's about it, if somebody's got some and they'll give it to any of us for free, we'll snort it up."

"Well, that's what I mean," Terri said. "Like Yakoub, he didn't go through three ounces by himself. He'd give it away and stuff, too, plus smoke it with everybody else."

Paul was not forgiving. "He was a dealer. He made his profits out of other people's miseries. That's why he was about to attract friends, so-called drug friends, because he had a quantity and he'd give it away and he'd have company. People used him for his dope and he used people for their money."

"What will coke do to you?" I asked.

"Give you a heart attack," Terri said. "After you do so much, you get like insomnia, however you say that word, and you get it so bad that you never sleep, and then once, by the time, you know, that you do feel like you can go to sleep, it's time to have to get up. So you just get up and do more, you know, to keep going all day or whatever."

I pursued the inquiry with Terri. "When they died, Ernie, Yakoub—do you remember your feelings?"

"Sad," she answered.

"When Yakoub died, he was like a friend of mine, too, but I was more or less sad for my girlfriend and Jonathan, the baby, you know, because now he doesn't have a father or anything.

"And he was Yakoub's little boy baby, and he loved him a lot. And Jonathan loved Yakoub a lot, too, and that's what made me more or less sad, too, because of that.

"And when Ernie died, he was just a close, close friend of mine and, you know, I'm always expecting, like when I see his cousin or one of his other friends, I'm expecting him to come walking in the door behind him. And he never does, you know, and I really miss him a lot."

I asked what he had been like.

"He was nice. He was always easygoing and happy, you could joke around with him, and I don't know, he was just really nice."

"When you think about him, what picture comes to your mind?"

"I don't know, really a lot of different ones. Just like the things we done and stuff, like we used to go to the beach all the time, and have a good time. Like mostly I can remember him is when he'd drink a load of beer, he'd be passed out in like five minutes. I can just see him, you know, laying on the beach, all passed out, with his boots on and stuff. That's all he had on, his cutoff shorts and his big jackboots, and that used to crack me up."

"Did you cry?" I asked.

"Yeah. Crying helps a lot, I think."

"When you feel bad," I asked, "how do you go from feeling bad to feeling better?"

"What I do," Terri said, "I call up my best friend down in Florida, and she always makes me happy. She's going to be having a baby. We just call and talk about her getting new baby clothes, and things like that. Which, when I found out she was pregnant, I just started crying, because of all the girls that hung around tight, out of like five or six, I'd say seven or eight even, that hung around tight all of our lives, I'm the last one left. She's the second last one left, she hasn't had it yet, but I just started crying and saying, 'Oh, no, my best friend's going to have a baby. What a drag!' "

I asked Terri to look at the preceding five years, talking about good years and bad years. That began, she said, with a year that was really bad. First of all, she had quit ice skating; more important, "I got into a fight with this chick and she shot me in a very personal place with a BB gun, so I took a brick to her head.

"And right before I got my court date, I went into Casa Magdalena because my mom, well, sort of put me in there, because I had truancy from home and school. And then while I was in there, my court date came up for that [the assault with the brick]—they called it a felonious assault, but really it was a self-defense. And I wanted to go to court to clear it up. And the home I was in [Casa Magdalena] wrote a letter to the court and my mom, saying that I wasn't mentally stable enough to handle any kind of court cases. And I wasn't in there because I was crazy, I wasn't crazy at all.

"So that was my bad year," she concluded.

The following year had been sort of half and half. In the summer Terri had run away from Casa Magdalena because of what they had said in the letter and because they were going to give her seven more months at the home; she ran away and hitchhiked to Florida, where she stayed for a while. When she returned, her mother placed her back in Casa Magdalena; Terri ran away a second time to Florida.

"So when I got back the second time," she said, "I didn't want to go home because she would just put me back in there and I didn't want to go back in there after I ran away twice, because they'd hassle you more and more.

"So I lived in a shed for from like October to December, and it was cold. I lived in a shed, and then my girlfriend came home—because she was off at school, my best friend, she came home—and I moved in at her house and when I moved in at her house, everything started going good."

"Did your mom know you were back?" I asked.

"Yeah, she knew," Terri said. "Because I'd sleep in the shed, our shed in the backyard, and then when she went to work I would just crawl through the window and stay in the house until she more or less got home. But she knew I was there because you could just tell.

"But she . . . really . . . didn't try, you know, too hard to find me or anything. Because . . . I didn't know, but my mom realized after I ran away twice that it was stupid for her to put me in there because it just made me worse. Didn't do any better. I was only, I turned thirteen while I was in there, and all the other girls were like fifteen, sixteen, seventeen. And you know, older. And they just taught me" —she laughed self-consciously—"worse things to do.

"Because I hitched, the second time I hitchhiked down to Florida with two of the girls, and they both, well, one was seventeen and one was sixteen. And they got me into more or less like harder drugs and, you know, things like that. And it made me worse. I was . . . I hated the world more, or whatever. And I really hated my mom for putting me in there."

This conversation was beginning to upset Terri. But she continued. "So we never got to talk. And she couldn't tell me that she was going to forgive me. Until one day she came home early from work, and caught me. I was in the shower. And then we sat down and talked, and then I started staying with her again."

I asked what had happened when the mother found her in the shower. Who had said what?

"Well, I about fainted. And she said, 'What are you doing here?' I said, 'I'm taking a shower.' And she said, she goes, 'Well, I've known you've been here for a while.' She goes, 'Where have you been staying? Have you been staying over at Janet's?' And I said 'No,' because like a couple of nights I'd stayed there, but Janet's mom—my mom and her was right next to each other [that is, tight friends], so Janet used to sneak me in if I ever did stay the night. So I just told her, I said, 'No, I been staying in the shed.' She goes, 'Well, that's stupid, you could stay here.' And that was it."

Terri stayed with her mother then, and after a while they moved to a new neighborhood. Soon living together didn't work. "We got on each other's nerves so bad, because when she first moved out there, she didn't know nobody and I didn't know nobody, and we were home together all the time. And my mom like acts ten years younger, and I act ten years older than my age, and we just kind of conflict that way." Terri had told me this several times before, that she and her mother ended up much too easily as rivals. "We just kind of conflict that way," she continued. "Because we're too much alike. And we go for the same guys and things like that. You know, it just doesn't work."

So Terri stayed with her mother for a while and then moved in with her friend Janet in the spring. She lived with the friend all that year, "and that's when I met Paul. Well, I knew Paul before that, because Janet was going out with him. But that's when I started hanging around with him. And that's when I got into, oh, white power."

That summer, she said, "was the best summer I've had in my life. It was so nice, the park was packed all the time, it was just white people. Black people went in there, they were ran out.

"Like I told you before, because of the parks and stuff—the niggers got all the parks, why can't white people sit back and party without those greasy . . . apes around all the time? Huh?

"It was my neighborhood, I was born and raised there, and that's when they started really getting down on *their* park, so everybody went to ours." There had been a de facto choice by the two groups, with blacks congregating at one park and whites at another. "And it was good," she recalled, "and there was never no violence. You know, once in a while, I'd say, once a month there was a fight, but you're going to get that with a bunch of people together that don't know each other and stuff. But most times, you know, it was good." Whereas, she said, had the park been half black and half white, there would have been fights all the time.

She recalled childhood times at this park, which then consisted of a dirt road along a creek. They had gone to play in the woods, shooting at what she called river rats with their BB guns. You could shoot a river rat four times and it wouldn't die, she recalled. She recalled further that river rats had killed one of her cats.

"My mom used to bring kittens home from Chrysler's all the time, because they used to have 'em in the trucks, and then when they were going to use the trucks, they'd just pull 'em out. So my ma used to bring home these kittens all the time. We had seven cats at a time, all the time." Since her mother worked and Terri went to school, they would let the cats out during the day. "Lots of times they'd come back all chewed up by a river rat."

The year that had followed had been neither good nor bad, she said. "I was getting kicked out of my mom's house and then she'd call me up—" Suddenly she remembered more clearly. "No, it wasn't that good, as a matter of fact. My mom was going out with this guy named Johnny Reb and he was an idiot—well, we called him Reb— anyway he used to sit back and say, 'I hate communists, I hate Jews, I hate niggers, and I hate Nazis.' And we'd say, 'Well, if you hate all these people, do you hate yourself? Because you hate everybody!' Because he used to get down on Paul and I for being Nazis."

Terri laughed a moment, remembering arguing with the man, but things had not been good. "My mom had him move in, and when he moved in, I had to move out. But as soon as he moved out, my mom goes: 'Oh, Terri, come back in and live with me.'

"That's how she is, when she's got a boyfriend, she don't want me around, but when she doesn't and she's staying by herself, 'Come on and move back in.' So that was kind of . . . a drag.

"And then the next summer," she continued, "I was going out with this biker, and he was a gross, sick thing. A gross, sick thing. And he hit me over the head with a pot. He gave me a fat lip and a black eye, so I never seen him since."

She didn't like to be beaten up, I suggested.

"No," she agreed. "The black eye and the fat lip didn't hurt so much, but when he hit me over the head with the pot, he dented the pot and broke the handle off it, he hit me so hard."

This had happened, she continued, in the house of a friend that was a Jew. She corrected herself: He was not really a friend, she had just been over there. "But he knew I was a Nazi, I knew he was Jewish, and we just had stuff to take care of."

The following year had had good elements—another stay in Florida, and her grandfather had sent her to a technical school for a while— but the year had also been the one in which the girlfriends had their babies. This brought us to the current year, which was "a drag! It's just so boring. No one's got any money, no one's working. There's no nothing around. Everybody just sits and watches TV. And we don't even have cable."

The parks, in previous years, had been great. "That's all I ever did. Woke up at four in the afternoon, took a shower, got some clothes on, stayed out till four the next morning, every single day.

"I didn't get too good of a suntan, though. I like to go to the beach and pass out on the beach."

Terri spoke further about walking through mixed neighborhoods and black neighborhoods. "My girlfriend Alison and I, we were walking, where her sister lives, it's really black over there. And we were walking down the street and these two black guys were up on top of their roof. And they were saying, 'Hey baby, hey baby!' And there was these two black girls walking down the other side of the street, so me and Alison, we didn't think anything of it, you know. We just kept on walking, kind of ignoring them. And then they were saying that and saying that, you know, and then all of a sudden we hear, '*Fuck you*, you white bitches!' And I said, 'Don't say nothing, don't say nothing. Don't stop, just keep on walking!'

"Besides, in that neighborhood, if you did say something and they decided to jump us—you know, all the blacks around there, they'd probably encourage it. So we just keep on walking, but we lifted our speed, started walking really fast.

"We never walk to the store around *here* anymore. I feel really sorry for her sister, because her sister's got to live in *that* neighborhood, and her and her husband are getting a divorce, she's got to stay there with her three little girls by herself. And the little girls are only six, four, and two, so they're not too much protection and . . . so I feel sorry for her. And the little girl that's got to go to school, she's the only white girl in the class, and there's only one other white person in the class, and that's a boy."

There was a pause.

"I've been raised not to like blacks," she continued. "Because my whole family, they're really against them. My uncle, he's a fireman. I don't know if I told you this before, but he was in a fire and two blacks were helping him carry the hoses in, the fire? And I guess they thought it was too hot, so they turned around and ran out, and left him in there, and he fell two stories down.

"And when you go in with a partner, partners are not supposed to split up whatsoever.

"My uncle always says, 'The best thing we can do with the blacks is to make Grand Canyon so no one can get out, put them all in there, don't feed them, and they'll eat themselves.' That's the way my uncle feels."

Terri said that a newspaperwoman who had come to interview her had "thought the whole reason I was in the [Nazi] party was because of Paul. But I was in the party before I even went out with Paul. I used to live with one of Paul's best friends that he's known for a long time. And he always used to try to talk me out of being in the party. 'Oh, you're going to get hurt,' this and that, just like my mom. But I haven't got hurt yet.

"And a lot of my girlfriends say, 'Oh, if you broke up with Paul, you moved to Florida, or you weren't going out with him, you wouldn't be in the party,' and this and that. And I tell them, 'Yes, I would.' You know, I'd believe in it anyway, regardless of if I was going out with Paul or not."

She would be like her girlfriend, she said, who had been the lover of another group member and now lived in Florida with a new boyfriend who didn't care for the party. The girlfriend, she said, still was handing out and putting up stickers, "and trying to keep in touch with the guys we met down there that formed their own Klan."

Those guys, she said, hadn't tried "to get in the Klan where there's a leader or whatever, like the Klan has Grand Dragons and things. They just went out to K Mart's and got their own sheets, and they'll walk around the neighborhood down there, and no one will say nothing to them, because they figure, 'Well, the Klan walking around here, the Cubans won't stay around.'

"Cubans are worse than the blacks around here," she continued. "They don't raise as much trouble, but they get down to the beach and they get five or six of their family out there playing the trash-can music. That's what it's called, I think. And it just drives everybody on the beach crazy because not everybody likes that music. And myself, I don't."

This is a kid talking, speaking in the same breath of a self-made Klan unit and trash-can music. It feels silly, until you think about the impact of racism on its victims.

The vivid thing for Terri was the personal gratification: She was alive to the pleasures she received from being a brassy participant in the encounters that were attended by the media; she was alive to the eagerness of reporters to interview her and to be startled by her intense responses; she was alive to the eagerness of TV cameramen to be sure she was visible in the viewfinder.

Participation gave her a chance to play a dramatic role. It certainly beat being subjugated as a biker's girlfriend. It gave her a gang of boys her age and a few men suitably older with whom she could buddy in her wisecracking way and find support and company. Most important, it gave her a resting place during the last part of the moratorium she was trying to draw, the slowing down of time that seemed critical to her. Each of the other young women her age that she knew had by now been caught by a pregnancy, had given up the autonomy and play of the early years and now answered to the total demands of their babies. Participation in the Strike Group allowed Terri to keep thinking of herself as a gang girl, to prolong the years of freedom.

Terri's racism was nasty and expressed the direct teaching of her family, as well as her neighborhood. She was heartless in her assumption of white privilege; she was blind to the pain of nonwhites. None of my sympathetic words make this less true.

Terri's story is fairly typical of the few women who are involved in this basically male enterprise. Despite her disclaimers, she really was there because of her involvement with Paul. She was a dependent girlfriend, taking on some of the pieces of her provider's life.

It's a very old role, and she slipped or was tripped in the oldest of ways. She and Paul failed in their efforts to prevent conception. I asked Paul, when I later heard of the pregnancy, what sort of birth control they had been using. "She had some pills from the doctor," he said, "but somehow had managed to miss them. For like about a month." I don't know what really happened. She could have run out of pills and delayed buying new ones; she might have fallen into a period of mindlessness; perhaps the pills just didn't work. Paul may have distorted memories of the incident. I was not able to speak with Terri at that time—Paul blocked my attempts to contact her. In any case, like her friends, she found herself pregnant.

For several months, according to Paul, they had debated what to do. Paul had spoken of raising the child, and Terri had delayed getting an abortion. Soon there was no choice. She had meanwhile left Paul, at the urging of her mother, and had returned to live with her. The mother kept Paul away once Terri had returned. More time passed, with Terri now postponing the next decision: Should the baby be put up for adoption? Shortly after its birth, she had it sent to a temporary foster couple, who took care of it while she recovered. After some weeks, she took the child back, and soon moved to Florida. In all this time, Paul had seen the baby only once. In Florida, Terri found a new boyfriend. I don't know what has happened since, but would guess that Terri's movement from protective man to protective man has continued and that she has more than one child by now.

Terri's story won't seem unfamiliar to those who work with urban youth. Though her mother had a technical job in an automaker's drafting shop, Terri grew up in a declining neighborhood in the midst of social disorganization. She ran a course from school to juvenile home to runaway to sequential coresidence with a string of tough, older men. Bouncing from mother to girlfriend to boyfriend, bouncing between Michigan and Florida, never progressing in school or picking up usable job skills, she was dependent on men for her security but able to go from man to man as she moved along. This more or less worked for her before she became pregnant, and may be working yet. Involvement with the Strike Group offered a certain amount of stability—the gang had some continuity.

Young women without money have to learn hard survival lessons early, have to go through frightening experiences, and have to deal with male power, often with almost no guidance or useful models. Life gets serious a lot sooner than it does for young men. This may be another reason few women are involved in these organizations at the fringe of society.

Our next case studies deal with representative young men in the group, beginning with a lost soul named William.

THIRTEEN

William

"It's about two and a half years ago now, my ma died. She had a heart attack. It's not really that bad, though, I don't think. Because the way she lived, she was really never happy, I don't think. I don't think she was ever happy. Because she would sleep where she could or—well, you know. So when I think about it, she may be better off this way. It's not that I like to see her this way, but . . .

"She'd come banging on the door—I was living with my sister— she'd come banging on the door in the middle of the night, drunk, and you know. And my sister would fight with my brother-in-law, because my sister wouldn't want to tell her to leave or nothing. But my brother-in-law was more or less not having as many feelings for her, you know. So they would fight. That would make them two fight. And then the kids would get brought down from it. I remember, because at that time I was living with my sister. Hearing all that. Just wondering, wow, when's it going to stop?"

That was William, at our first meeting; the theme would haunt all our meetings. A badly traumatized young man who had been taken from his alcoholic mother at an early age, a person with no firm center of his own, a representative of perhaps a third of the people who are attracted to white racist organizations, but also a type who could as easily flow into a cult—or into the various addictions that have marked his life thus far. Let us look first at his racism.

William had told me early in our talks that his family did not like black people. Each time I asked him to expand on this, I heard that blacks brought the city down. "I was brought up not to like them," he said. "I mean, if I was to go out—just saying this, I'm not saying I would—if I was to go out with a black girl, my dad would disown me. Definitely. [Actually, his father was dead.] But I would do the same if my son did that, I would think."

I asked why, and he said, "Just the way they live. They don't live right, I don't think. The way they live, it's just so dirty."

More than this, the black people his father had met at a welfare-related training school "wouldn't learn anything. He said the blacks just had such a low mentality."

Beyond this, there was the question of that deep inner nature of blacks that caused them to want to take things rather than earn them: "All the blacks that I know, more or less, the only thing they know is, oh, *take*. Not make something. Just *take* or, oh, harass. If you lived where I used to live, it's just three whites and then you see all the rest of the block is black. And you walk down the block, a nigger will come up to you and say, 'Let me have them cigarettes, white boy.' And you have to fight him.

"They ain't getting nothing from me. I just don't like the way they live. Just the way they are.

"If I walked down by Cass Corridor or Greektown or around there, all by myself, what would my chance be of not getting robbed or whatever? But then if a nigger came out to where I live, he could walk right down the street. And no one would say anything. Know what I mean?

"The NAACP, they're looking out for the blacks, we're looking out for the whites. The niggers wave their banner. Jews wave their banner. I don't think there's nothing wrong for the whites to wave their banner. The blacks wave their banner and it's just like, 'Those poor niggers, they've been through so much, look at them.'

"I think they should ship them. Ship them back to Africa. Yeah, they can live their lifestyle there."

William's family had moved a number of times, trying to keep away from black people. They had gone from Detroit to its immediate suburbs, and William's grandfather had gone all the way to a town

I will call Rumbolt, an industrial town fifteen miles west of Detroit. William lived in a trailer park with the grandfather and had worked for a while at a factory in the town. There he had met Paul and been led into the Strike Group.

Paul remembered this. "We just started talking at work," Paul said, "and being friends about different stuff, like rock and roll and house parties and things like that. What everybody did after work and who knew who was from what cities, and whatever. And I don't know how the subject came up or something, somehow we were just talking about problems, somebody mentioned the niggers giving somebody a problem or something, and one comment led to another and the next thing we were talking about how white power was the answer to all that problem." The subject didn't come up again for another month or so, Paul said. Then, "we were opening up our second bookstore. Couple of months after I met him. And I think William had seen a sticker or two or some literature that I had had from the first store. And was asking questions about it, what was that all about. So I said, 'Come on down—we're going to be opening up this weekend—and meet the people at the store.'" Two other people from the group also worked at the factory, Paul continued, "and they were all saying, 'Yeah, William, come on down, come on down. Bring your friends. We're going to have a beer party at the weekend and open up Saturday morning.' So him and his girlfriend and his girlfriend's brother, all of them came down and spent the weekend from Friday till Sunday. William met more people there."

William remembered: "Picked up some of the literature, took some home with me, checked it out, and more or less, I liked it and understood it and felt it was right."

William, twenty-one years old when we met, had been involved in white power since he was "about sixteen or seventeen. And more or less I had been living in Detroit and the niggers would more or less run over you and treat you wrong, you know. I was always against them. My whole family was always against them. So more or less when I found you could stick up for your own race, I was willing to join."

William developed these feelings further for me in a later conversation. I had asked him what it took to be a good member of the group.

"Stay white," he had said, "and do what you can to help all other white people out. And just . . . unity. Helping each other out and stuff."

I asked what it meant to say "stay white." I teased him: "Every morning I wake up and I'm the same color."

He didn't understand the joke and talked about the dangers of "race mixing." He also talked about liking the chance at rallies to "speak your piece," feeling good if even a couple of people really listened.

He wanted people to hear why the Strike Group was for white power. "A lot of them think we're just terrorists and stuff that just run around with the swastika and burn down houses. But that's not really it. What it means to stay white and to keep your family white. I would be totally bummed out if someone in my family had a mixed-breed child. It would mess up the whole family tree later on."

There was a long silence. I had been trying to find out what these young people actually felt when they thought about interracial coupling, and why they felt it. William seemed open; I tried to uncover his feelings. I told him that I did not understand emotionally what it would mean to him, what it would feel like for him.

"It's hard to explain," he said. "Just like it's hard for you to question it right, it's hard to answer right, you know. I mean, I could sit here, probably after you leave, I'll think, wow, I could've said this or I could've said that. I don't know. It's just how it goes."

I told him again that I just had trouble connecting to what he might be feeling. I decided to mention an example. "I've got a good friend," I told him, "who's black, and he's married to a white woman. And they have a very beautiful baby. All three of those people are physically very attractive and they're real nice people. And I just don't . . . What does it mean emotionally to you when I tell you that right now? Right now, this minute?"

He was surprised. "Just emotionally, I don't know, it just makes me feel good to be able to have someone sit down and listen. I don't know," he said, "it's hard to explain. Why, how would you feel emotionally? Isn't it a question and a half?"

"No," I replied, "I mean, I'm sitting here thinking, what in the world does that mean to William? Why does he care? I'm trying to think—"

He interrupted: "I just, myself, I just can't *stand* race mixing."

"That's what I'm trying to get hold of," I told him. "What difference does it make to you if that woman and that man love each other and have a baby? I mean, what's it to you? Why?"

This was getting to him. "Inside, it's just . . . I don't know, I just don't like it. It's a feeling inside, I don't know. It's real hard to explain."

I tried to lure him out. "Well, what does that feeling look like, what does it taste like? What color is it?"

He was perplexed. "It's like even colors that don't have names, it's hard to explain. It's like you could throw five colors together and it wouldn't be one color—you know what I mean?"

I tried again. "Okay, well, just try throwing words out when you think about it. What are words that come to mind? Close your eyes and just let her rip: What comes to mind when you think about it?"

He couldn't keep dealing in depth with my probes. He tried for a minute. "It makes me think that if everyone starts race mixing, all right, and they keep race mixing, you tell me if there's going to be one single pure white person, if everyone starts race mixing." Now he fell into the familiar raps. "Because when they race mix, then that kid's half and half. And when he grows up, he's going to go with whatever. And I just want the white man to stick around. Race mixing's going to kill the white man, I think."

We almost had found a way for him to express the unease he experienced over sexual contact across racial lines. But I hadn't quite found the words that would help him communicate with me, and he hadn't found words or else couldn't identify his feelings. Like all the folks I pressed on this, he reverted to a rote answer; pressed for a direct examination of his actual feelings, he withdrew into an abstraction distant from feeling.

William said that he would want his grandchildren and his great-grandchildren to grow up in a world that was all white with the blacks living in "their Africa or whatever." Much of his extended family lived on Michigan's Upper Peninsula, where blacks are rare.

"Part of my family's up there now because they don't like the scummy blacks down here. Just like my dad. First he lived on Tireman Avenue. The blacks invaded that, so we moved to Madison Heights. Blacks invaded that, we moved to Royal Oak. Blacks came in there, we moved to Livonia. Then we moved to Rumbolt. But we kept moving away from there and where you going to run? Where you going to move next if they're all over? I don't know."

I asked William what he made of the group's connection to Hitler. William, who said he kept a swastika and a skull emblem over his bed, said that Hitler "more or less, he took the bull by the horns. I don't know, I don't know if all that stuff is true about him, you know. I mean, they say he killed all those Jewish people and all that. I didn't see it. I mean, there's propaganda all over this world. I guess the only way I would believe something like that is if someone in my family stood there and told me they saw it."

His father, William said, hadn't liked the swastika "because he fought against it [in World War II]. But he didn't like the blacks at all. I mean, at all. And I was brought up that way. Move away from them. 'We've got to leave this town now, they hit this town.' So I thought the white race would just run, keep moving and run. And then I was very enthused to find that there were a few white people that did stick up for it.

"And I wanted to check it out and see what it was all about. And if I thought it was right, I would join it. And I understood what they were saying, it made a lot of sense to me, and I just started coming over more often and getting more into it, picking up a little literature, reading it. I was enthused."

William's feelings about Jews were much less intense. Jews struck him as snobs, based on his experience working at a pizza parlor. "I don't know," he said, "I haven't met all of them, you know, but what I have met, it's them and no one else. They only care about themselves. I mean, for two dollars' worth of food, they expect you to give them your life. I mean it, man. They're stuck up, you know? I mean, they're just very inconsiderate."

William thus was a young man who could be brought into the racist fold and was seen for years at demonstrations. But that was far from his central concern. The story that William carried around in his own head, the story that persistently reverberated inside him and held his real attention, was not about racism but about abandonment.

William began to tell me about the family at our initial meeting. I had asked whether he had been able to see much of his father after his parents had split up.

"Well, for a couple of years I didn't see him," he said, "and then he picked me up on weekends. Every Saturday was my dad day. I saw my dad every Saturday."

What was his father like?

"Tough. Tough. Yeah. I don't know, if you looked wrong, he'd . . . more or less, he didn't hit me, because I was so young, but my sisters . . . he was just more or less, I can't explain it, but everything had to be done right. Real strict. It had to be done right, or you'd do it over and over and over until it was done right, you know."

I asked what they did when his father picked him up on Saturday. The father owned a little shop, William said, where they worked on cars and sharpened blades for saws and stuff like that. When William was seven or eight, he got to work with the father sharpening saw blades and liked it a lot.

What was his mother like?

"Oh, she drank a lot. That's more or less why they split up.

"See, they didn't have really a divorce, they separated, when I was about five and a half, six years old. And then I lived with her for another year, year and a half, two years. And then my dad came back and saw how—how worse she was than when he left. And he had a social worker come over and the courts decided to take me away from her, and I went to my sister's."

"Did you see your mother after that?" I asked.

"Well, for about four years I didn't see her at all. I never talked to her on the phone or nothing. And then she finally called me and we started getting together a little bit, but she more or less lived here and there. She never had one specific house or something."

His father had died of cancer a year before we met. "It was in his spinal cord. And it went up through his spine into his brain, and he got mixed up and everything, you know." The father also was a diabetic.

William's mother had died two and a half years before our talk,

of a heart attack. And this was the point in conversation at which
William had told me that it was really not that bad, because, given
the way she lived, his mother was really never happy. He had spoken
of her coming and hammering, drunk, on his sister's door in the
middle of the night. I could picture William sitting in his room,
listening.

He elaborated on the central story a year later. "You want me to
start right from the beginning?" he asked. "Way back?

"When I was seven years old, the court said that my ma was drinking too much, which she was, she was an alcoholic herself. She drank
too much and she took care of me, you know, real good, but then
again, she'd go out on these binges and drink, you know. And I'd sit
home all by myself.

"So I just stuck with her, and then I turned eight, I was in school,
I went to the bathroom, this ain't no kidding, I came out of the
bathroom, I was sick from all the depression and stuff, you know. I
was throwing up in the bathroom. And I came back out of the bathroom, and here's my sister and the social worker from Pontiac [an
industrial suburb]. My sister Jenny, the younger one. They just
scooped me up and took me right out of school, just took me away.
And, ah, that's when I moved in with my grandparents.

"And they took care of me and everything. But you know, I still
missed my ma."

I asked how he had felt the day they picked him up.

"Bad. Real bad. It was on Easter, too. My ma brought a basket
and a bunny rabbit and everything to court, and I was kicking the
policeman in the leg because they wouldn't let me leave with my ma.
And the judge's name was Pontoon. And I was just kicking the policeman in the leg, and I could see the policeman had tears in his
eyes.

"And they put me in a little room so I wouldn't do nothing. They
locked the door and just gave me a piece of paper and a pencil. So
I sat there and drew."

When this was over, he had "felt real bad" and gone to live with
his grandparents. "And anyways, I was just staying around there,
and my ma would call me on the phone and all that, this and that,

you know, trying to talk to me, and they wouldn't let me and stuff.

"And she was drunk and out of her mind. And she was with a guy and all. And this guy was shooting up and stuff, you know. So . . ."

There was quite a pause then. William didn't like what he was saying. "I don't know what to say now," he said. "You want to know everything and then again, you know, a lot of stuff I remember, and I don't, you know. I do and I don't.

"Hard to say it on tape, you know. This is my personal life."

We sat quietly a few minutes. He told me then that after a while his older sister had decided that he should come to live with her, and he had done so, "and the social worker was in and out, making sure I was all right." And his sister had treated him well. "In fact, she was treating me too good because she knowed what I was going through, she treated me better than even her stepkids, you know." So he had been living with her and going to school, but felt that he couldn't handle his sister's stepkids and her own kids. "I just felt out of place, you know. I didn't have my own home. You know."

He had then moved to his younger sister's home in a trailer park. He was fifteen and "started getting messed up in drugs and stuff."

He spoke of his mother's death. "I got a phone call that my ma went to get a bottle of whiskey at Booster Drugs, it's right in the middle of Royal Oak. Eleven-Mile and Long Road. Okay, she had a heart attack and was in intensive care." At the same time, William's girl-friend had been rushed to the hospital. "My girlfriend, the one I was going to marry. Sally. Busted down in the middle of work and had, what's that called, appendix. Her appendix had all poison in them from worrying about me. So she had to be rushed to a hospital in Pontiac, before she died. If they burst, she would have died.

"Okay," he continued, "so I'm confused. What do I do? Stay with this girl that's went through everything with me, okay, or go, you know, see my ma that I haven't had time to be with, that the court said I couldn't be with.

"So here I'm confused, what do I do now? I drank, you know, just drank. Just to slow myself down."

He ended up spending one day at the hospital "through my girl-friend's operation and everything." Then, "without sleeping or nothing, right from there," he had gone to the other hospital to see his mother. He spent two nights in a row there.

"Okay, seeing her in intensive care—you can ask the doctors or anything. My ma was almost dead. I walked in her room, doctor was standing right next to me. Her blood pressure went to normal, I'm not lying. Her blood pressure went to normal, her heartbeat went to normal, everything went to normal. Because I was there."

William had not slept, he said, for four days. He was dirty and smelly. He went home "just to take a shower, call up Sally, see how Sally's recuperating. I get out of the shower, I get a phone call, and—" His voice became very still. "My ma died."

There was a long pause.

"You know, she died. I got a real sneaky suspicion—she went to normal when I was there, she went to sleep, they gave her stuff to go to sleep so she would stay normal. And I left, she got up and called my name, and they said I wasn't there, and she died."

"Do you know she got up and called your name?" I asked.

"Yeah, the doctors told me. My sisters were still there, and they told me. She asked for William. See, when you have a heart attack, you're half there, you can hear stuff, but it doesn't register." For this reason, William felt, his mother hadn't realized he had left or why, hadn't known that Sally was also in the hospital. His mother had loved Sally. But there was Sally, "in the hospital and stuff, so I call her and everything, I get off the phone with her, and then I get the phone call that my ma's dead. So I'm—I went under the bridge and, ah, cut my wrists, drank a fifth of peppermint schnapps, and I cut my wrists.

"Then I gave up. Just started drinking, drinking, drinking, drinking. That's it, you know."

At first, when she died, he had "hated everyone. No one could even talk to me. Because I just more or less blamed everyone for her dying."

In a later interview I asked William to describe his mother and father. He had vivid recollections of his father. He could give few details about his mother, I could get no sense of her, but he liked talking about his father. "Oh, my dad went to all kinds of schools. He was the *smartest* guy, you wouldn't believe what he could do. He could take apart an engine and put it together blindfolded. I'm not kidding. He could do *everything* to a car. He'd say, 'William, when you time a car, you don't use a timing light. You use your ear. You *feel* the car. You don't use lights, none of that stuff. You *feel* the car.' It's hard to explain, but he taught me."

His mother "was a real, real nice lady. She always worried and cared about me and stuff. She just drank too much. Just drank and drank and drank. Her and my dad split up."

But what did she do? I asked. How should I picture her when he was little?

She would just be in the house, he said, "cooking dinner and stuff." And then he went on to talk about how his father would be at his shop, putting together little engines and motors, and how everyone knew his dad.

What did his mother like to do with him? I asked.

"She would more or less like to be with me . . . happy or sad, either way. My ma was happy and sad, happy and sad, either way, you know."

When had she begun her drinking?

"Oh, way back, I heard, way, way back. See, that's—the doctors told me that the reason I'm so small is because when I was in my ma, she was drinking when I was in there. That's why I was born a blue baby, that's what they tell me." His parents had had another male child before William, also a blue baby, who had died three or four minutes after birth.

William had been in the hospital, he said, for his first thirteen or fourteen months. "I don't see the sun for the first year, you know. I was in the hospital. In my incubator. I was real, real small and tiny."

William's voice was very small at this point.

"My dad said I was so small, he could put me, he could seat me right in his hand."

William tended to become unstrung when things went badly. I heard a lot about collapse and addictions and treatment centers. I asked at an early meeting with him what he did to go from feeling bad to feeling okay.

"What do I do?" he said. "Call my sis . . . well, I'll spend hours on the phone, and just call up people and talk to them, you know. Talking just makes me feel better. Like my aunts or my sisters, you know. Helps me out a lot. Well, I had a counselor, too, I used to, you know, tell my problems."

I asked whether that had been a counselor at school.

"No, just a separate counselor. After my ma and dad passed away, I . . . I don't know, I kind of lost it for a while.

"Sometimes I'll go out working on my car, just pulling things apart, you know, because that's what I do for pastime. That's what my dad always did, so I kind of follow in his footsteps. Or I'll smoke a joint.

"But sometimes, it depends on what kind of down mood you're in, sometimes if you smoke pot or something, you think about it even more. So it depends. What you're thinking about.

"My doctor was giving me these pills," he added. "I just call them happy pills. I swear to God, if you take them, just like you couldn't look down on anything. I mean, if you, I don't know, if you got in an accident, you'd probably still—I don't know."

I hadn't expected to find young men in these circumstances receiving counseling. A year later, we got into a much more detailed discussion. William was telling me that bad hearing had affected him from birth; it came, he said, from having been a blue baby, from his asthma, and from his drinking. He was going at this time to a clinic named Deeper Soundings. "It's a psychiatric place. They got, like it's a small place with about eleven doctors, regular doctors. They do brain scans, brain waves, just to see how you are inside. And all my liver. They inject you with this dye and they take pictures, you know; make sure I'm all right.

"I was drinking heavily every day for two years, two and a half years. Every day I'd wake up shaking and depressed, and I'd walk to the store and I'd drink, you know. Drink it right down just to try and forget about stuff."

Now, he said, he was putting his life together. He had decided this since I had last seen him. He was going to get schooling; he had stopped drinking. "It's all coming together for me. I just got a bunch of girls that keep goofing around with my mind, you know. All they want to do is play with my brain. I just got to find one to settle down with, you know."

He spoke more about the treatment centers at our next meeting. Again he blamed his drinking on having been separated from his parents by the courts. The reason he had quit drinking, "what turned me around was, I was just thinking about how my ma died from it, my Uncle Eino died from it, and my Uncle Rusty died from drinking, and I was just thinking about it, and then I just stopped." He had gone, he said, to Heron Court, to Deeper Soundings, and several other centers. Heron Court, he said, was "an in-patient place, it's like a motel, you work a couple of hours and then you have classes. Like you talk to a guy about your life in front of everyone. Then you have a Bible class, then you have another class. It's just a bunch of classes about drinking."

He had not drunk at that point for three months. Deeper Soundings had helped him as he dealt with quitting: "You know, you get —you shake a little and stuff. And that's what Deeper Soundings does. They give me, more or less, their—slows me down. So I'm not so . . . anxious, you know." He thought the pills they had given him were Valium.

I asked for clarification. Why had his lawyer sent him to a treatment center? Had he had some trouble with the police?

After more prologue about his mother, he gingerly approached his offense. "And I hit a couple cars and got in trouble and stuff, so my lawyer told me a couple places to go. So I went there and straightened me out."

That was the point at which he had gone to Heron Court, which seems to have worked with a confrontational peer pressure model. He had spent six days there. "They got this thing that's called a hot seat. You sit in front of everyone and they all bitch at you and tell you all this stuff. It's hard to explain, but it gets you really scared, kind of. That's why it's called the hot seat."

I asked whether this was the kind of thing in which other people in the group confront you, tell you you're not facing your life. He said yes, and added that there were about eighteen people doing that. I asked how that had felt.

"Shaky," he said. "You don't know what to say. You don't know whether to stand up, sit down, smoke a cigarette, or nothing. You didn't know no one, you were all by yourself, you were just one person, kind of scared."

He had seen this done with someone else and hoped it wouldn't happen to him. "And then, boom! The next day it was my turn, and I went, 'Oh, God!' "

He said he had liked talking to the different people at the different places. "You just talk to these people, like one guy I talked to, De-lessep, that was at Beaumont Hospital, I was up there—see, I cut my wrists, you know, because I just thought it was all over, I kind of gave up." This seemed to have been around his mid-teens. "Kind of just gave up on everything. But then again, once I talked to them and everything, turned out all right. You know."

Those sentences were characteristic of William. He would drop on you a drastic note that called out for help—such as "cut my wrists"; it would be located at some time you couldn't really pin down and its relation to his life events was obscure; and he would end with a most unconvincing claim that the clinic visit had cleared up the problems and that everything now had turned out all right.

Having someone working on his case was like having someone concerned about him, I think, and the clinic visits did give him support that kept him afloat for a while. He probably felt relief at being part of a structured setting. He liked to phrase his descriptions as though problems had been solved, as though his life now was under control and going in the direction he wanted. It was disturbing to watch him mistake brief support for lasting change.

We spoke of it all one last time a few days later. I was asking him to list the four clinics and hospitals he had gone to for help, when he remembered another: "I went to one in Pontiac, too. You know, I don't stay at them all. I just checked each one out to see which one's the best. This one in Pontiac was the one where I O.D.'d.

"By accident," he rushed to say. "By accident. I didn't mean it. I'm serious. I didn't."

I asked what he had taken.

"Placidyls. They're downers. See, this girl—I'm going to tell you everything. All right, this girl was hanging around with me and stuff, and see, she goes to a psychiatrist, and this psychiatrist gives her anything she wants. So more or less, the way she lives is high all the time. I mean, how can a doctor do that to a person? All the time, she's just . . . nowhere.

"Anyways, I was shaking and stuff, you know, from drinking. I took a couple. And I went out of my mind. It was a real downer effect. And somehow I got all mixed up and I ate too many of them and I went to the hospital, Lister Medical, and when I woke up there was a couple priests next to my bed asking me if I had seen a light at the end of a tunnel and all this stuff. And I had tubes down my throat and down my nose. All that stuff. I think I slept for seventy-two hours. Something like that. I was in intensive care.

"But at that time, you know, it was no death trip or nothing. I was just trying to slow my heart down and it hit me too hard, I guess.

"So I went in the hospital and they gave me a lot of help. I talked to them and stuff and I met a girl there and talked to her and everything. And I came out of there."

William, who had an uncle who was a suicide, one more time had made a suicidal gesture and received some support; again he had found professionals who would talk with him; again he had found a young woman and talked with her. He used his difficulties as a basis to try to create caretaking relations.

He ended this conversation with a picture of his sister's devotion and with the usual conclusion that everything now was okay. "My sister sat by my side all through the day, twenty-four hours a day, crying and stuff. You know, when you're in a coma, you can hear everything, but you're not awake, if you know what I mean. You hear what's going around, you know what's going on, but you're not awake. And I guess I put her through hell, you know, but it's all right now."

William ran away from home for more than a year in his mid-teens and set up an independent life in Detroit. This story was important to him. He told it to me twice, in radically different versions. The first version, recounted early in our acquaintance, was extremely dramatic: He had run away at age thirteen; he had lived in abandoned houses and basements. The abandoned house was next door to his girlfriend's house, so he had been able to climb up knotted sheets to her room when it was bitter cold. When he left home he had weighed about a hundred and seventy; at the end of the year he weighed a hundred and ten. "I remember I didn't eat for like . . . I think it was about two and a half weeks. I didn't eat nothing. Nothing at all. And the first thing I ate was a whole box of chocolate cookies. Boy, did I get sick!" He had been afraid: "Yeah, I was scared. Wake up and a rat's crawling over you or something. You know, you can get rabies and shit from that." In this version William's purpose had been to be able to be on his own, since he couldn't live with his parents.

A second version, much less dramatic, came in a later interview. In that version, most of the initial period was spent in the girlfriend's room, with only occasional nights in the basement of the abandoned house next door; also, in that version, he was soon taken under the wing of a woman named Mary, the daughter of his father's girlfriend. Mary came to see him and told him that he could come live in the basement of her home. She was buying William cigarettes and food and helped him find a job; they set up a good room for him in her basement. In this second version he is fifteen.

The fear and the hunger that are striking in the first story probably did happen; even with the opportunity to sleep most nights in his girlfriend's room, he would have had to spend a good amount of time in the abandoned basement, and it would have been frightening. Equally, there could have been a long time before decent food. So the fear and hunger were real memories, but the duration and his age probably were remembered wrong or misrepresented.

The striking thing about the second, probably truer version, was his reason for running away. Right after his grandmother's death, he said, "I got messed up with a guy in school that was selling me marijuana. He said it was good marijuana, which it turned out to only be stuff he grew in his backyard." The dealer put the home-grown marijuana in William's locker, but told all his friends it was good stuff. William packaged the material and sold it "for the price that good pot is worth." The students smoked it and returned, demanding their money back and leaving him with half-bags. The dealer student came for his money—$200—but William had had to give people refunds. So the dealer was going to beat up William.

"And my brother-in-law, he's from the projects in Hamtramck. You know, bad—strong, and bad. Okay, Max is his name. So this guy walked in the house after me, and Max said, 'This is *my* trailer and no one else's, this is *mine.*' So he threw the guy out the door.

"I didn't want my family getting messed up in my trouble," William concluded. "So I just run away. I went out to Detroit." This was his introduction to the second version of the runaway story.

William ultimately was apprehended; a policeman recognized him on the street from a description, and he was taken to the juvenile detention center, where he spent several difficult weeks. He spoke of harsh treatment and humiliation there. He was brought to court, where his father surprised him by demanding the right to take care of him: "I'm taking care of my son, heck with everything. I'm going to take care of him." To William's further surprise, his father did not punish him for this escapade, but seriously wanted to know what had been happening and why William had felt this compulsion. William lived intermittently then with his father and grandfather in the grandfather's trailer, ultimately helping his grandfather care for his father when his father went through a final illness.

The runaway story is troublesome. I had thought the first version spoke of the minimal claims William felt he could make on the world. The second version is more striking for its portrait of the luckless William messing up in his involvement with the drug dealer, caught between the customers and the dealer. But it also says odd things about family ties. On the one hand they seem weak—the kid flies away. On the other hand, the network of support is there, in its fashion. His girlfriend is taking care of him, and, more importantly, the daughter of his father's girlfriend takes care of him. (Curiously, William never mentioned this second woman again, in the many hours of conversation that we held.) I have always been struck by the lack of support that the young people in the Strike Group experienced, but William's family did throw life rafts to him again and again. Perhaps he was smart to make clear his neediness.

William was unemployed during our acquaintance. He had held one or two jobs earlier in small factories; he had just been laid off from a pizza parlor. He was supposed to have been training for a mana-ger's position and worked remarkably hard, but was laid off as soon as he had shown the actual new manager the ropes. Characteristi-cally, he had not noticed for some months that his hourly pay was one fourth less than he had been told he was making, and, charac-teristically, he was unable to collect the $500 he was owed.

He spoke often of trying to prepare himself for the GED exam, to acquire a high-school equivalency, but took no action. He had gone through one semester of tenth grade. This left him "kind of nervous" about trying to do the exam or trying school. "Because most people quit eleventh or twelfth, you know. They've got, they're a little more smarter."

He would get plaintive, thinking about trying to pass the GED exam, and talk about how his parents would have been proud to see him graduate, should he manage to. "Because they tried talking me into doing it for so long. When I was younger, I was more wilder. I used to say, 'No, no, no.' But I quit because of the fad, believe it or not. Everyone was quitting, man, so I had to be bad, too. 'William quit, too, man.' And *now* I think I was *so* stupid. I could be done with it now and have a year or two already at the community college."

He did not lack role models. One of his sisters had completed high school late, despite working and having children, and was doing well. Nevertheless, every conversation we had about night school or GED preparation courses drifted quickly to images of his dead parents or drifted down lines that signaled to me that nothing was going to happen. "I'd like to go through it with a friend, though. I know this girl that lives down the street from me that wants to go, too. So it'll be a little easier knowing that there's someone with me." Was she really going to do this? "Yeah, she says she is." Then he looked rueful. "I'll believe it when I see it."

In other words, she wasn't really going to, and so he wouldn't really have to. We were still in the world of never-happen.

By now you have a sense of William as I had come to know him in the first two years of our talks: a fairly troubled young man involved in the white racist work of the group. The picture began to change at the end of the second year. We had had a pair of long interviews a week apart in which he spoke about his life and the way he tried to make sense of it. I had listened well; he had begun those interviews with a quiet but clear sense of warmth toward me. We held a third interview a few days later, during which he suddenly revealed his disaffection with the group.

We had been talking about relations between black and white people. Blacks lived in bad conditions, he said—dirty houses with rats and roaches. Blacks preferred to take rather than to earn—80 percent of them, he estimated. Blacks couldn't be fired from jobs and blacks had all manner of TV shows of their own. I then began to explain to William the impact of slavery—what conditions had been, what it would mean to be a mother and to lose one's children forever without having control over their sale. I hoped this example might lodge in his mind. I attempted to explain the movement north—the mechanization of agriculture, the displacement of the Southern farm-worker, the conditions into which blacks had been confined in the north. I began to discuss with him the statistics on comparative life expectancy and the statistics on median family income. He had thought that black and white families enjoyed about the same income; I explained that white incomes were almost double. (The actual statistic is that median black family income was 54 percent that of white family income in 1950, 55 percent in 1960, 61 percent in 1970, 58 percent in both 1980 and 1990, and 57 percent in 1991.)

The numbers meant nothing to William: Black people had to learn to live right. I explained again that urban black people were penned in, confined. I reminded him that I had spent years interviewing black families and that most of the black people I had met would fit right in where he was. He said that he just wanted to be able to walk down the street anywhere. Good, I said, just change the country so that for several generations black people got a square deal, and then he would be able to walk where he wished.

That could be fine, he said, but when was it going to happen? When people worked so that everyone got a square deal, I responded. His group, I pointed out, was going in the opposite direction: They were preaching that black people should be held down.

His thing, he said, was that there should be two separate places.

Why couldn't there be two countries, a black country and a white country?

First, I told him, we all needed jobs. Second, I added, it was more fun when things were mixed. That idea was new to him.

Encouraged by his warmth, I elaborated. He had mentioned earlier that my kind of work looked like fun, and I pointed out that it meant getting to meet all kinds of people. I spoke of the boredom I had felt in Augusta, Georgia, when I was in the Army—the sameness of the accents; I spoke of the excitement of visiting Brooklyn and hearing a variety of accents and languages. I told him of my distaste for the segregation in the Texas town where I had grown up. When I saw a black and white couple walking down the street, I told him, I loved it. "I think it's wild," I said. "Let it all happen! I love it. Let everything be going on." I talked of the fun of getting to knock around with the Finns I had known (his family was Finnish); I told him I'd been to Africa and how interesting it had been, how gentle the people had been. He was quite startled: "In *Africa? Honest?*" Yes, I assured him, and told him illustrative stories. "Someday," he said then, "this world might make it."

He had been getting into a lot of things lately, he now told me, and one was the Bible. He'd been "reading the Psalms and stuff. Watching all them movies and stuff about Jesus, how his disciples and stuff. To me, I like it a lot. Really understand it now. I never knew what it was about before."

We chatted a few minutes more, and then he suddenly asked me who else heard these tapes. He had me turn the recorder off. He asked whether Paul was given a chance to listen to the tapes. I assured him again that Paul wasn't.

With that assurance, he let me turn the machine back on and spoke haltingly of the new thoughts he was beginning to have. "Well, it's just what I was trying to tell Paul. This is what I think, okay? All right, there's a Chinese, Japanese, black, white, Mexican. There's one of every person. Then a white is only one person, if you know what I mean.

"That's what I've been trying to tell Paul," he said. "if you brought all of them together, one of every person, a white is only one person. You know what I mean? I've been trying to tell Paul this. It's so hard to explain."

I told him I didn't quite get what he meant. He said again that if you took a Japanese, a Chinese, a Mexican, every single one altogether in one group, a white would be only one of them.

"Out of that group, you mean?" I asked.

"Yeah," he answered. "Yeah, that's what I'm trying to tell Paul. Paul thinks white is superior. You know what I mean?"

The group was based on the idea, I reminded him, that white was superior. It seemed, I said, that he was saying that white "was just one more."

"Yeah," he said. "I mean, I been trying to say that to Paul, but he just laughs."

I reminded him that he was reading the Bible now, and that there was some suggestion there that all of us were God's children. He agreed it did say that, that "every living thing is made from God." He had tried to explain it to Paul, he said.

I suggested to him then that the Strike Group, while claiming it was *for* whites rather than just *against* blacks, did not actually *do* anything for whites. What did it accomplish, I asked, to hold rallies?

He became inarticulate: "Well, more or less, it's just like . . . I don't know. You stand there and, oh . . . I just stand there and see if, ah, I don't know how to explain it."

Then he suddenly said, "See, what I was trying to tell Paul is that . . . what are you going to do is ship them all out?" He was referring to the group goal of deporting all blacks. "I mean," he went on, "what are you going to do, get rid of every single one of them? I mean, there's no way. It's like a losing game. There's no way to win. You know what I mean? That's what Paul says the party position is, ship them all away."

There was a pause. "You don't think that'll work?" I asked.

"No."

"How come?"

"Well, *jeez*, how *can* it work? We can't just ship people away and just say good-bye, you know."

I laughed. "What's happening to you, William? Better start drinking again, you're seeing things too clearly."

"No," he said. "No, I know what's going on. That's what Paul said, too, better start drinking again, you're seeing things too clear.

No way. Never, I have to see things clear. I mean, you just can't get them altogether and say good-bye, you know."

William, having said all this, now again said that his desire was to see that whites didn't get hurt by blacks. He wanted to be able to walk in any area without being harassed. I suggested that one had to know a little bit about how to speak with people, how to meet people. I told him about taking different members of my family into unfamiliar neighborhoods in Detroit and meeting people. I talked about the ways that one could reassure strangers and get to know them well. "It's out there, William," I told him. "There's just a world of people who want to be happy. They want to have dignity and they want to be happy. And for every person who's been turned vicious, there's a hundred who haven't been."

William listened hard. What about Jews, though? he now wondered—I think he was trying to put a lot of things together at once. "See," he said, "another thing I don't understand is, what's wrong with the Jewish people? I know you're Jewish. I don't understand this, though."

What's wrong? I asked him.

"Paul tells me that . . . Jewish people are . . . taking over. I don't understand that."

I waited for him to carry the thought further.

"And if they do, they do, you know," he said. "I'm living my own life. They can do what they want. They're people, too. That's what I keep trying to tell Paul."

I told him we weren't taking over, but to go ahead.

"I know," he said. "I know you're not. Or they're not. Or whatever. You know. It's just . . . I don't know."

He was stuck. He didn't quite know what was bothering him.

I asked him what Paul was telling him about the Jews. He told me that Paul had told him about the little kosher marks on canned goods and things like that, and that "they all get a cut and everything." He asked whether it was true, and I told him it was not. He pleaded earnestly: "Can me, you, and Paul sit down sometime? I want to see what he has to say!"

I told him Paul and I had been over this stuff a hundred times. He said he had to do it once, anyway.

Suddenly he sounded quite centered. "*I want to know what's going on!* I don't want to mess around with a group that—I don't want to mess with no one. I don't want to be no *bad* guy walking around with this, you know, black boots out to kick someone's ass, you know."

It was an amazing moment.

I told him that I had been a bit surprised as I realized he and various others in the group were rather gentle people. "What you're doing here with black boots on and a skull on your collar beats the hell out of me," I told him.

"More or less," he said, "I just, I'm just sick of being beat by them. I am. I'm *sick* of it! It's just like, I'm *afraid* to walk down in Detroit. I don't want to be. I want to be able to walk down there. I want to walk where I want to walk."

"All right," I told him, "I'll tell you one thing I'll do with you, to move you toward there. I'll take you someday, and we'll go do some interviews in a black neighborhood."

"Will you?"

"Absolutely. I want you to have the experience of walking into a black home where you don't know a soul, and finding that if you just act like who you normally are, that they're going to like you." I assured him that we would do this.

"Definitely," he said. "Definitely! Don't forget me."

I told him that I would be glad to share the experience with him, that I would love to communicate to him that it was a bigger world than the group thought.

"Show me, show me!" he cried.

I agreed we would do it. Just for the hell of it, I said. "And Paul will bust a gut," I added.

There was a slight pause. Then William spoke in a small, scared voice. "The hell with it! I don't care. It's my life, not his," he continued. "I'm starting new now. This is *my* life, no one else's."

He was beginning to remember lessons he had heard in his therapies. His voice gradually became firm. "I should have started way back, way back when I was being thrown around from here to there." He reverted again to the story of the runaway years. "People were, the courts were telling me I have to do this and I have to do that. And I'm trying to tell them, why do I have to do this and this and this, when here I've been on my own for two years, on my own making a living and supporting myself, and here you've put me in Juvenile, and I know how to take care of myself. You know."

And again he spoke of the absence of his parents—that now when he felt ready for them to be there, they were dead. "Now I'm old enough to be with them, and they're not here."

I told him that there was a way to make up for this—that in four or five years he could have kids, and that he could make for his kids the kind of love he wished had been made for him.

"Yeah," he enthused. "Yeah, the kid that I get, that I make? That kid's going to be so happy, he ain't going to know what sad is!" He laughed. "I'm going to show him—" Then he brought up the child that Terri had had, saying that it was sad that Paul hadn't had a chance to keep the child, but that it had been Paul's fault that Terri had left. Then he asked me to come out and meet his grandfather.

"No matter what anyone says," he now said, "my own mind is my own mind.

"Paul's very smart, though," he added. "He knows a lot of stuff."

I said Paul worked hard in his role as leader.

"The thing is, though," William said, "I told Paul . . . I wanted to just be myself and not be in the group. And he says we can't be friends."

I asked when that had been said.

"Couple of months ago. See, my family don't like me in this group."

We ceased recording at that point, as Paul had just returned to the house.

We met later that week; William was spending several days at Paul's house. William wanted to know whether I would be going to people's houses that day. If he was free, I told him, I wanted to go do some fieldwork. "Let's go!" he cried. "Let's go!"

I agreed, but talked to him for a while first. Paul came to the house during that recording and then left again; with much reluctance, he left a key so that William could also go out if he wanted. William did not mention to Paul that he was going to go interview with me.

"I'm so happy," William kept saying as we drove eastward to the neighborhood I had in mind. It must have been stultifying sitting around at Paul's—normally not being allowed a key, sitting in place until Paul came home.

I was nervous about this venture. I really wanted to show William that he could be accepted readily by a group of black people who did not know him. I had decided to go to a mainly black neighborhood adjacent to the blocks that several Strike Group members came from; I wanted a sense of black lives in the homes alongside those of the group members. I hoped I would succeed in making a good contact.

I cruised the selected neighborhood a bit and found a likely cluster of young men standing about and talking at the edge of the street. I circled back to them, parked, and walked over. "Hey, excuse me," I said. "You could help me if you could spare me a few minutes." I smiled and held out my hand, gave them my name, and shook hands. "I'm a teacher at the University of Michigan," I said, "and I'm coming out to different neighborhoods in the city today to talk to people in the different neighborhoods." William was at my side. I introduced him, telling them that he was working with me.

"Like what do you want to know?" asked a young man in a black shirt with Japanese characters painted on it in red.

I started in about the economy—had things really picked up, as the government was then claiming? The young black men jeered, and then became serious, talking about work and their lives. The fellow in the Japanese shirt explained that he was thirty, that it was hard indeed, that he had been out of work for six months, but that his wife had a pretty fair job, thank goodness. There were no luxuries, however; they were just getting by and had had to cut way back. "Soon there will be no workers," he said. "They are being replaced by robots." He noted that everyone was having to make concessions to keep their jobs, that everyone was falling further and further back.

We had a fine conversation, but soon this man had to drive his brother to work—the brother was standing near us in a white shirt with a hospital I.D. tag. We all shook hands and said thanks.

William was terribly excited as we climbed back into the car.

We stopped again two blocks farther down the street. I led us onto a porch where an older woman and a middle-aged man were sitting, both of them African-Americans. Again I asked for their time, and they and William and I sat on the porch talking, joined soon by the man's twenty-one-year old son, who had ambitions to attend a technical college.

It grew late, and we took off, stopping to buy William a new pack of cigarettes. Heading back to Paul's, William cried out, "Why didn't I learn? My mother and my father tried to teach me this. But I couldn't hear." William was excited, happy, and buoyant.

We arrived back at Paul's some fifteen minutes later than William had been due. Paul had had to use his "emergency" key to get back in. He lay on his couch wearing only cutoffs, the fan blowing at him. He was reading the paper and listening to rock radio. "Where were you guys?" he said in a grumpy voice. "Did you record in the car?" Paul was suspicious and angry.

On the way home William had asked, "How can one person like you make me so happy?" He liked attention. Maybe he also was finding that the world was less dangerous than he had assumed. He had told me with excitement on the way out how a black man had shaken hands with him the day before; he had been at pains all this afternoon to copy me and to go through the many handshakes I had initiated.

That was all to the good. At the same time, I had my own misgivings. The signals I picked up from Paul were that he found himself in competition with me for William—that he needed William's dependence and needed to feel that he had control over him. I asked myself why Paul drew all these young men in and needed to keep them. "If you leave the group," he had told William, "we can't be friends."

I also found myself thinking further about William's dependency and his formlessness. I wondered whether his was the sort of unanchored soul that sat limply, that was drawn to whatever came by.

Hesitations aside, I was gratified. I had wanted to let one of the young men try perceiving the world the way I did; I had wanted to let one of them experience an open world in which one reaches out and is met with a normal warm, human response. I was pleased that

I had been able to present that experience. I hoped that there would be good long-term results.

I attempted to keep in contact with William the remainder of that summer, but found opportunity for little but hurried visits to his home in the trailer park. I drove him to the doctor several times. The next autumn he called to ask that we get together. We agreed not to work at Paul's place, which he said he found "too confining. I already had one threat," he said. "Paul told me, 'You been talking too much to Rafe. Watch it.' " William was concerned that I not repeat things to Paul.

We did not in fact meet each other again until spring, and then in poor circumstances. I was at Paul's place one day and the woman Paul was then with, Cindy, kept phoning her apartment, trying to reach William, who was supposed to be minding her three-year-old. No one would answer the phone. Cindy fumed angrily, "What is this shit, William? Answer my phone, dammit, William! Don't fall asleep on the floor; show a little respect, William!" She was more and more worried about her child. I drove her over to her apartment. We found William on the floor, drunk and passed out.

I heard a good deal from William in the following winter and spring. He called in January to say that his grandfather had left the trailer, had gone to live with one of William's sisters. William was not working, was drawing disability. He had told Paul that he was going to call me, and Paul had acted as though it were a bad idea. William said he was not involved with the group, and he asked me not to let Paul know that he had called. William told me that he had again stopped drinking—hadn't drunk for six months—and wanted to get together.

I called repeatedly over the next weeks, but no meetings could be arranged, usually because he was sick. He hadn't seen the group members for some time. About the group, he said, "I gotta ease up on that, I'm growing up."

Finally William telephoned. He cried out desperately, "I need to talk!" A girlfriend had died a few days before, had been hit by a drunk driver while she was walking. William asked whether I was taping him on the phone. Paul had told him not to talk to me anymore. "He can't tell me who my friends are," he said. "I feel like *drinking!*"

I told him I would come out, but would phone first.

I telephoned the next day at noon. He didn't want me to come just then. "I . . . sort of . . . got a girl here. How you set for time? Call me at two. That will give time for me and her to shower. She has to go to work anyway."

I telephoned back at two. He yelled into the phone, "What the fuck do you want?" I told him who it was. "People are throwing rocks, Rafe," he said. "People are throwing rocks at the trailer. The cops are coming!"

He said that he had turned in some neighbors on dope, that they had found out, that they had "put a shotgun in [his] face."

He told me to call at five. I did, and he said to come on out. "I've been drinking."

I arrived at the trailer at seven. William had passed out. He was on the floor, drunk. I left.

William phoned a few days later. He spoke of an assortment of illnesses and of a plan to get baptized and to see a therapist. He didn't care who laughed at him, he said, Paul or any of them. "I look different," he said. "My hair is not straggly. My face is cleaned up. I'm happy. I don't have to have a bottle. I was with the wrong people," he said, referring to the people from Rumbolt. "They want liquor."

I reached William on the phone the next week. He said he was vomiting blood, had an ulcer. He needed to check in at the hospital and get tests; the doctor had told him his liver was large and "foamy."

William's phone soon was disconnected, and contact became difficult. I stopped at the trailer after a month and had a brief visit with him. He was on his way to see a psychologist. He was sick and lonely, trying hard—he felt—to remake his life.

He wanted to move back near his family. A specialist had told him that he wouldn't work on his stomach, that it was too messed up. He had been in the hospital for a while after our last talk, with tubes in his stomach.

He was out of the Strike Group. "Don't have nothing to do with that now." Paul had told William that if he wasn't in the group, Paul didn't want anything to do with him. William was hurt; he had thought they were friends, "but if that is what Paul wants . . ."

A series of missed connections followed—William would be out when I drove over to keep a date, but the notes he left on the trailer door seemed genuine. He then phoned, to see whether I would drive him up to the Bavarian Festival in central Michigan. The Strike Group was going to be up there; William couldn't drive up with them, since he didn't want to be part of the group, but he wanted to be on the scene, to see what Paul would be doing there. I was not free to help him.

At midsummer, finally, I phoned the home of William's sister to find out whether William or his grandfather had succeeded yet in selling the trailer, as they'd hoped, or whether William still lived there. A young girl answered my call. William was no longer in the trailer, she told me; he was somewhere in Pontiac. I asked if there was a phone number where I could reach him. "Maybe you want to talk to my grandfather, he was closer to that."

The grandfather came on the line. I reminded him of our several meetings when he had still lived at the trailer. Fortunately, he remembered me.

"Yeah," he told me. "William is at the Pontiac mental institution." I asked when William had gone in.

"About two weeks ago Monday," he said. "He was on dope. He tried to commit suicide. He was in a lot of trouble."

The grandfather said that he had sold the trailer and that William had been evicted.

What are the doctors telling you? I asked.

"The doctors there said he needed help real bad," the grandfather replied.

When I had talked most recently to William, I told the grandfather, he had had the feeling that he was doing much better, that things were looking up.

"Yeah," the grandfather said, "but things weren't good. There was an old fellow there. William wanted a car. He can't ever get a license again, with his record, so I don't know what he wanted a car for.

That old fellow had helped him before. William wanted him to help him get a car. That fellow said no, he wouldn't sign a note. That old fellow had a truck, a camper; William set it on fire, burned it. He said he didn't do it, but two girls saw him do it.

"I think he wanted to go to the nuthouse himself," the grandfather continued. "I drove him there myself. I drove him from the trailer. I think he wanted to go to the nuthouse himself. I think he was afraid of the authorities."

I told the grandfather I was sorry. I told him I knew he—the grandfather—had had a lot to deal with, in his life.

"Yeah, I've had a lot of trouble from that kid. I think he wanted to go to the nuthouse himself."

William was dismissed from the mental institution before I could visit him; his grandfather did not know where he had gone; I could not tell whether William had wanted to go to the institution because he was frightened by his own instability or because he was afraid of arrest—or both. In any case, the pattern of the four years was clear: drift and deterioration, feeble attempts at integration, a search for fathers, a deepening spiral of self-destruction.

At a rally, William, standing with the others in his black uniform, holding his wooden shield with its swastika, suggested danger. As an individual, however, he was dependent and empty, looking to the organization for friendships and a fleeting sense of purpose. Paul took care of him in some ways and also demonstrated the harsh strength William had loved in his father. For the most part, however, the group was not of much use for him. The Strike Group was a gang; its purpose was good feelings for those at its center, not for people like William.

He began to drift from the group toward the end of our acquaintance. My attention played a slight role in that movement, but there was no positive alternative awaiting him. As he became detached from the Strike Group, he fell increasingly into the chaos that waited in the local youth drug culture.

FOURTEEN

Raymond and Rosandra

It's a big leap from William to Raymond, a leap from fearful hesitance to arrogant ignorance. Raymond was a noisemaker who didn't know himself. He had to keep moving, keep talking. You knew his kind in junior high school, the kid who broke other people's stuff and ran his mouth, talking trash.

Raymond styled himself a country boy from Arkansas. He had done a lot of drinking; he had helled around on his motorcycles. He showed me a photo of his last girl back home; she had a great grin, standing bare-chested astride his Harley. They were both too strong-willed to really get along, he said, but he liked flashing the picture.

Raymond appeared rather suddenly in the first spring of my interviews and was quickly a prominent group member. He had arrived from Pennsylvania, where he had been involved with a survivalist bunch in the Appalachians that had begun to steep itself in the doctrines of Christian Identity. He had left because he couldn't deal with Identity, he claimed; I wondered after a while whether they just had thrown him out. He had connected with the survivalists when he and they were at Jim Ellison's paramilitary compound in Arkansas called CSA—the Covenant, the Sword, and the Arm of the Lord. (It is no accident that CSA also stands for Confederate States of America.) Before that, Raymond had spent a few years in Chicago, working with several Nazi organizations; he had come to know the Strike Group by reputation at that time, which is why he had made Detroit his destination when he left the survivalists. Before Chicago, Raymond had created white racist organizations of his own near Memphis and St. Louis; he boasted to me of the violence of those groups. He was twenty-five when we met and had been involved in Nazi activities for about seven years.

Raymond spoke in a number of interviews about the role of his grandfather in his education in racism during Raymond's youth in Arkansas. His father and mother were still married to each other—a rare occurrence for this group—but his father had lived at the other end of Arkansas from Raymond and his mother, working in oil fields near the Louisiana border. Raymond had had one brother. "He got a tour of Vietnam. And they shipped him home in a box. I hope these government assholes that got rich off the war appreciate it, too." He did not mention the brother again in our many interviews.

Raymond was tall, with brown hair and brown eyes. He was angular and unfinished, his manner jarring. He demanded attention and violated boundaries. When I tried to talk with others in his presence, he quickly interrupted, verbally pushing them aside, trying to be sure that I kept looking at and listening to him. If I told Raymond to wait his turn, he reappeared moments later—he would sit next to me, his voice in my ear as I tried to question another member, directing me to look at the photos in the album he flipped in his lap. "And look, Rafe, here's a picture of me in my Brown Shirt uniform, that's my buddy Leo and that's Jerry, he nearly killed a guy one time, you got to look at this—" The group members didn't know what to make of Raymond.

Raymond had taken an upstairs apartment in an old wooden building on the southeastern edge of the city. Very soon he began a relationship with a woman named Rosandra, a dreadfully myopic eighteen-year-old. Rosandra would stoop over the sink in the gloom, doing dishes. I have never seen a dish sink so poorly lit; there was perhaps a fifteen-watt bulb. Given that bad light and her terrible vision, she would have to bring the plate within a few inches of her eyes to see it well enough to wash it. Rosandra became pregnant almost at once; Raymond "didn't believe in" contraception.

Raymond was almost clever. He had attended (without being affected) a branch college in Arkansas for a while; he knew nothing, but he saw himself as a person of ideas. He was fascinated by the sound of his own words. He had never thought, beyond shallow catchphrases, about his own life, although he was twenty-five.

Raymond's racism had almost no connections to experience or daily life. One could easily and mistakenly write off a fellow like Raymond. He had taken part, however, in a long string of organized activities; Paul was delighted to have him around and active; Raymond was like many people who come to white racist organizations to find scope for their blustering energy and sense of drama.

Raymond at some level was lonely. He desperately wanted attention and approval. He, finally, had many thoughts that involved guns and killing.

There was a mindlessness to Raymond's racism. He really didn't know who he was or why. Violence mattered, but so did foolish games, one-upmanship. He had the deep ignorance of the self-educated who think they know something.

The most important image he ever drew for me came as we talked about the group mission and the future as he saw it.

"When the race war breaks out . . ." he began. "You run into this average middle-class American on the street, he's seen all these years of TV or he's had an uncle who fought in World War II or something, and they'll hand you back the leaflet and say, 'Oh, I don't want this.' When I meet someone like that, I reflect into the future. When the race riot breaks out—there's a date, it's already been predicted by some of the prophets of the white Christian churches, that it's going to come down in the near future. Okay, if I was in the city and say like the guy handed me back a piece of paper, my leaflet, I'd say that would make me feel bad. Because I know he'd know who I was when the race riot broke out, and I had my .22 or whatever and I'm trying to survive, and that same person that handed me back and said, 'I don't want to have anything to do with you, you people disgust me'—that same person will be expecting me to bite a bullet for him when the race war breaks out.

"And it makes me feel bad. Because as much as I hate to see a white brother die, I'm not going to bite the bullet for somebody like that."

It depressed him, he claimed smugly. Blacks were proud and unified, whereas whites had no pride, were "practically turned against their race by the propaganda they see on TV and in the media." But the race war would come, the ultimate race war. And the white masses simply wouldn't even think about it.

"They're so worried about their color TV and their new Cadillac or their new suit, that if it ever comes down to the war, when the electricity goes out and the power plants are blown up or whatever and their color TV goes off, they'll sit there in their living room and they'll kick back in their easy chair and wait for their TV to come back on.

"And when a race war breaks out, the first thing the masses are going to do, they're going to loot the big arsenal on Eight Mile Road, the first thing the masses are going to do, there's going to be mass looting. And if any of the black mobs ever get into one of those arsenals, get ahold of those M-16s and the grenades and whatever else they keep in there, you know, there's not going to be—he'll say, 'Oh, there's a riot, but the National Guard will handle it.' The police could be dead! The National Guard will probably be dead if they're crazy enough to come into the neighborhoods!

"Because the population—they can make all the gun laws they want, the gun laws will stop an honest man from getting a gun. But the criminals and the *degenerate* elements of society will always be able to find firearms.

"That same white person that sat up and said, 'Oh, you people are full of shit. The race war will never happen. I don't believe anything you have to say.' *I think about what that man's face is going to look like when he turns around and looks out his window* and he sees a black nationalist standing there, and the *last thing* he sees is the flash on the M-16, when it rips his guts out and sprays them all over the back wall!"

This fantasy wraps it together: the white who won't listen, the violent black who acts, the speaker himself who is vindicated as the white sees his guts splash across the wall.

Violence in real life delighted him in memory. I was asking about happiest and saddest moments. "One of the happiest moments," he said, "was when I cranked up the first unit I'd ever cranked up. *My first street activity!* Cabaton, Missouri [not the real name]. You heard of Greensboro where five communists were killed? *We* nearly took out a Red at Cabaton. Just outside St. Louis. Our group and Storm Troopers from Chicago."

He was crowing with pride in his story. "This Red was on top of a Storm Trooper and he caught a steel helmet four times in the back of the head. They didn't think he was going to make it, but he pulled—you know, damn it to hell, he pulled through.

"We could have got rid of a Red—*first rally I ever went out on, we nearly take out a Red!*"

An important occasion. "*I fired up my first unit!* And I had my address published in the old paper—before it was the *New Order*, it was the *N.S. Report*. And I've got the first copy I was ever published in. The first envelope.

"I went to the post office box, I took out the first envelope I ever received in an *N.S. Report* post office box. And it was from, I think, [a top leader]. 'Congratulations, Comrade!'

"And he sent me a few leaflets, said, 'Here's some master copies. Give it hell!' "

"You were getting congratulations for having formed a unit?" I asked.

"I had a blond-haired, blue-eyed friend of mine," he said, "that was about the same size, he was younger, but he was as big as I was. And we just got—me and him built the whole thing, we got about six or seven good people."

Raymond's happy thoughts about hurting people came up again later in that interview. He was talking about a fight that allegedly had taken place in Chicago. "There was eight Storm Troopers who went to Daley Plaza. And there's three Jews who ran up and grabbed the first Storm Trooper off the truck, and they were going to beat him up. And they didn't know how many more was in the truck. And the other eight come piling out.

"Two of the Jews managed to run off, but the first one that got up there and grabbed that Storm Trooper, the Storm Trooper grabbed him, too, and managed to hang on to him.

"That was back before they had the ban on poles in the street, and they had these big poles [on which signs were mounted]. And they worked his head over.

"He's got a steel plate now, and he's sitting in some little private hospital somewhere, playing with his toes."

This way of speaking pleased Raymond; he figured it made him sound knowing.

Raymond spoke a lot about what he called "race mixing." "You see some ugly white girls hanging out with these black bucks. The white men won't have anything to do with them. This black guy will have her because she's a white woman, but a white man wouldn't have her because if she walked up to a mirror she'd be so ugly she'd break it. But the nigger wants her so he can brag about 'Oh, I have a white woman.'"

I spoke of an interracial married couple who were friends of mine. The woman, I said, was both white and quite beautiful.

He was taken aback. "I'd be surprised," he said weakly. "What she's doing disgusts me." That came out stronger. Then he began to recover himself. He didn't believe in it, he said. She might be beautiful on the outside, he said, but on the inside she had no racial pride. He moved into the usual rhetoric: The babies, if she had any, would be half black and half white. More than that, "in the dog world, everybody wants a Doberman. Everybody wants a purebred German shepherd or a purebred collie. Nobody wants the mutts. They gas them at the pound because nobody wants them."

The reference to gassing the undesirables came to him readily.

He wanted to explain white sexual involvement with black folk. "Maybe it's a deviation. I think it may be a form of sexual deviation because you get out and you see these white women here in Detroit who like to sleep with blacks. I'd have to categorize them with the homosexual, someone who'd be into bestiality or something like that. They get maybe into some kind of a weird sex trip. She wants to picture herself as some kind of a slave to the—she's on some kind of white guilt trip because her ancestors owned slaves and she thinks she's making up for it by sleeping with the big black buck.

"There's no way I could ever see myself going to bed with a black woman, you know. If I, if I ever reach that point, that I, if I ever lose my racial pride and I reach that point that I'm that insane that you catch me in the bed with a black woman, I hope that one of my movement brothers is considerate enough and cares enough about me to give me a bullet in my brain.

"I don't hate black people, but the thought of having sex with a black woman, it disgusts me. It's just something that's not, if there is a God, like I say, people say it's against God. I believe there is some Supreme Being and I don't believe—you know, that's, that's like homosexuality. God created Adam and Eve, he didn't create Adam and Steve. It's just, it's not right."

He was working to build a world, he said, in which his unborn child would never have to come home from school and say, "Daddy, some black kid beat me up and took my lunch money away at school." That would not work, he said; he would be in prison. He would go find out who the kid was, look up the kid's father, and say, "Hey, you know what your kid did to my kid? Better put a leash on the monkey."

The Strike Group, if it gained power, would rid the country of non-whites. "We believe in repatriation," he said. "If we got political power, the black man would go back to Africa. The Jewish people would be sent to Israel. America would be for the white people who founded it and built it."

I asked what would happen with communists.

"Communists would be charged with treason against their race. If it was a white communist. If they were guilty of doing things which were against their race and against their country, they'd pay the penalty for treason."

"What," I asked, "is the crime of treason against the white race?"

"Having sex with a non-Aryan."

I looked at him. "And they should be killed for that?"

"Yes. Death penalty. I believe in some of the old principles. If a white woman slept with a black man, like I say, the black man, I'd repatriate him back to Africa. I wouldn't shoot him. The black man would automatically be on a boat. The woman who slept with him, she'd get a bullet in the brain.

"She'd still get a trial," he added.

This fantasy came out easily and forcefully. I thought I had better bring him back to earth. I pointed out that I had been talking about a real person, in fact a sweet and fine woman. He began to back down. He made up an escape clause for himself—maybe he would want to say that she was not worth the bother of a bullet. Then it would be okay to let her go back on the boat with her husband, join him on the trip to Africa.

I wasn't ready to leave it at this. I pointed out that on one level "we're just having a bullshit conversation, okay? On the other level, if we think about the real world, real people involved—I guess my question is, Raymond, what leads you to feel it's your business that these two people live together?"

"I told you my wife [that is, his woman friend] was pregnant with that baby?" he answered. "I don't want him to even see an interracial couple walking down the street."

"Why not?" I asked.

"I don't want him to see that."

Again: "Why not?"

"If he ever sees something like that, I want it to be in a history book. 'Great Degenerates of the Past.'

"The fact—what she's doing disgusts me. If she had any racial pride, interracial marriage is wrong. That's treason. It's wrong in the eyes of God, it just wasn't meant to be. It destroys two races. Like I say, I don't believe in killing off all of the black people—"

I interrupted: "Wait, wait. For a moment I don't want to hear that level of statement. I want to hear in terms of your own feelings."

"My own feelings?" he asked.

"Your own feeling is . . ." I prompted.

"Disgust," he said flatly. "It makes me want to, it just makes me want to throw them both in the gas chamber. That's my first impulse."

Again, the gas chamber.

"But I try and put myself in the position like, you remember Klaus Barbie, who was the Gestapo officer in charge of Lyons, France? He probably had to do some things he didn't like to do, but if I was in a position like that of leadership I'd try and do good things, I'd try and concentrate on doing good things for people. But in trying to clean the society and trying to remove the degenerate elements and the bad elements, you'd have to do some things you wouldn't want to do. You have to do some—when you're changing something so drastically as we're changing it, you may have to do— Like I say, we're going to have to, the repatriation of the black people and the nonwhites to their own country. But there's also going to be a lot of bad white people. When we get into political power— Like I say, if I was in a position of leadership, I'd probably have to do some things I wouldn't really care for."

This childish man, remember, is twenty-five, not eleven. This is not talk on a playground. These images of power, these fantasies that one is responsible for making social program, have been nurtured in seven years of movement work. Nothing in his life in the movement stops him, nothing demands realism.

The movement encourages this fantasy of power—here are the powerless drifting off into daydreams of power, as you and I drift, pressed by monthly bills, into daydreams of winning the lottery. But not so innocent. Note that the Klaus Barbie image wraps together virtue and violence. Note the martyrdom of the justice-seeker who must do things that are unpleasant—and who, in the case of Barbie, eventually was cornered by the unsympathetic world. Again and again, my respondents in interviews have pictured themselves as victims. Note particularly that Raymond's fantasies pair sexuality, or at least interracial sexuality, with murder: "a bullet in the brain."

Raymond had a heavy anti-Jewish agenda. Telling me about grave health issues that he had in his teens, he talked about having been saved by a Jewish doctor, but he drew no lessons from that. I pointed out to him one night that the movement literature he and I had been looking at was deeply anti-Semitic, but that in my contact with Strike Group members I mostly heard about black people, not about Jews. He agreed, saying that most of the group members had grown up in the inner city with blacks and had had little to do with Jews. They hadn't known much about Jews, he said, until they came into contact with the Nazi group. "So I guess you could say we're responsible; you could say, if we could make a reference to the Garden of Eden,

we gave these young people the apple. We gave them the knowledge."

He himself, he said, was "more anti-Jewish than I am anti-black."
He could more easily accept blacks, he said, if he had to choose;
blacks were typically poor and uneducated, were less dangerous. "I
don't feel that they pose as much of a threat to the National Socialist
movement or to the cause and goals we're fighting for.

"But you ask where I learned this, and I say my grandfather. I told
you he was a States Righter back in the sixties, when the Freedom
Riders were coming through the South. He was with Fields' and
Stoner's National States Righters. And he spoke to me often about
the Jews. He spoke often about them.

"When I'd arrive at his house and I'd sit there and I'd go through
his stack of papers, *Thunderbolts*, and read his literature, I'd ask him
questions. And he didn't care for the black people. He was very
bigoted towards the blacks. But I have to say he was equally if not
more prejudiced against the Jews. And he was vocal about it. He
would speak his mind and tell people what he thought."

I asked what sort of things his grandfather had told him. Raymond
replied that when he had asked about the Holocaust, his grandfather
had told him that he didn't believe it happened—but that "if it did,
Hitler made one mistake: He didn't get rid of every Jew in existence.
So that pretty well sums up his feelings in one sentence."

I asked what else the old man had told him.

"Well, the usual part about the international banks, finance, the
control of political power, control of the media, control of the
money.

"He tried to impress upon me that you were all crooks. You know
all the stories that are supposed to go along with the Jewish people.
I think I've heard ninety-nine percent of them."

"What are some of the things you really do believe about Jews
that he taught you," I asked, "that are important?"

Raymond said he believed that the media were controlled by the
Jewish people and that the Jews controlled communism.

"What else I believe about the Jewish people?" he went on. "Well,
I know you don't come out from under mushrooms; that's one of
the old children's tales that used to be told."

I happily told him that this was the one thing he had been told that was true. "We do, Raymond. We come right out from under mushrooms." Then I again asked what he believed that seemed important.

He had to think for quite a while. Then he said, "I believe the Jews are dangerous. Anything they want to do, they have the people in political power. They have the media and they have the finance."

They were better educated, he said. He had noticed that kids in Jewish families were constantly told to study. But basically, he said, they were a political force. This turned out to mean that Jews were much to blame for the fact that the white racist movement had not gotten any further politically in the country than it had. Here he particularly laid the blame on "all the movies that have come out of Hollywood, about the evil, killing Germans, and all of the anti-National Socialist and anti-white propaganda. You look at the producers' names: Silverman. Goldberg. I watch a lot—not a *lot* of television, but I watch probably quite a few hours of TV a week, and I read the subtitles at the end of the movies. Check out who the producers and directors are."

What else did he believe? He spoke of the Holocaust as having been a hoax. Then there was a pause. He had been taught, he said, about ritual murder. "Jewish ritual murder. I didn't get to read up on it as much as I wanted, but part of the Jewish ceremony, the book said that they kidnapped children. Drained their blood for use in the ceremonies."

I asked which ceremonies.

"God only knows," he replied, "but I can show you some cartoons that—"

I interrupted that citation of "evidence" and asked whether he believed it.

"I *wonder* sometimes," he said, with a nasty tone of implication. I struck him, he said, as a fairly nice person, but he had "seen some of those rabbis in their long black coats with the hat, and, *you know*."

Did he think, I asked, that they might kidnap children?

"Devious-looking characters," he replied.

"You halfway believe that may be the truth?" I pressed.

"I halfway believe it," he said.

I asked what else he halfway believed.

"This isn't halfway believe: I believe Israel would like to rule the world. If they can get financial power in enough countries. There are French Jews, German Jews, Polish Jews, Russian Jews. A lot of the stuff that's happening, I believe it comes from—just like it was planned—*The Protocols of the Learned Elders of Zion*. And I believe that to be an authentic document. I just believe the only reason that the *Protocols* weren't fulfilled is because World War II kind of put a damper on the plans."

One of the most powerful images arose a few moments later. I asked him to look at his statement that Jews had gotten so much education in America. Did he suppose, I asked, that Jews were smarter than the Aryans genetically?

"No," he said, "I believe they're better organized. If the Aryan families would push their young people and do the same thing the Jews were doing, there's no way the Jewish plan would make it. But like I say, we're going to have to—"

Now he interrupted himself. I guess he was about to say they were going to have to impose some sort of restriction. In any case, the thought led him to this:

"That's why the laws in Germany were passed about Jewish doctors could treat only Jews, because so many of the older German people were disgusted. They'd see some pretty little blond German girl, twelve or fourteen years old, going into the Jewish doctor, and you know what went through their minds."

"No," I said. "What went through their minds? I *don't* know."

"The usual . . . nightmares. They saw the little German girls being deflowered and felt and poked and felt out and—"

I interrupted his blossoming fantasy. "Why would a Jewish doctor do that any more than a Christian doctor?"

"That's one of the old cartoons I've seen," he said. "I'm not stating that that happened in all cases."

Somehow that didn't quite cover it. "Why would it happen *ever*," I asked, "any more from one than the other? Are Jews by nature more lecherous than Christians?"

He didn't know the word. "You mean 'sleepier'?"

"No," I explained. " 'Lustful.' "

There was a pause. It would depend, he figured, upon the individual Jew. "But I've noticed that the pornography business, the sex business, you see all those shops around?" He went on in an insinuating tone: "Wonder *who* makes all of those pornographic movies?"

He presumed the answer was obvious. "Jews. The right wing is giving the credit to the Jewish people. I halfway believe it. Nobody's proved it to me on paper, just on instinct, I halfway believe it."

Note this example of logic. Jewish doctors had to be restricted because of fears they violated Christian German girls. Why should they have been feared? Because Jews are pornographers. How do we know that? Nobody has proved it, but we can know it's true just on instinct. This set of thoughts has at its center a powerful nugget of emotion: the scene of the Jewish doctor and the little flaxen-haired girl. Remember that Raymond's source for this image is "one of the old cartoons I've seen."

Raymond had another image for me. "I know one rumor that I heard. The Jewish rabbi who performs a little operation. That all the male members of the Jewish faith are supposed to have, the circumcision? We heard a story about how they do this surgery. After they cut the skin, something about kissing, or the blood, or something. A drop of the blood, they have to kiss it." He snickered. "Or basically give the kid some head, you know."

Later that same evening, Raymond and Rosandra were discussing their coming baby. I pointed out that they kept assuming it would be a boy, but that it could equally be a girl. That would be fine, they said, they would get it pink dresses and a stroller and it would still grow up with a National Socialist education.

I said I hoped the baby would get over it.

"She might marry the next Führer, who knows?" Raymond said.

"She might marry a Jew, too," I suggested.

"I don't think so," he said, "when we're done with her. If she does, if she marries a Jew, there's a rope in her future. I'm dead serious. If she ever comes home to me and said, 'Daddy, I met a nice Jewish boy today,' I'd ask her one question: 'Do you have a death wish?' "

"Wait a minute, Raymond," I said. "You think I'm a nice guy, right?"

"True."

Okay, I said, what if she met one of my grandchildren?

She wouldn't have the opportunity, Raymond pointed out. "We're not planning on you guys being around twenty years from now."

I laughed at him. Look here, I suggested, suppose she's on a tour in twenty years to Greenland and runs into the place where we Jews settle when the boat drifts the wrong way and she falls in love with one of my grandchildren? "I mean," I raved on, "if you think I'm nice, you ought to know my kids, because they're super nice. And my grandchildren will be out of this world!

"And she's going to fall in love with this really nice, really nice guy named Abraham Ezekiel out there in Greenland. Come back home and say, 'I met this beautiful man, Daddy. Loves music, sings all the time. Really funny, really intelligent. Down there in the lost Jewish colony in Greenland. And we're going to settle in England where nobody cares one way or the other.' What are you going to say then?" I asked.

Raymond was quick. "You're under arrest!"

We both laughed. Then he went on seriously, "She would definitely have to go to one of the reeducation centers. But I doubt seriously that would ever happen. The way we educate our daughters—"

Rosandra interjected: "Or our sons."

"Or our sons. If he were to meet one of your grandchildren in the future . . . hmmmm. He'd probably speak and be courteous. But, I don't know. He'd probably be dreaming of a little oven somewhere in back of his head."

I was jolted. Raymond was conjuring an image of his unborn child burning my not-yet-conceived grandchildren. I demanded and received an apology.

What do you say after this tour through Raymond's mind? Why had Raymond ever concerned himself with Jews? Probably the answer is his education at the hands of his beloved grandfather, who had served under old-line racist stalwarts such as Fields and Stoner. But what is even more strange is his language—he speaks as though the Third Reich still existed and he held a position in its forces.

What's in it for him? It reminds me of kids much younger falling into roles in Dungeons and Dragons. He doesn't distinguish reality and fantasy well.

In Idaho, at the Aryan Nations compound, a picture of Adolf Hitler rests in a place of honor on the wall. The artist's rendering shows deep, intense eyes in a sensitive face, a face that is strong but suffering.

Raymond, like Paul, kept a picture of Hitler's face in his room. It had fallen down one day as we spoke; Raymond said it had come unglued. I suggested that Hitler had come unglued long before. Hurt flickered across Raymond's face, but he kept silent. Later in that interview, he expressed his adoration of the Führer.

"I almost consider Adolf Hitler to be a god. When you said that —I don't think you want to know some of the ideas I—I had some thoughts about you that would've probably scared you.

"That's my hero. One of my heroes. Hitler. One of the greatest leaders who ever walked the face of the earth.

"They said Christ came to preach salvation and save the world. It's not just me, there's many people who feel the way I do, many of the old Germans, like the ones who came and shook hands with us when we went up to the German festival at Frankenmuth, looked upon Hitler as—you know, there's a lot of people who they say Jesus Christ was a Savior. The Messiah, the prophet, come with the message.

"I know some German people who if they heard you—being a Death's-Head man, I didn't like the words, but like I said, I'm not going to, as much as I wanted to—I wanted to feed you your words, was my first impression. But I know some of the older German people who if they heard you say what you said about Hitler, would do their, would probably do their utmost to try and blow your candle out for you. They feel that strongly. You know, in their heart, just like in my heart, he will always be the Führer."

I pointed out that Raymond was the first in the group I had heard become passionate about Hitler.

"You mean almost idolize him as a God?" he said. "The SS runes and the Death's-Head aren't just on my shirt." He thumped his chest. "They are in *here*. My heart. If I were taken—if the communists came into power and they took me out and shot me tomorrow, the last two words out of my mouth would be, 'Heil Hitler!' He will always be the ultimate leader to me."

I suggested that others in the group did not have this intense attachment; he claimed not to know, not to have discussed it with them. He allowed that they probably weren't as involved. "Close as we are as brothers, you know, I'm not a mind reader. I do believe that they admire the Führer, but I still look upon him as the ultimate leader.

"If we were to come into political power, I would build a statue of Adolf Hitler five hundred foot—I'd build a statue of Hitler larger than the Statue of Liberty.

"I doubt whether any of the other brothers, that they feel the admiration for the Führer that I've felt. If he were to come back today, I would be the first person to salute him and say, 'God bless you, my Führer!'

"Like I said, he gave an ideal for our people. He gave us the pattern to follow. And I'm just trying, I'm keeping, his goals and his ideals are alive, you know, and his ideal will have a chance of coming back again. And you talk about I'm unemployed and the position I'm in? I don't even consider myself good enough to shine that man's shoes. He was the ultimate, you know. Like I say, I almost consider Hitler to be a god."

I spent a long time trying to find the roots of Raymond's attachment to Hitler. First I asked how old he had been when the feeling had become real for him.

"Believe it or not," he said, "before any of the members of my family educated me. I was sitting and I was watching the speeches on TV, the old Hitler speeches, and I was just a kid. I knew there was something about that man I liked. It was just the personality and the forcefulness. It was almost—you know the power Hitler had over the German people, it was almost a hypnotizing effect. Forty years after his death, thirty years after his death, watching the old tapes, you could still—the dynamic personality, you know. It's like the book says, when you can make an accomplishment sometime and get people to unite to do something sometimes, you're a leader; when you can do it every single day, you're a great leader. He did it every single day."

I asked again how old he had been during these experiences.

"When I was six and seven, five, six, seven years old. My grandfather spoke to me a little bit. But I'd sit in front of the TV and watch the German troops marching by. I got to see some of the old movies of the rallies. And I sat there and clapped my hands: Yeah! Yeah!

"It's nothing I could put my finger on, but I knew there was something I liked. And then when I got old enough where I could understand, I found out what he stood for and what he really stood for. And I got my first copy of *Mein Kampf*, and I got to read the thoughts. The thoughts of my Führer down on paper and see what he really felt. Then I could say, hey, this is it, this man has got the plan.

"But that was one of the proudest days of my life, when I got my first copy of *Mein Kampf*, when I actually got to sit down and read the words of the Führer. You know. It's almost like even though I never got to speak to him, when I read the words, I, in my mind, I pictured the Führer saying this. And I said, okay, even though the Führer in his body may be physically dead now, his ideals are still alive. This is the message he left for me, right here.

"I was a reader when I was a kid. I don't read as much as I did when I was a kid. I loved history, all types of history, particularly the Second World War, though. There's always been something about the National Socialist movement. At one time I got off on a kick on prehistory, and I studied the prehistoric forms of man and the genetics. And I saw what man evolved into. But then when I came to the books on Hitler and I started reading about Hitler—this is one of the ultimate human beings, I said, this is as close as we're going to get to God walking this earth right here. This is one of the ultimate human beings we're going to get."

What does Raymond's attachment mean? As with so much else, it suggests someone at a younger age, an eleven- or twelve-year-old, who feels alone, perhaps abandoned, and shaky about his own worth, who focuses on a distant figure that can be loved, a safely unavailable figure, one that overcame odds to achieve great acceptance and power. With a certain amount of self-abasement that affords some relief, the eleven-year-old can safely acknowledge the love object and merge with it, trading adoration for (often imagined) approval.

As I pressed Raymond about his involvement with Hitler, his grandfather, who had died two or three years before, became more and more our subject.

"Well, one thing, my grandfather had a lot to do with it. When I seen the Führer speaking on TV, I knew that I liked the way he spoke. And the dynamic—the personality itself and the way he conducted himself. I just always looked up to him, almost like a father figure. And then, I knew I always admired my grandfather. My grandfather, back in the forties and fifties, my grandfather always wore a Hitler mustache. He did up until about a year and half before he died, when he had the cancer and he wasn't able to take care of himself. Then we had to take care of him.

"He wore a Hitler mustache when it wasn't popular. And my grandfather always spoke highly of Adolf Hitler. He said the only mistake Hitler made was not getting rid—my grandfather hated Jewish people—he said the only thing Hitler didn't do right was not getting rid of *all* the Jewish people. But he always spoke highly of the Führer. My grandfather's the one who told me, read *Mein Kampf*. 'You really want to know what Hitler was about, the man wrote a book. Read it.'"

Raymond's father had not minded him receiving these thoughts from his grandfather. Raymond said his father "was racist, even though he was nonviolent and he believed in live and let live." He said his father had taught him as a kid that "we were better than the black people, taught me the same white supremacy." But his father "wasn't as much up on the Jews."

Raymond's father was a veteran of World War II. "He fought in Belgium with the American field artillery. He was decorated, so you could say my dad was an American war hero." His father's side of the family was German, and his father had told Raymond, "Be proud of your German bloodlines. The war happened. It was a terrible thing. But don't let these people make you ashamed of your German bloodline because of it." His father had taught him that the Germans were a great people, "and were descended from the Viking warriors."

Raymond had asked his father about the war, and his father had said that he didn't hate the German people or Hitler, but that he was born an American citizen, that his country drafted him and ordered him to fight. He was loyal to the country. As Raymond saw it, his father "doesn't really agree with everything that Hitler believed in. But he didn't disagree with all those things, either."

Raymond had spoken, I suggested, as though strong bonds joined him and his grandfather. He agreed with passion. I asked how one fit his father into that picture. He had to think about that a moment. Then he said that he was close to both of them. He looked up to his dad, he said, respected him and loved him, and they were fairly close—"but I'm going to say I was just as close to my grandfather as I was with my dad."

There hadn't been as many activities with his father; they would do something every once in a while, "but every time you turned around, I was fishing with Granddad or walking along beside him when he worked his garden with his little garden tractor."

This grandfather was Raymond's mother's father. The family originally had lived some 140 miles from the man but would see him once or twice a month, and in the summer Raymond's mother would leave him there for months at a time.

Raymond had been given a little white hat like the one his grandfather wore as an electrician. Raymond tried to do everything just like his grandfather. "Tried to copy him to a T. I'd even sit around and roll—if he wanted a cigarette, I'd say, 'Let me roll you one.' He rolled Bugler. And I'd roll him cigarettes. I'd say, 'C'mere, let me do that for you.' And I got to where I could roll a mean cigarette. I wanted to be just like Grandpa."

Raymond told me then of his grandfather's death. "When we finally moved near him, he was dying of cancer. He worked—he had government clearance—he worked on some of the bomb projects. He worked on the bomb project at Hanford, Washington, and was exposed to the radioactivity. He had cancer in every vital organ of his body. And I had to carry him around like a little baby. And eventually I had to—I had to sit and watch him get ate up with cancer. He didn't believe in drugs, so he wouldn't take any; you had to just about slip him the pain medicine.

"We moved when I was twenty-one, when they found out he had cancer. He died when I was about twenty-three. He lived for two [more] years. I watched him go through two surgeries. And carried him around like a baby.

"I fed him. I sat besides his bed and I read to him from some of the old newspapers. He got to where during the last days he didn't even recognize us. All he knew was—the electricians used, you know, the old expression, 'What do you know, Joe?' And I'd come in and I'd look at him, 'What do you know, Joe?' And he'd look up at me —I'm not going to say his name, but anyway that wasn't his name. And he'd look up at me and smile and he'd say, 'Just hanging around.' He'd smile because he remembered that.

"He got to where he didn't even know us. But anyway, I'd sit and read to him, and I'd go to the store and get him treats. He lost his appetite, but he'd eat better for me than he would for anybody else. I'd fix him a bourbon and Coke, and I'd take a plate in, even if he was in one of his moods where he wouldn't eat. I'd say, 'If you'll eat this, I'll give you this.' And I'd get him to eat.

"And anyway, one day I took my father's truck and I went to the store to buy him some doughnuts. I went to a doughnut shop. And I got him three chocolate glazed doughnuts and three regular. And I got back to his house and I looked in. Nobody was there. And the house was empty. His bed had been stripped. I figured, well, they must've took him up to our house. I went up to the house and they weren't there. I had the feeling when I seen it. I called the hospital and I said, is my grandfather there? And they said yes, he had a heart—the cancer had weakened him down to where he had a heart attack.

"I said, 'Well, he's all right, isn't he?' I said, 'Tell me that my mother and grandmother are bringing him home.' And she said, 'I'm sorry, but your grandfather is dead.' And I said, 'Don't lie to me, bitch,' I said. And she starts, 'Sir, sir, I'm sorry, I'm sorry.' And I hung up on her.

"And—hmmmm. That was a bad day. I kind of—that was the

day, I kind of come unhinged that day. I took my Ruger 10/22 and I went out in the backyard and chopped up some hills. I went out and started beating on trees."

"You took your what?"

"I took a carbine and I went out in the backyard—I didn't think —when my grandfather died, I—hmmmm. I didn't think it would be true. I wanted to believe it was a lie. And I was actually crying. That was—my grandfather was one of the people my world circulated around. There's very few people I'm going to say I've ever been really super close to, but my grandfather had to be one of them. I idolized him.

"And—I got mad. I said she lied to me, and I said I got to get out of this house, I'm going to go—I got my carbine. I said, I'm going to go out and shoot. I said, you know, I went out and started chopping up the hills in the back of the yard. And I mean, I went out, I walked on out into the forest. I threw the gun down, I started beating my fists against the trees. And then I fell down against the tree, and I just sat there. And I wanted to, I was just wishing the whole world would go ahead and blow up and I could go, too. And I finally got myself pulled together and I came back to the house, and my mother and grandmother finally got back, and I pretty well devoted the rest of my attention to my grandmother that day. Anything she wants is good enough for me.

"I carry three pictures in my wallet," he said, beginning to choke up, "aside from my young lady friends, who are back at the back. See the first picture: That's my mother. That's his oldest, my grandfather's oldest daughter. My mother is his oldest girl. That second is a picture of my father. And that third, I don't think I have to tell you who that man is."

There was a pause.

"That picture . . ."

He couldn't talk. He began to weep.

After a few moments, he breathed deeply and resumed in a shaky voice, "That picture . . . will be in there . . . till the day I die.

"That was—hmmmm—that was a knife in my heart, the day he died.

"My world definitely rotated around Grandpa, he was number one. So. Hmmmm. Anyway.

"What else can I say about that? The man took me flying. I loved, I've always loved airplanes. That was a man, the first man to take me up in an airplane. Say, 'Here, boy, take the controls and hold her steady.' Hey, who else will grow a beautiful garden and pick you vegetables and then peel them and . . . you ask a lot about my political beliefs and the way I feel. You know what he taught me, and now you know how I felt about my grandfather. That's probably about three fourths of my political beliefs right there. But like I say, there's still the one fourth on my own. I still always looked up to the Führer and the white racist cause. My grandfather was a States Righter. He always—the one thing he always taught me: Do what's right."

As he recovered himself, Raymond spoke a good deal more about the old fellow—how healthy he had been, how he had been a boxer as a youth, had owned a pool hall, could work hard physically even in his later years, and how drastic the physical effects of the cancer had been. "We watched him go from a hundred and seventy-five pounds to, when he died, I doubt he weighed a hundred pounds. It was just skin stretched over bone. Looking at his face, it was just a skull with some skin stretched over it, and the eyes were sunk back in deep. And the cancer was causing him great pain, so as much as I hated to lose him, the heart attack he had, in a way, it was almost a relief.

"Anyway. I watched him go down to a skeleton. What really hurt me, even, like about four months before he died, he would still have his moments when we would be there and I could sit and I could read to him, and he would be receptive to it. And he would listen and he'd say, 'Yeah, I like that, I wish I could do that,' or something like that."

We are left, then, with this strange confounding of Hitler and Raymond's grandfather, and Raymond's real attachment to his grandfather. I could learn almost nothing from Raymond about his father and mother, other than his mother's rough ability to handle Raymond's teenage behavior. Little was said to suggest attachment to either parent. Hitler and Granddad were playing in an uncrowded field.

———

Rosandra's mother, who lived in a small town in northern Michigan, was heavily involved with the Klan, which wanted her to organize a chapter up there. Rosandra had met Raymond when she and her mother attended one of the periodic gatherings at Bob Miles's farm. I was teasing Rosandra and Raymond one evening and asked why Rosandra's mother hadn't kept a better eye on her, not to let her wander off and run into Raymond. Rosandra said that her mom "didn't have much to say in it," and Raymond said, "That's the only type of person her mother would even let her associate with, Klan or NS [National Socialist]." Rosandra agreed, and pulled out a photo from the gathering showing herself in what she called a Klan shirt, with thunderbolts on the collar and little flags.

Raymond said that Rosandra had picked him out from the group—that he had been, along with Paul, one of the only older members present, and that Rosandra's mother had been impressed because he, Raymond, happened to be the flag bearer that day and the banner they had chosen to bring was their "Führer's standard, Adolf Hitler's standard," and that Rosandra's mother had a great admiration for Adolf Hitler.

After Raymond told me how to distinguish a "Führer's Standard" from other Nazi flags, I said, "Oh, okay. So there you were with the Standard, and Rosandra's mother saw that and said, 'Go, daughter, that man's got a pretty flag!'"

"No," Raymond said, "I broke the ice. She was sitting at a table with her mother, and my armband had come unpinned. The safety pin came open. I pulled it off and tightened it back up. That was my excuse, anyway.

"I said, 'Could you assist me with this?' We took a walk. We held hands. We wound up giving each other a smooch or two. We started looking deep into each other's eyes.

"And I didn't have to take and teach her things about the movement," Raymond continued. "Starr, my girlfriend of two years [the young woman of the motorcycle photo], was anti-black. She was very anti-black, but she didn't know a thing about a Jew. I had to teach her what little bit I knew about Jews. But I didn't have to educate Rosandra. Her mother—"

I interrupted to ask Rosandra what her mother had told her. She was reluctant to answer—"It's kind of hard to explain"—but finally quoted what her mother had said: "Don't go out with them. You bring one home, you got a shotgun!"

Raymond added, "If she brought a Jew home, her mother is anti-Semitic to the point where if you went up there with us to that area, you would very probably leave the property on the end of an assault rifle."

I asked whether the mother had taught Rosandra about blacks as well. She said yes. And what had she been taught?

" 'Don't hang around with them.' It's like when I was in high school, I had this colored girlfriend. And me and her would walk back and forth, but if my mom ever seen us, she'd tell us to get in the car or get in the house."

I said I was surprised that there had been a black girl up in those northern woods.

"Not there," Rosandra said. "We were in Indiana, a town next to Hammond." She had spent her life there, and there had been many blacks, "lots of them."

Had her mother told her to watch out for them?

"Yeah. When I was going to school, I had a nigger pulled a knife on me. And the school system would not do a damn thing about it. So my mom just said, 'Go get your papers, you're quitting school.' And I said, 'Oh, good.' "

This had been the ninth grade, and that was the last she had seen of school.

Her father, who worked in a die-cast factory, had left the family when Rosandra was seven; he lived now in South Carolina and was remarried. According to Rosandra, her father "really didn't care who I hung around with."

Her mother lived now from Social Security she was collecting for Rosandra and her little brother, Rosandra said, and mostly stayed home. The Social Security came because of Rosandra's acute nearsightedness—her glasses were extraordinarily thick, she could not drive a car—and because of a finger that was crippled from birth. The finger, with a tendon that was too short, could not be straightened out. "I had an operation on it," she said. "They said all my cords and veins up here to my elbow are all tangled up together. It come out to a twenty-thousand-dollar hospital bill, just the operation." Rosandra claimed not to be bothered by the hand.

I asked what she had done after dropping out of school—had she taken a job or stayed at home?

"I was staying at home. Sleeping till noon, getting up and watching my soaps. All I did every day."

"What were your favorites?" I asked.

"*All My Children, One Life to Live,* and *General Hospital.*" She was still keeping up with them "once in a while."

She also did a lot of reading. "Usually, I'm reading romance."

Rosandra was usually in the apartment when I came to interview Raymond, but she would stay in their bedroom reading, with very occasional forays out into the living room. She would offer coffee and sit and smoke a minute, but soon go back to her reading. She was eighteen years old and very shy. It pained me, as I have said, to watch her hold the dishes to her face to see them when she was cleaning up after their supper.

I doubted that she was eating well enough, and I was worried about her pregnancy. One night she interrupted us an hour after midnight because she was having cramps; she needed to get to a doctor. I drove them to the hospital and waited for quite a long time with Raymond. Raymond had talked a lot about this pregnancy and his pride in it; nevertheless, he was insensitive and self-absorbed throughout this incident. Fortunately, the trip was a false alarm, not a miscarriage.

Rosandra was quiet and easily cowed. She was glad to get out from under her mother's domination. She seemed dazed by the pregnancy; life had changed a lot more than she had expected.

Several days after the trip to the hospital, I went away for a few weeks. When I returned, I began receiving phone calls from Raymond, who had gone back to Arkansas. He desperately asked what the group members were saying about him; he believed that they were trying to incite Klan assassins to get him.

I asked Paul what had been going on. It turned out that Rosandra had needed to get away from Raymond because he had been beating her. Nolan, a group member, had helped to spirit Rosandra away from the apartment; she had stayed with Nolan's mother briefly and then gone north to her own mother. Raymond had left town shortly after Rosandra's escape. On the way out of town, Raymond phoned the Secret Service, Paul said, and reported to them that Nolan and others whom he named were secret Nazis who were plotting to assassinate the president.

According to Paul, Raymond had been cut off welfare a month before he left town; he had refused to report for the eight days a month of work that Michigan required.

Contact with Raymond and Rosandra ended there. Raymond was working at a motorcycle repair shop in Arkansas; Rosandra had gone north to have her baby.

Raymond will find some new uniform for some new play-acting; Rosandra will be bent over the sink at her mother's house, washing dishes and listening to the cries of her child. And the child?

FIFTEEN

Francis

Raymond was visited frequently by a young man from the neighborhood, a fresh recruit named Francis. I wanted to find out what had brought Francis in and what the group had taught him, and we spent a long night at Raymond's house talking.

Francis was a native of the desolate area in which Raymond was renting an apartment; Raymond was passing through, while Francis and his family had lived for years in the violence-ridden slum, a run-down splattering of wooden houses waiting to burn. Francis felt the poverty sharply. He believed, bitterly, that people with money did not care what happened to people like him. He considered "rich people" and "Jews" synonymous. The group was teaching him vicious contempt for Jews.

"My name's Francis," he said at the start. "I'm nineteen. And my family, my ma is from Germany, my sister and brother, Dieter and Karen, is from Germany. Me, Frederick, John, and Timmy was born in USA. Brother Timmy got killed at the age of five by a car, he got hit. And we ran home and told my mom about it and she ran out the door as fast as she can, went down where my brother got hit, a block away from my house. And he was dead.

"So my ma got very upset, so did we. But I was four, he was five, so it really didn't affect me more than it did my ma, because I was young, at the age. We . . . had a funeral for him."

His mother "took the money that the city had give her, wasn't that much," and bought new furniture for the whole house, but then the family had to move because there was a new and disagreeable land-lord. Rent was cheap in the new place, "the only thing we had to worry about was those cockroaches."

This next house caught fire one night. "We had to move from out of there to my dad's house, and that was a bitch there because my dad is a prick. It's no difference from my stepdad. He damn near give me a broken knee, all this, but you know you get tired of it.

"My real father, he be telling us to get a bag of chips while we were watching TV. If we didn't jump right when he told us, he'd throw a boot at us. Now, my stepfather, none of us would listen to his ass, so he gets my ma to tell us. You know, since he's our step-father, we say what the fuck, you know, we ain't going to listen to his dumb ass. But my ma, she's our real blood, I'll listen to her, she tells me not to do that, I'm not going to do it, you know."

His brother, he said, "called the president four times, threatened to kill his ass. He used to have a picture up there on the wall, every time I come in I turned the fucking picture over, because I can't stand it. I don't want to see it, man, you know. He's a prick. He ain't doing shit for this USA. Can't control the niggers. Can't do shit with them.

"If I was up in the White House," he said, "the fucking niggers and Jews be out of the USA right now."

He talked about seeing houses in the neighborhood burn; the night before, "the two apartment houses on the street was burning, the whole inside you couldn't see *shit,* but flames, fire, smoke. They de-stroyed that house, niggers, they don't give a fuck. Every night. To-night is the only night I know there ain't a fire."

He told of a recent neighborhood shooting. A black man had come into a neighborhood house at five in the morning looking for one of the men who lived there and begun shooting at everyone in sight, killing several people. Were he the judge, Francis said, he would "execute his ass, I'd just execute him, put him in the chamber, do something, hang his ass. Because, fuck, one of us, you know, if I found out Raymond had killed somebody, you know, I wouldn't be by him for the rest of my life, I wouldn't, I would disown his ass;

same for you, I wouldn't be talking to you if I know you had killed somebody. If my *brother* killed somebody, his ass is out, I won't even talk to him because I think it's wrong to kill somebody.

"I think it's wrong to kill somebody in your race, you know. Fuck with the niggers, you know, we can just blow them away. That's one less nigger in the city. But these were white people.

"My brother," he went on, "got set up in jail, you know, he's doing time right now, my brother John. Somebody—it was attempted B & E, somebody busted a window, I guess, that's what he had told my mom, and they found the footsteps from the gas station to his camper, that's in Florida in wintertime, and they caught him on that, he broke out of jail twice. Caught him, and the police shot him in the arm, that's how they caught him the second time."

I asked whether his brother had really committed the B & E.

"I cannot tell you," Francis said, "because he never did tell me." He had been traced by the footprints, and the state had wanted a bond much higher than the family could have come up with. He had been in jail for several years and would be out by the end of the year if he could find a job and make parole.

Did Francis miss his brother?

"Of course. Wouldn't you miss your brother if he was sent up? If you were used to being with him all the time, and he leave, you know, you miss him. Just like my sister, she's in California, I miss the hell out of her. She writes every day."

Strange stories popped up as Francis spoke. "I was standing at the bus stop," he said, "this nigger asked me, 'Do you mind if I snatch this old lady's purse?' He was half white, half black, and he said, 'Do you mind if I snatch this lady's purse?' And I said, 'You can snatch it as long as I'm not around, you know, otherwise leave her alone.' If I see someone snatching somebody's purse, no telling what I'd do, no telling. Probably kill his ass or hurt him real bad.

"I see somebody doing that, I'll do more than slap his ass, I'm going to hurt him where his nuts is at. I know he won't do it again, 'cause he got his lesson from that one time.

"Stomp his ass, beat his ass first.

"No, I don't want to kill the boy, just stomp his ass into the ground, you know, and go up for manslaughter then. Beat his ass, that's what you going to do."

Francis had been talking about Jews before we started recording. I pointed out to him that he hadn't spoken about them a month before. He agreed, said the group members, "not only Raymond, it's Michael, Nolan, Lane, all of them, they got me so I look down on Jews."

I asked whether he had ever thought about Jews before.

Yes, he said, "when my ma was working for them. She was housemaid, when she was working for Jews. And the way she was telling me how you guys, instead of using a mop, you guys believe in a scrub brush. And my mom's not used to doing that. And they worked her so damn hard, you know, and she got blisters all over her, her hands and shit.

"But it didn't affect me to hate them much, Jews, you know, they made me sick but that's the only thing my mom had to do at the time. She doesn't want to get on ADC. But now she has to, cause ain't no money coming in."

His stepfather, a painter, had had work for a while, but was currently laid off. The painting contractor had placed the blame for layoffs on the customers—"you guys," as Francis put it, which seemed to mean either the rich or the Jews; the customers were choosing building materials that didn't take paint, and so his stepfather didn't have work.

I asked what the group was teaching him about Jews.

"You guys," he responded, "well, a couple of things I heard, you guys got money, you know, you got this stuff, you don't give a fuck about the poor.

"In the Bible," he continued, "you guys are all in the Bible. Jews. Jews this, Jews that, you guys are Jews everywhere. Even on TV, Jews. You guys want to win the wars and shit, you guys doing this and that. The population get sick of it, what you guys do sometimes. Like spit on the revolution flag [the Confederate flag], half of the people do.

"You guys want the money. You probably living out there, Fifteen Mile or Twenty-six Mile Road, in a nice big-ass house, built-in swimming pool, you know, something like that. We got a fucked-up house. No built-in swimming pool. And we got glass on the street. House is run-down, not because *we* do it, but it's the neighborhood. Some houses are kept up. It's the old Polish people around here. They're behind us. Yugoslavians. Keep their houses up."

"But you figure," I asked, "all the people who have more money than you are Jewish?"

"No, no," he said bitterly, "all the people who got money more than me are bastards!"

"All those bastards are Jewish?" I asked. "Tell me more about the Jews, man. I want to know what the group's teaching you."

Francis said he didn't want to go on about Jews, that he was afraid of offending me. I insisted.

He continued, in some confusion. "You guys are hypocrites. What else? There's different other things they been telling me about that slip my mind. You guys want all the stuff. Inflation." The group had some stickers, left over from an earlier period, that read INFLATION IS JEWISH. "Inflation. You guys leave things behind. That's inflation. You guys buy up shit, you know.

"You got something—not the pope, but you guys, you wear your beanies. The rabbis. You know. Rabbis, rabbis get into Congress, you know, this stuff.

"You ever saw a rabbi—now listen," he suddenly said, "you ever saw one ride a motorcycle? My mom did."

So what?

"So what? He ain't no good. He rides a motorcycle, he's supposed to be in a Lincoln. A limousine. Something like that. Rabbi, he gets all your money, all our money. You guys take the money from us, give it to him."

He couldn't remember, he said, what else they were teaching him, so I asked whether blacks or Jews were more dangerous. He said Jews were, and I asked what ought to happen to blacks and to Jews.

"What ought to happen? Well, the blacks they could send back to Africa. Jews, they could send you guys where you guys wanted to go, as long as it's not in the USA. Follow the niggers. If you guys wanted to follow the niggers, you follow them. They want to follow you guys, follow you guys."

"What if we don't want to go, man?" I asked.

"What if you guys don't want to go?"

"Yeah! This is my country. Suppose I don't want to leave my country."

"We build a brick wall," he said, "between here and the ocean. So you guys have a ship. Maybe that's how to do it, you know. You guys can climb over a brick wall, we have dogs."

I looked at him. "Now here you are," I said, "you never heard of a Jew before—"

"Shit!" he exploded. "You ever hear of a speck of shit?"

"What?"

"A speck of shit, you ever heard somebody saying a speck of shit? That's what I think a Jew is." He laughed with scorn. "It's a speck of shit!" Words suddenly blasted from his mouth in a clutter: "It's a speck of shit! You know. Fly, shit, flying away, you know. Nigger shit fly, just fly away, you know, Jews fly, just fly away. Be airborne. Your bodies come down."

He was too angry and excited to quite make sense, but I got the point of the explosion.

He leaned forward in his chair, bent at the waist. When he spoke, the words were pronounced oddly and indistinctly; I had to strain to tell what he was saying.

Had he ever known any Jews? He had met a couple. "They treat me like shit, so I treat them like shit. You know. I think they should stick with their people."

The point was, Francis said, Jews wanted to "make one of us work so hard. Like my mom, like other people." How come? "Because you don't feel like getting off your ass and do it yourself." More than that, there was hardly any work out there, and the Jews would take care of their own before taking care of the other people. "Some of *us* barely make it on the streets. Some got maggots eating their foot off. Some, different things, angry and all, don't want to get amputated because they can't afford the doctor bill. Winos on the street. Niggers bumming cigarettes off you, robbing you."

Francis was getting to me. The Jews in America did advance their position a lot after World War II. The distinction between that new Jewish wealth and supposed institutional Jewish power was invisible to Francis, who was quite ready to have a "racial" scapegoat for his humiliation. Because I thought he was a real victim, I was embarassed and defensive when he equated Jewishness with class exploitation, and I lost my cool. Persistent poverty in his neighborhood, I told him, had to do with long-term changes in the economy, with automation and plant relocations. Changes were being made by people who ran the great corporations "who are not Jews and could care less about your ass. And you waste your time on this *racist* bullshit!"

He heard only one word. "I don't care about your ass," he said.

"I don't care," I replied, "whether you care about my ass. But I do care about poor people in this country."

That got to *him*.

"Why don't you show some consideration, then?" he cried out. "Why don't you do that and tell the rabbis, your people, to help some of us. Because you guys got rich fucking homes out there and you say *fuck these people in Detroit,* eastside, south, west, and north of Detroit. You probably live in Hamilton, Birmingham, Highland Park . . . one of those places out there. Grosse Pointe. They *don't give a fuck* about us! Like I said, a nigger moves in your neighborhood, you guys try to get him out. You either tell him to get out or you're going to burn his house down. Because you don't want him in there. It's an all-white neighborhood. You don't want to start making it race-mixed like this neighborhood here.

"You guys are not letting a nigger move up in there, I bet. You guys are not. I bet there ain't a nigger in your neighborhood in the first four or five blocks."

I contended that he and his friends should be trying to acquire some economic power "instead of listening to this racist bullshit," that in dividing poor whites and poor blacks they were playing into the hands of rich people who exploited both.

He did not understand. "They don't want us. If we go out there in a uniform with a fucking Nazi sign on our backs in a rich neighborhood, they'd probably kill us."

Yes, I told him, he was not welcome in that neighborhood, but his organizing in the streets was welcome. "Man, they *love* race hatred. They *adore* it. When you have poor whites and poor blacks fighting each other, that's what they love. It's all through history."

He could not hear this. Race is a much more compelling idea in our culture than social class. I argued in crude populist terms for class solidarity and for class interests; it went past him. He ended right back with race. "One day," he said, "we all be rich and you guys be out. We all be rich. If it's not this life—they always say you got two lives coming—if not this one, be the next. But this earth will be back to all white again."

"Do you figure," I asked at last, "that white people are real different from black people?"

"A *lot!*"

"Do you think that, inside, your souls are different from black people?"

"A lot," he repeated. "Because their souls is black. Our souls are white. They ain't got the same kind of blood we got."

At this point Francis suddenly remembered another piece of his recent education about the Jews. "Now I remember!" he shouted. "You guys got the fucking bomb! You guys got the bomb. Yeah, you guys invented the bomb! That's what Paul had told me that day. That's what slipped my mind. You guys got the bomb!"

I hardly knew whether to laugh or to sing. How come, I asked, an inferior race like the Jews would be smart enough to invent the bomb and a superior race like the whites couldn't? Why were people from the superior white race living in poverty?

"Give us time," he said. "It's going to take a short while, for you guys to get out. You guys watch. You'll hear about it in the paper: Jews, move out of USA."

I wasn't leaving, I told him. "It's my country. I'm not going to leave it."

He laughed. "You'll have to be executed, too."

I asked him what he had said.

"You'll be executed, too," he repeated.

"That's life," I said.

I moved our conversation to calmer ground. Francis had left school in eleventh grade: "too many niggers." He was studying for the GED exam from a large book and attended prep classes. He found the practice tests hard. "They got some rough shit up in there that I never saw in school. And I say, damn, what is this, you know. Fuck, I don't know this."

He hoped after the GED to go into the Army and learn a trade, perhaps diesel mechanics. "Working on diesels you make money. I just want to get something where I know in the future I could make a lot of money." He would avoid the Air Force or the Navy for fear of dying in the air or the water. "I don't want to die that way. I want to die on land. So I know they could send my body back home to my mom."

Threats, reputation, and fights were a big part of his environment, and Francis thought about them a lot. "Nigger ever punch me," he said, "I'm going to try to damn near *kill* his ass with my fists. If I can't succeed killing his ass, I see that nigger again, he will say hello, how are you doing, and walk away. Because he'll know I put up a battle that day. Even though I get my ass kicked, I'm punching his ass back. One, two times, if I punch him, punch me three times, he could walk away. But I'm going to punch his ass back.

"Fuck that. I have this dude, huge dude, punch me dead in the face, sucker-punch me. I flew back about two or three feet, and I got back up and I went to go punch him, four nigger friends of his grabbed me from behind. I didn't even know they was behind me. I was going to stand my ground. That's what you got to do, stand your ground against these niggers. You cannot let no nigger push over you. A nigger punch you, you don't do shit but walk away, he's going to punch your ass again, and again, and again until you fight his ass. Until you fight him.

"You don't want to get your ass kicked every time you see that dude. You do not want to get punched. One time's enough, two or three times, you got to beat his ass."

I told Francis that he was right, that one had to be tough in his sort of neighborhood. "That doesn't mean that you have to wear a damn swastika, and it doesn't mean that you have to hate a race. You're living in a beat-up neighborhood where people are full of hatred and anger because they're living in poverty. Right?"

"Go ahead," he said.

"People have a lot of anger, they got a lot of shame, and they take it out on each other."

"How do *you* feel?" he cried. "How do you feel? You live in a neighborhood you guys don't get beat up, you guys don't do shit but stay at home, watch TV, do this, it's peaceful. How do you feel if you were living in *this* neighborhood right here? You'd get the fuck out, that's what you would do. You'd get the fuck out!"

I agreed, and asked whether he was living there because he wanted to or because he had to. When he said that he had to, I suggested that he not run crap on me about why wasn't I living there. "I'm not stupid. I don't want to live in poverty," I said.

"You want to live like a *king*, though," he charged.

I was startled. "Like a king?"

"Hell yeah, you guys are living like a king out there. I don't know shit about you, where you live or what you do, but I know you live in a nice neighborhood, because your ass wouldn't be here.

"What *we* have to do to survive in this neighborhood is kill and fight one another. You just don't have to do that. You guys don't have to do that."

I agreed. There's a lot of hatred, I told him, because there's poverty.

"It's not because of that," he said. "It's because they want to have all the hatred in this neighborhood. It's just like, like me. If you punch me, I'd be damned if I won't try to punch your ass back. I might get my ass kicked, but I will try like hell to punch your ass back. You step in it, I'll punch your ass. Just like that. You never saw me fight, but I tell you, I'm a strong motherfucker.

"I could fight," he went on. "You just, you think I look like a fucking burnout, you know. You know what a burnout is? You think I look like a burnout, but I'm not. I be watching my back every fucking night, man, I watch my back. So if the crazy motherfucker's trying to sneak up on my back.

"I can not leave my home," he said. "This is, this ghetto right here, what you want to call it, whatever—cribs, burned-down shacks, burned-out neighborhood, mixed-in, which I cannot move from here because my body's adjusted to this area.

"Like I said, I'd like to see you move over here, just for two or three weeks. You go up the avenue there, they'd probably think you're a cop and shoot your ass. You look just like one of these fucking pigs up here. Just like one."

We talked further of the death of Francis's brother—a drunk had driven up onto the sidewalk and hit him—and that led to a discussion of his father. "He would kill anyone else who fucks with us. We don't look for him to back us up, but if we really need him, we got him, you know. He's a son of a bitch."

"Does he live in Detroit?" I asked.

"No. Moved," Francis said.

"Where to?"

"I don't know. Fuck him. Don't know." Francis had not seen him for two or three years.

I asked Francis to tell me about his father.

"He stands about seven feet tall," Francis began. "He has to bend over to get in the door. But the doors we have at our house are kind of short.

"And when he told us to get him a bag of chips, go out to the store and get a bag of chips, we didn't move right then, he'd throw something at us until we did get up and go. He left my mom while I was in the hospital, when they were taking half my liver out. And he come up there and saw me, but he didn't tell me that him and my mom broke up. And I offered him something to eat, and he took a bite, I wish it was poison that I offered his ass. After I found out that my mom broke up, everything.

"At first, you know, it was hard on me because I was in the hospital down there halfway dead. And when she told me, I was still in the hospital, they had broke up. It was kind of hard on me, but I guess I pulled through, you know."

He was six or seven at that time. I asked whether he had had hepatitis. "No, I had bad liver when I was born. And they had to take a half of it. I only got half a liver now."

Before the breakup, "him and my mom always got in a fight," and his mother and the kids would evade his father by leaving the house through an upper window. "One day he caught us going out the window. He beat all of our asses, all except for my mom's. He said, 'You don't go with your mom, you stay here with me.' And I said fuck that, you know, I'm going with my mom. I ain't going to stay with his ass."

His father would throw his mother out of the house—her house, as it happened—when he got mad. "He tells her she can't come in the house because she's not home on time that he wants her to be in. Sometimes she has to work overtime or something like that. She wasn't on ADC. She just recently got on ADC, because she lost her job."

She had been working as a maid "for the Jews. She'd come home, blisters on her hands, sore knees. Right now the doctor said they doubt she's going to be able to walk in a couple of years. They're going to have to put some plastic kneecaps in her legs. Because her legs got water in them, you know, from working so hard on her hands and knees."

This was also from running; his father used to chase his mother up and down the street, he said.

His mother and father were each about forty-seven. His father had been working at a glassmaking company. "He was working there and he got, I guess he got laid off, I don't know. That's when my mom and dad got divorced. My mom's still seeing him, you know, but they wasn't . . . having any relationship, you know, they're just . . . seeing."

I reminded Francis that he had said that he wished he had fed his father poison in the hospital because he broke up with his mother. I asked whether he wished the two had stayed together.

"No, I'm glad he did leave, glad. Very glad, you know. But it hit me, you know, like it would hit your son if you left your wife if he was the age I was.

"I haven't spoke with my dad after they got divorced for a while. But he made us work like a fucking dog, man, he made us work every day. He was putting in a swimming pool, it was like twenty-four feet out, ten feet sideways, ten square. And he made me, after he dug the trench, you know, for the bottom of the pool . . . he made me put glass around the pool. And then I was what, eight years old, man. That shit got heavier and heavier every time I pick up glass, you know. You know how the artificial glass is, you know. That shit was heavy for me, you know. And he made me do that shit for two days. It took me two days to go around that damn pool. And he sat on his ass drinking a fucking Stroh's. That's how come I hate Stroh's. Stroh's beer. I can't stand that shit. He was sitting on his ass drinking that Stroh's beer. I guess that's all the fucker worried about, Stroh's and his woman. Bitch."

"Is that the woman he was living with then?" I asked.

"That's the woman he's married to," he said. "He was going with her when he was going with my mom, but they got married after my mom and him got divorced. He tried to . . . get . . . us when he was older, he tried to get custody over us. But my mom lived down the street by Marge's house, it's a neighbor we knew for a long time, we still know her. She was crying and I asked her, what's the matter? She said, 'Your dad is trying to take you guys away from us.' So we had to go in front of a judge and shit, you know. And the judge asked each one of us, five kids, who do you want to live with? All of us said our mom, you know. So the judge give custody to my mom. And ever since then, he never pays child support for us. Never. My mom tried to get him to court about that and he'd stand there and lie his way out of it, every time he lied to the court. She never got a penny since they was divorced for us. Never got a penny. Those was hard times on my mom, very hard times."

"How," I asked, "did she support you guys? Five kids, man!"

"Working. Working her ass off, man. She work seven days a week. You wouldn't believe it, you know, my mom *worked,* too."

I remarked how impressive it was that she had taken care of five children.

"Not only five," he said. "She adopted three kids. We got three adopted kids, in fact."

"Why did she adopt them?" I asked.

"Because she loves kids."

Did this mean she was earning money to feed eight kids?

"No, no, no. She—after we grew up, she adopted three more. That's the three that Raymond said, the day he woke me up to go to the rally, he said, 'Francis, I thought I saw a black girl sitting on your couch.' I said, 'You did.' "

"What?" I said.

"I've got a black, half-and-half sister that my mom adopted. And I love that girl more than I would love fucking Jews on the street because, you know, I'm not for Jews."

Raymond, who was with us during this particular conversation, said, "That shocked me to see a black girl in there. I said, 'Where'd you get the nigger?' And he said, 'My mom adopted her.'"

Francis added, "I liked to punch him when he said that, but he didn't know. He saw her around my house every time he comes, see, but he didn't know it was my sister. You know, my stepsister. It's not my mom's blood. It's just that she went in front of the court and all of this and adopted three kids."

I asked, "And one of them is this little girl who's half black?"

"Half black and half white," he said. "The boy—we knew the mother of the three kids. She was white, her name was Loretta. She, the boy, she had, she called up to the bar and said—my mom was working at a bar at that time—said, 'You want this little bastard? He's sitting on the back porch with his clothes.' My ma went over to the house and picked him up. The boy was sitting on the back porch with his clothes. That's the first boy we got off the bunch. Okay, like two weeks later, she sent the girl over, half black and half white girl. She sent her over. She was pregnant with this girl named Louise, is her name now, but she didn't have a name before she was born. And we got her. Now, that makes three my mom adopted."

This seemed to have all begun about five years earlier. Francis did not know what had happened to Loretta since. "She tried to come and see the kids, but we won't let her. The kids disowned her."

Raymond asked, "What happens when it comes time for the blacks to go back to Africa?"

"She ain't going," Francis said. "'Cause she's not black, she's white."

Raymond pointed out that she was half and half.

Francis disagreed. "She's white. No, she ain't black, she's white. She's living with a white family, she's white. She grew up with us."

I think this was Francis's real position, that his sister was now a white and to be treated as one. What he said next was that she should be given a choice as to whether to go to Africa. He talked about what would be done with those people who did not choose expulsion. "All the niggers that don't want to go to Africa we take care to them. Build a big wall around this city where they can't climb over it. Put them on the other side of the wall. Jews could be over there, too. They could have a race-mixed country over there like we got over here.

"If you ever saw that movie *Escape from New York*, ever see that? How they had the president over in New York and nobody could come back over on this side, or if they come over they got shot? That's what we should do to his ass, right there. Send the president, send him over there, shoot his ass, execute his ass. *Kill* the mother-fucker, that's what we should of said."

I was more interested in Francis's mother than this talk of regicide. "Francis," I said, "your mom sounds like a very interesting woman. First of all, I'm impressed that she took care of all you five. And second, I'm impressed that she would take on these three additional children."

"She'd do it," he said. "I guess when they grow up, she'll probably get some more."

"What did she think of Loretta?" I asked.

"Just what I think of Jews. They're sluts. That's what she would think. She's a slut."

"A slut?"

"That's exactly what she is. She opened her legs to anybody that come right by her."

Loretta did not work with Francis's mother. Was she a neighbor, then?

"No, Loretta wasn't nothing, you know, but a street person. She rather run the streets than take care of her kids."

Francis said he was happy to have these kids in the family, happy they were being given things they would not have received from their mother, indeed, things he and his siblings had not received. We were just speaking of this and of his mother—"She loves people. She loves to work when she can"—when the session had to end; this was the night that Rosandra was having pains and we had to rush her to the hospital.

The interview with Francis was difficult. The sudden revelation that he had a half-black sister whom he loved was delightful. But the bulk of the meeting disturbed me: the brutal energy he brought to his racism, the nastiness of his attacks, the ease with which he had been directed into anti-Semitism, all of this against a backdrop of unfortunate lives in threatened homes.

I thought of him a lot in the months that followed. His anger came from real circumstances; no one should have to live as both black and white must in his neighborhood. An emergent fascist regime in America would find him and his peers ready recruits for its strong-arm squads. A regime that presented itself as championing the disadvantaged against the advantaged could readily aim his sullen hatred against the targets the regime nominated.

SIXTEEN

Joey, Eddie

Families that live in poverty, regardless of race, get slapped around by chaos. Some of the Strike Group members had been hit hard. The most difficult story came from a young fellow named Joey, whom I met for the first time one summer night when I interviewed a number of members until two in the morning. I had asked each of the seven members who were present to tell me both happy and sad memories from childhood. The atmosphere in the room slowly grew quiet and warm. We all heard things that we had not heard before—none of the members knew before, for instance, that one of them had been sent to a foster home for part of his childhood.

Joey was sixteen, an unemployed ninth-grade dropout. His parents had been separated several times; his father was an out-of-work boiler maintenance worker. Joey had two sisters and had had four brothers; two of the brothers were dead. "One was in a car accident down south. Down in the boonies. Flipped over a hill, chopped his head off. Car accident. And the other died, couple of years ago, suicide . . . guess he got tired of life."

At the end of the evening Joey told the story of his brother's suicide. His brother had earlier been hospitalized for a year as a schizophrenic and was heavily into drugs; Joey mentioned mescaline and acid. His brother had just come back from four months in California when, after several days at home, he went up to his room after breakfast and put a shotgun in his mouth. No one had noticed the report of the gun, and Joey had discovered his brother several hours later, when he looked through a hole in the wall that separated his room from his brother's.

It had been no accident, he assured us. "Accidents just don't happen like that. You don't just be looking down the barrel of a twenty-gauge and the bullet goes off, you know. What he did is just triggered it with his toe. And that was it. Because the way the shape of the body was, you know, I could tell what he'd done. Because I seen the blood all over the walls and brains hanging off the walls and strings and everything. It looked thick, it looked like . . . I don't know, I can't really talk about it.

"I looked in there, and that was it. He was gone. I seen him laying there with no head—he had a head, only his face, but from here back, he was gone. You could see part of his skull laying on the floor. All his things, his eyes were missing, his back teeth was gone, roof of his mouth was gone, and the whole back of his head was gone.

"It hurt me bad because I had to find him. And then when I went downstairs, broke the news to my mom and dad, it was just like—they were sitting there tripping out, 'No, don't be playing these games.' And they go upstairs and kick down the door, walk in and see him, then walk back out, his blood and everything was just dripping off the walls.

"My dad, he almost died out on the front grass because of a heart attack. Because when you have a heart attack, you got to take nitroglycerine pills. He didn't have any on hand at the time. And they had to borrow some from somebody around. And he had three heart attacks in a row."

Joey had decided, as I say, to share all this with us after having sat through a number of stories from others in the group. I had not pushed him, but apparently the evening had awoken a desire to talk about it. He had memories and regrets.

"Real strange how he did it. I wonder sometimes why would he do it. He should have just come out and told us what the problem was or something like that or anyways try and work it out. My ma and dad should have just had him locked back up. Maybe they could have done something, a brain scan, something like that, run those on him and see what the deal was.

"But normally, for schizophrenics, that's what'll happen, going to break down, schizophrenics, people like that. Go off in their own little world. Start tripping out. He used to sit there and tell me, I used to listen and he would come up with some shit. 'Yeah, I hear the next-door neighbor talking about you, man. Don't you hear him, man?' I'm saying, 'What?' He'll say, 'Yeah, I hear him talking. You hear that bitch talking to me, talking about me?' I put my headphones back on, and it was his trip, you know. I thought it was funny at the time. But now when I see someone doing it, it kind of scares me."

Joey had not come through this unscathed. "That's like one of my worst things, one of my worst experiences. It didn't . . . at the time it didn't bother me for the first couple of days, but as each day went, it seemed like I got more depressed about it. When it first happened, it didn't seem like it bothered me all that much, but each day went by and I got more and more depressed and I was just getting more down and down. And I was just tripping out and shit. Getting all freaked out. Finally locked me up. That happened in August, and I got locked up in December. December second. I didn't get out until like end of that month.

"The night that I got locked up, I cracked up. I started swinging a bat through the house. Busted up the whole upstairs. Went right through a paneling wall. Just like made my own door. Went right through that. And then I went outside and beat up my sister's car with a pipe. I guess that was good enough reason to lock me up. I was kind of glad that they did, you know, because I thought myself, I was going to crack up, too, and do something dreadful or do something drastic. I was glad they locked me up.

"And I did something that I never thought I could do in a lifetime, that was to try to blow my sister up.

"It ain't funny. I swear to God, what if I had done that?

"I turned on—while her and her girlfriend was upstairs, they were just smoking a joint, you know, like most people, after they smoke a joint they'll light up a cigarette, right after that. I turned on all the—blew all the pilot lights out. I had gas all through the house.

"I went through the house with a baseball bat, and then after that, I just turn on all the gas. I was trying to blow them up and everything.

"I was going to do it, but she had to do it, too. She had to strike the match. I was filling up the house full of gas. When they come downstairs, they come running out of the house choking, I said, 'Damn, they didn't blow up.'

"At the time, that's what I thought. 'Man, they didn't blow up. They didn't do what I wanted them to do. Why didn't you do what I wanted you to do?' I was saying shit like that. They're sitting there, 'You're crazy! Get away from me.' "

He told stories of the hospitalization. He had been handled with strictness and force and he had been uncomfortable because "you got all these nuts in there, you know, coming up to you, messing around." He mentioned in particular a black kid who he thought was gay and a white kid who played with himself; he had been afraid they were trying to get near him and had threatened them to keep them away. His sister had come to see him along with her friend when he had been in a week or two and had started calming down. "I apologized to them. Man, they were looking at me kind of strange, though. Asking me was I okay and everything. I told them yeah. They said they could understand. I asked them would they forgive me and they said, 'Yeah, you haven't did nothing to us.' And they said, 'We understand, you know.' "

Joey was very bothered by this memory. "I wish I'd have never did it, man, you know. I just think what happened, you know, at the time. It was terrible. I'm glad she didn't get killed, you know. I'd have probably killed myself if she had of killed herself."

A seriously disturbed individual is not likely to last a long time in an extremist organization, but may be drawn by the language and the air of such a group. I had run into two members, Nolan and Michael, in the park one summer evening and took them and a new fellow named Eddie over to Paul's to talk. Eddie monopolized the first hours in an increasingly wild monologue. He was loud and strange. I could not tell whether some substance was increasing his oddness. It was one of the few meetings that made me nervous.

I had asked Eddie when he had left home, and he replied, "You want me to tell you what made me leave home? Right there on my arm, buddy. I want you—you're a professor in college, you tell me, I am not imitating a serious burn."

He showed us a nasty scar on his arm and continued, "And I'm here. I am still living. It is a stroke of God that I am still living. This burn right here is ten times over a third-degree burn."

What had he been burned with?

"A cross. A solid, iron steel, bloody red cross, man."

I asked who had done that. Had it been his father?

"Niggers! Bingo. I have to say it."

I asked when it had been done.

"This was done exactly about—you want to know when this was done? Right after our Lord Jesus Christ was born on this earth, which was Christmas. And that is a sacred holiday. For somebody to do that, they got to be nuts."

He talked about having been grabbed and held. "When they put it on, I just kind of freaked out and I just shook them off of me, buddy. I got up, man, I reached up, bam, like that! I hit him, I hit him in his jaw, man, I swear, I hit him in his jaw. The other dude, man, he's coming out with a .38, coming out with a .38, pow! Okay. Listen, listen. And these are blacks, man. And these blacks are dead, brother. And I'm here, bud." (The pistol doesn't recur in Eddie's later versions of this story, nor do deaths.)

Shortly afterward we were talking about family, and I asked about his father.

"My dad was a warlord of a motorcycle gang which had two thousand chapters in the United States. That's more chapters than any club has got.

"He worked at Ford's, he worked at Chrysler's. He boxed. He's golden state champion boxer. He went to Jackson [state penitentiary] when I was born. He boxed. He boxed for our survival sometimes, he made maybe a thousand dollars a fight."

Why had he been sent to Jackson?

"He went to Jackson for being somebody that shouldn't be. Well, he went to Jackson for all kinds of things, buddy. You know what my dad did to somebody, man, when they got smart with him? He

took their eyeball out and he stepped on it. He went to Jackson, but
you know what they say about Jackson. You know about prison life?

"He just got out of the place. He's settling down. He's the nicest
person in the whole world, man."

We returned to the incident of the branding.

"I was walking, minding my own business. Up comes somebody,
Young Boys, Incorporated. I know you have to know them. [Young
Boys, Inc., had been a notorious Detroit youth gang.]

"Can we shut this door, man? I hate people listening to me. All
right. Young Boys, Incorporated, man. They wanted me to buy heroin. Listen, I ain't no drug addict. I said, 'No, I ain't buying your
damn heroin, buddy. I don't want none of it.' I smoke a good joint
any day. And I'll drink beer. But I don't mess with no hard shit. And
he goes, 'Well, I'll fix that, white boy.' I said, 'Buddy, you don't call
me no white boy. Because I ain't no fucking white boy.' And when
I said that, bam! I flattened him right there.

"I hit him. And when I hit him, his friends were behind, right
behind. Grab me from both sides, drag me over there, you know,
struggling and everything, they got me in the house. That's when that
happened.

"They heated it up, buddy, they heated it up. A cross, you know
what the cross was for? You know what the cross was for, you know
what the cross was for? You know what the cross was for? They
know I stand for white power, buddy, Klan, Nazis, everything. They
say, 'Well, we're going to put one on you.' "

I asked whether they had known he was involved with the Klan
and the Nazis. He said, "I believe they did. Because they had their
secret sources."

How could they have known? I asked. Had that been in his
neighborhood?

"They—we're kind of famous, man. We're getting there, anyway.
This Death's-Head is starting to make headlines."

The elaborate recounting continued, and then he went to the Gospel.
"Listen, give me a Bible. I'm going to show you. You know what it

said the Jews are. I'm going to tell you something, let me. The Jews. They own this country because they're smart. But you know what helped them be smart? The Devil, buddy. Because they want this country. Right, they had this country. All us poor folks, that are run by the Jews, but we ain't going to be here because our home is in heaven. Listen, listen. The Jews, right. They got their education, they got everything they want, but God says this land, be it known, ye is the father of the Devil himself. He was talking about the Jews. The Jews was his chosen people. But it's going to be the end. God, it's going to be the end. The Jews, right. They had, they're smart, they are smart, they are smart people. They have billionaires, trillionaires, and millionaires. They pay the president, they do everything. They own the country. They tell you when you can get a dollar, right?

"I don't want to say nothing else. I'm just saying out of my heart, man. The Devil has got us, man. I'm speaking as a true Christian.

"*God wants you to believe, buddy.* He wants you to pray every moment of the day because he can come down and whip your hide!

"Look at this. I'm going to show you something else that I think is based on numbers, buddy. You break this down. My mom is a computer technician and she shows that these fine lines right there mean six." [Eddie was pointing to the Universal Bar Code lines on a Marlboro pack.] "And all of them equal out 6-6-6 in computer language. And my mother is a computer technician.

"Listen, this right here is going to a computer Antichrist. And they know everything that we smoke, we drink, and we eat. If they want to, they—you know what they want to do? You know what they want to do? They want to try to put brainwashing things in our food. When they say preservatives, it's brainwashing. Communists. Because God, he says, if you got the Holy Spirit in you, you can drink poison. I mean, you can poison me. And if I got the Holy Spirit and he don't want me to die, it'll cleanse my system. And the Lord speaks through that, buddy. And I'm done. And I ain't lying.

"Right now, God is speaking.

"Now, listen here, can I say something about the United States? If the United States would be smart, the United States was like they're supposed to be and following our traditional fathers, but you know what? We came here because we fought. We fought for our freedom, right? Now all these money-begging motherfucking thiefs, money worms, they can't wait to get a hold of it. They helped build this country, but they're trying to ruin it, too, by letting *piggy-ass, scummy-ass* communism walk in *our* United States."

Eddie had said before we began recording that Hitler was the smartest man in the world. I asked him about this.

"Adolf Hitler was a very smart person. Because he wanted his, what he wanted, he changed Germany around. He gave his people a chance, right?

"And he tried to take on communists and he tried to take on Jews that were already over in the United States. And they just smashed him together, buddy. Now, if he didn't have that—if he would've had some more support around, right now we'd be saying, 'Heil Hitler.' Because he tried to take on everybody. He took on Russia.

"But Theodore Roosevelt was a Jew. Theodore Roosevelt was Jewish. He sold us out to the Japanese, buddy. Pearl Harbor.

"Because you know what the Jew wants to do? He wants to prove, he wants to— Listen. Can I say something? Can I say something, bud?

"The Jew. Okay, and Adolf Hitler. He killed all them innocent Jews. The Jew killed all the innocent white folks.

"They say fuck with the white folks, buddy! We come from the mountains and we can shoot. Pop! And we are a democratic nation. But I believe that is it: *The Jew is Antichrist!* And he wants to be another Hitler.

"Who killed Jesus? The Jews do not believe in Jesus. They don't believe he's already come. But Jesus, Jesus, our Savior, Jesus is the one that got His hands put on the cross to shed our, he shed his blood to redress our sins. Jesus did. And I have faith in Jesus and the God, and our God, the Almighty Father, that created me, you, him, and all them communist scum, buddy. And I'm going to leave my case closed right there, buddy. And I'm telling you, buddy, I'm speaking the God's honest truth about this Book.

"Now you boys talk. Because I'm with *God,* man. And I'm for— do unto others as they do unto you. And I've been fucked around with niggers, Jews, whites, Puerto Ricans, pinks, blacks, fucking on-the-moon kind, man, every other kind."

All this went on and on, Eddie raving in the hot little room. After a long time I asked him to tell me about good days and bad days.

"I was down in Kentucky. I fucked five women the same day! That's my good day.

"Bad day for me was when I got in a fight with about five dudes, and they said they were going to try to cut my throat, and they were wrong. And that was in Jerry Ben's bar in Williamston, West Virginia. Dude was on acid, man, he was going crazy. He was on acid. Which I will not take the stuff. He said he was going to beat me up and stuff like that. I said, no, you ain't going to. See, I come from a pretty rough part of town, buddy. But he didn't believe me, so I had to kick him in his face about five times. Then he tried to throw a garbage can through my bedroom window. Went back and got him a twelve-gauge shotgun, I come by, I had me a caliber. Forty-five caliber. Thompson.

"Well, the guy, I didn't use the gun on him, but I had a fight with him. That was a real bad day because, you know, they wanted to jump on me, and I just didn't want to jump on them. I took it from there.

"Is this interview almost to a close? I'm getting kind of sleepy. I want to go home. You give me a ride, I'll pay your gas money.

"I want you to tell me why the Jewish people do not believe that Jesus came. Why do people mock Nazis and Ku Klux Klan because they're for the white people and not for everybody else? Can you explain that for me?"

At that point, several other people arrived looking for Paul. They left after a few minutes, and Eddie took a ride with them. Nolan and Michael were looking quite strained, and said they wanted to explain to me. Nolan said he wanted to tell me "how Eddie's scar had really gotten there."

"See," Nolan said, "when I got my tattoo, he was jealous about it. He was jealous because me and this other guy that used to be in the group, before he got kicked out, we both got tattoos, and . . . I don't know why I got mine. But Eddie, he wanted a tattoo, but his dad wouldn't—his dad would get mad if he got one.

"So, after he moved, these guys burned a cross—I mean, see, he had these guys who were going to give him a tattoo, and these guys told him that they had to *burn* the shape into his arm first, and *then* tattoo around it."

Michael looked disgusted. "You don't give a tattoo like that, man."

"I mean," Nolan said, "anyone who could fall for that deserved it."

"So his friends burned his arm for him?" I asked.

"Yeah," Nolan said. "And he made a big production out of it. And all that other stuff, that stuff on that scar, is because it got infected. That was where the doctors had to cut all the infection out. They had to do a skin graft on him."

This had all happened about a year ago. "I don't know why he made that story up, though," Michael said. I asked whether he generally told that same story, or told different ones. Michael said that he generally stuck with the one we had heard.

Eddie had been trying to get active, Michael added, and the group had been keeping in touch with him. Michael himself had not seen the fellow for about a year. Nolan said that he had known him for close to three years. "I've heard some of his wild stories."

"Well, then," I asked, "did you hear him when we were driving up here, talking about how there's a crate of submachine guns—"

Nolan said, "You know what this is? His dad owns a Thompson. I've seen his dad's Thompson. And he acts like he can touch that Thompson anytime he want to. If his dad ever caught him touching that Thompson, he'd break his arm."

"Well," I said to them, "you guys had better watch out. I don't want your group to succeed; but he is disturbed. He has a serious disturbance there."

I cautioned Nolan and Michael to be sure that Eddie was not taken into the group as a regular member. I feared that he would hurt some innocent person if he were present at one of the highly charged encounters between the Nazis and counterdemonstrators. I further urged this view on Paul when he returned to his apartment. Paul was quite sheepish about the association.

I saw no more of Eddie. Several years later Michael told me that Eddie had died. Eddie and his brother "had been fooling around with a shotgun." The brother had accidentally fired the gun, and killed Eddie. Michael had gone, on his birthday, to view the body. Half the face had been replaced by wax, Michael said. As he told me this, Michael looked quiet and ill.

Eddie was far from average for the group. However, an organization with symbols and goals that appeal to sadistic impulses can be made up of fairly normal people and still attract people who are dangerously disturbed. What is worse, those people may readily be used by organizers who are complacent about the risks. Paul would have been glad to have had Eddie as a member.

We will close these portraits with a closer look at Nolan, a young man who was in far better mental health, but enchanted by racism.

SEVENTEEN

Nolan

Nolan fascinated me. He was the healthiest of these young men emotionally, but completely happy in his association with the group. At our first meeting he seemed wild: His long hair streamed from the sides of a fatigue cap drawn low on his forehead and his eyes blazed with a cold glare. He looked downright evil when he told me that his father had left when Nolan was only two. At our next meeting he was infinitely more accessible. He no longer seemed furtive. His hair was caught by a bandanna across his forehead, a hippie style modeled on the Apache look of Western movies. His bearing fit the style; he seemed tall and loose, a spirited kid.

He was seventeen when we met. He had left school ("too many niggers") two and a half years before, at the start of tenth grade. He had been in the Strike Group for a year, having heard about it from a neighborhood friend who was a member.

His father, he said, had done "everything guys do that work on putting girders up on buildings and stuff. My ma, she has Social Security." His mother "used to work in a restaurant until her back got messed up. She was working as a cook and waitress. A small restaurant, only two people working there." Nolan had six brothers and one sister; he was the second from the youngest. He and two brothers still lived at home.

———

I asked Nolan what he liked about being in the Strike Group.

"Mostly the same things my friends do," he said. "Go out, get face-to-face with the Reds.

"I got even with them the last time. Saving the American flag, swastika banner, and the Confederate flag. They'd come trying to grab them and I'd beat them back."

I asked whether he meant with his poster stick.

"Yeah," he said. "But I had a light one. I wanted a heavy stick. It would have hurt more."

How long would he stay in the group?

"The rest of my life. As long as I live. Stay in white power and this group as long as it's around. If this group's done, I'll go to another group. That's how it is."

"What do your brothers and sister feel about your being a Nazi?" I asked.

"They all hate it," he said. "They saw me going to rallies where there'd be fighting. They're all scared that I'm going to get hurt."

They also were bothered by the swastika, he told me when I asked. Why? "Because of six million lies. Lies. About the Holocaust or Jews, whichever you want to call them. They say Nazis killed six million Jews. It's all wrong. It's just the way the Jews can get away with everything they want. They make up a big lie, and anything they ask for, it's theirs. There was no six million Jews in there, living in Israel."

I explained Israel wasn't the place in question.

"Well, wherever Jews come from. Wherever the Jews supposedly come from. It doesn't make any difference." And he took up a semi-fact that has circulated in the movement. "It takes two hours to cremate a person, and you're talking about six million Jews, all burnt? That would take one hell of a long time, to burn that many people." He laughed. "They'd still be burning them today.

"Yeah," he said, "there was people killed during the war. And the Jews that did die are the ones that died from the war diseases. I don't even care, really, what happened, because I wasn't born at that time, you know."

"Nolan," I asked, "if you could have your way, how would you deal with black and white relations in this country?"

He got into the question with energy. "Send all the niggers back to Africa. All spics back to wherever they come from. Give Indians part of the country, because it was their country at first. Give them part of the country. So they wouldn't be mad at us, because we took their country from them. Give them part of the country. Give the whites the rest of the country."

What if the blacks and Hispanics didn't want to go where he wanted to send them?

"There'd have to be a revolution then, after this. Kill them all off and just say, this is our country, you're going back to your own country."

What if the blacks said that they had contributed to building this country and they'd been living here for three hundred years, and it was their country, too?

"Well, you'd just have to, you just, the whites just have to start shooting them off. Maybe, sure, they'd get guns and come after us.

"Communists in this country, any communists in this country, I'd rather hang them before I send them back to their country."

Nolan brought up homosexuality a lot.

"Can we talk about gays again? Faggots? I like putting down faggots and commies the most because those are the two I most hate.

"It even states it in the Bible, I'm serious, that God is against—I believe in God, Jesus Christ, myself I also believe in my race. And gay people, man, I mean, God made man and woman to breed and make other men and women, right? He didn't make Adam and Adam to breed, to make other Adams.

"Homosexuals—they're tied with communism. Slap them all on an island and let them all catch AIDS.

"You just got to keep them out of the system. Because homosexuality, it's all in the genes. It's all in the genes. Because if you got a bisexual, one who likes a man and one who likes a woman. All right, he goes to bed with this chick and gets her pregnant. Her kid pops out, the kid turns faggot, man. How else do they get here?"

I asked Nolan to compare himself to "the typical white person," but he said that he couldn't do that. "See, if I don't know the guy, I'd have to sit down and talk to him. See what he's like, you know. I don't like to judge anybody that I don't know. I might be wrong about that person."

I asked him, then, to think about rich whites and poor whites, what he liked about each and disliked about each.

"Well, the rich whites—there's a lot of half-poor white people, you know, that's just barely making it along. These rich people, they don't care about us, they don't care about us *poor* white people, all they want is their money and their fame and stuff like that, big mansions and stuff, driving around in their fancy cars, burning up all the gas that we have to use to live with, to live on. We need that gas to get around. Drive our old clunker down to the store or something. They're burning it up left and right in their big limos.

"*Poor* white people, they can't help being poor, you know. Poor people—poor whites—it's hard because *I'm* not so—it's hard describing what I don't like about a poor white person because I'm not so rich myself."

I asked whether he thought that rich people respected him.

"Respect me? I doubt it. Because I ain't as rich—probably because I ain't as rich as them. I can't go out in public wearing a nice three-piece suit. If I wanted to, I could blow my money on a three-piece suit, but I ain't got much use for one. I don't go to no big fancy places.

"I've been in the supermarket, I met a few rich white people that don't like me because my hair's long. So what if I got long hair? I mean, anyone could have long hair. Why do you have to hate them because their hair's long? Like Paul, he's a pretty cool dude and his hair is long. Ain't nothing wrong with long hair."

When Nolan came to the question of interracial sex, he quickly lost his cool. "I mean, seriously, how could a white chick or a white dude go to bed with a black person? I tell you, if I was going to kiss some nigger, *I might just as well kiss some fucking dog!* It's just like kissing a nigger.

"I seen some disgusting race mixing. I was in a doctor's office and there's this one terrible old, I mean she was an *old* white lady, I mean real old. And she was with her boyfriend, big black dude, big seven-foot-tall guy walking around in a three-piece suit and everything, and here's his girlfriend, she walks along in some scagged old dress, looked like it came out of the Dumpster. I don't know how she—maybe that nigger was using her for something."

Done with this lurid image, he came to a question I hadn't heard for a while. It's the question the racists in my hometown always had to ask the white anti-racist. "How would you feel, Rafe," he asked, "if your own wife betrayed you for a black man? What would you do? What would your reaction be?" He asked, "Would you kill your wife or the nigger, which one?" He giggled. "Got to be one of them, man, you know. One day you come home from work and you see that black man up in your bed with your wife?

"In bed with my old lady," he said, "I'm going to shoot them both right there."

I asked Nolan to describe the events of an ordinary day. He spoke of long hours sitting in his room listening to the radio, long hours sitting with his mother and keeping her company while she watched soap operas, and long hours rereading the newspapers in his foot-high stack of old movement literature. He didn't recall conversation or activity with his brothers who lived in the house—they sat upstairs watching TV or listening to the radio, his mother sat downstairs in front of her TV with her soaps, and Nolan sat in his room or with her. Sometimes he read one of her books—love stories, romances.

"I talk to my mom a lot, you know. Like when I sit down and watch soap operas, we'll sit and talk about them."

I asked him to describe his mother. "She's nice. She's more or less a hillbilly. She was born in Tennessee. Just outside of Nashville. That's where most of my family comes from."

His mother was forty-nine. She was usually, he said, "in a good mood. Except on the days when her back's hurting her and stuff like that. Like today, when it's raining out? The rain, the moisture in the air, bothers her back because of her arthritis, you know." Though she could stand and walk if she could sit down periodically, she had had to quit work. "She was working in a restaurant, you know, had to pick up heavy pots of water and stuff like that."

He had spoken of his large collection of white racist movement literature, and I asked how he acquired it. "I don't have them sent to my house. When Paul gets them, then I'll get a copy from him. Because Paul always gets big bundles of them and stuff, you know. Calls everybody in the group and then when we all get over there we all go through boxes full of newspapers and stuff."

During the week Nolan would leaf through part of his stack of old movement papers. "I just read the old ones to see what they've got in them. Read about old rallies and stuff that we've had. Stuff like that. Just have a few good memories about them."

For a few months Nolan had a good job with a roofing company. He worked hard and enjoyed it. He talked of the pleasure of carrying heavy rolls of tar paper or heavy bundles of shingles up the ladder, the pleasure of swinging the heavy tar brush, or of flinging shovelsful of gravel from truck bed to roof. "I don't know why, I like the work. I don't like work that's real easy. I like, you know, it's a little hard. I like to work. I like my job. Everybody's going to need a new roof put on their house sooner or later. And I thought about it a lot, doing this for a career. Because, see, what I want to get into most is hot tar roof." He talked in detail about the task; he described intense physical labor. "Then the next day I went back to work and all that pain went away from flinging all that rock up. I like being on it! I don't know why, I just like hard work. I like hard working."

We spoke of his father, who had left when Nolan was two. Nolan had not seen him since ("only pictures") and did not know where he was. I asked whether he had had daydreams about meeting him, and how he might feel if he did.

"I thought about seeing him again, a few times. I just couldn't figure out whether I'd be happy or angry to see him. Near as I could figure it, I'd probably be mad at him. But in a way, I wouldn't mind seeing him, either.

"That took up a lot of my time, thinking about that. Because it used to bug me a lot. What would I do if I seen him, you know. I still didn't figure it out."

He thought he had been starting seventh grade when he began to think a lot about this. "Because I was seeing all these people with their fathers, you know. And just realizing that I didn't, I didn't have one, you know.

"And then, then after a couple of months, I realized that I'd probably never see him anyways. I don't think I'll ever see him."

There was a pause. "I can't do nothing about it if he don't want to come around and see us, you know. I can just return his feelings. If he don't want to see me, I don't want to see him, you know."

His father had had a good job and had been making good money, "but he just couldn't keep from getting drunk. He was always drunk except when he went to work. When he'd get off work, first place he'd go was into a bar." When he got home, his parents would "always fight, you know, and he'd hit her. Always be yelling."

I asked how he knew of this, and he said his mother had told him. He and his brothers and sister never spoke of it, nor of their feelings about their father. He had spoken to his mother because, at one time, he had wanted to find his father, at least to meet him. His mother did not want him to go looking for the man. "See, last time she heard anything about him—she didn't hear from him, it was just, you know, *about* him. He was always staying drunk and he was starting to lose his mind, or something. And she's just probably afraid of what he would do if he found out I was his son."

When I asked Nolan to distinguish parts of himself that came from each parent, he saw little that came from his mother, and felt most came from his father—but knew little about him. There seemed to be a gap here.

His mother had offered him signs of her support. He was too young to have noticed, or to mention, her day-to-day support, but he did remember a dramatic piece of protection. A boyfriend of his mother's had hit Nolan when drunk. "I was about seven or eight. He was trying to tell me to go to my room and stay there. I wouldn't do it, though. He slapped me in the face. He came up and hit me in the face a few times. Then he left and my ma went out looking for him and ended up stabbing him in a bar." Nolan had liked that, and his mother had ended the relationship.

Nolan liked to talk tough. "The race war could start next year very easily. If the race war breaks out, believe me, I'm not going to turn chicken shit and run. I'm going to kill me a few of them mother-fuckers. I ain't going to start it."

He became ignited one day about the Jews. "Most of the time, I just sit home and watch the TV and see how the Jews are trying to brainwash the people. I mean, you look, you look at them, and on TV, all right, that nigger Farrakhan, he may be a nigger, but on TV they put him down. Because the Jews run all that shit on TV. They do not want, they do not want him to speak the truth to all these people. See, Jews, Jews are slowly working on the boneheads. Niggers ain't the real problem. Because if you really look at it, Jews are behind most of the problems. I mean, you look at it, and look at it, and Jews just about control everything. And they won't let the truth get to the people. That's what we're here for. We're going to get the truth to the people. But of course, you do have your gullible, your gullible white and black folks sitting at home all day watching their TV. You try and educate them, they say, 'No, no, that ain't what it says on TV.'

"We do have one big fight ahead of us. Just educating people. See, first of all, all right, our biggest problem's going to be the Jew. Because the Jew's got a tight grip on everything. I mean—if we could get, if we could get a president that wouldn't baby the poor fucking slimy Jew—a president that would stick up for this country and keep his nose out of Israel's business, we wouldn't have so many problems."

"Tell you the truth," Nolan concluded, "I'd rather have Farrakhan in the White House than you."

Nolan's outspokenness at this interview flowed from several previous meetings at which I had asked him to speak of his feelings about Jews. He had claimed both times that that was most difficult —that it was hard, because I might "get offensive," by which he meant get offended. When I kept pressing him, he turned out to have little to say. In general, he seemed to have no concrete thoughts about Jews, either before or after coming to the group, other than that they were "greedy little pigs" and that they used the Holocaust as a crying towel and an excuse to get everything they wanted. He had little detail or organization in his thinking about Jews.

I pressed him again several other times.

"What do I think about Jews?" he said. "I have no use for them."

I asked him to tell me more. He said it would be hard to talk about Jews to a Jew. I kept reassuring him that I wouldn't get mad. He said that made it even harder. "But most things I'd say about Jews," he said, "you know, if we're just sitting around talking, you know. We're sitting around, we'll make, we'll think of jokes we've seen in newspapers and stuff about them. I mean, like this one old Jew, this one old Jew on one of our leaflets, you've probably seen him, he's sitting there, he's sitting there crying and he's pointing at some numbers on his arm, talking about he was gassed six times. He goes, 'I was gassed six times, no, eight times, no ten times!'

"You know, because I don't believe that Holocaust shit. I think it's a pack of lies because I ain't never seen no true proof of it. I've seen pictures, I've seen pictures, but I've also found a way of proving them pictures fake."

I said, yes, I heard him saying that he didn't believe the Holocaust happened, but I wanted him to tell me what it was he felt about Jews and what it was he thought about Jews, "what Jews mean to you inside your head."

He had trouble. "When I think about Jews . . . I think they are liars because they lied about the Holocaust."

There was a long pause. Then he said, "They're greedy."

There was another long pause. Quite a long one. He was trying to find something to add. Then he said, "I don't too much myself, I don't think about Jews, you know. Unless I'm sitting there reading an article in the paper about them. And then I think of them by what I'm reading."

He had never had a friend who was Jewish; he had known a few Jews; he hadn't liked them. Several had gone to his school.

The violent language comes from a head with a nearly blank image of "the Jew." The detested enemy arouses contempt and hatred—or rather, the name of the detested enemy does, the idea of the detested enemy does. The concrete objects out in the world, the actual Jews, have little to do with the viscerally experienced idea of the enemy. As usual, intense prejudice has more to do with the inside of the person who harbors it than with outer reality.

When Nolan first joined the Strike Group, his mother claimed to him that his grandfather on his father's side was Jewish or part-Jewish. It is impossible to tell whether she was serious. Nolan says that he is finally convinced that it could not be true. I don't know what he really believes.

Nolan was an unhappy man at our final interview. He hated the heavily black neighborhood into which the family had had to move. One of his brothers was in the Strike Group along with Nolan, but two of his brothers had become friendly with neighboring black people. "I sit up in my room and read my papers and stuff that I got up there. That's mainly what I do if I'm not looking for work or going out putting out literature. Sitting there and this one nigger kid, I went in to use the bathroom, he goes into my bedroom, and I had one of my *White Patriots* sitting out there. I come in there and here's this little kid reading my newspaper. He didn't have too much to say on it, but I just asked him what he was doing. 'I just come in here.' I said, 'Get the fuck out of my room.' He turned around, walked out. . . . Can't have no peace with niggers around. They always want to go in your house, rummage through all your shit."

Worse had happened, however. I had begun the final interview by mentioning that Paul had told me that Nolan's older brother agreed with the group basically but felt opposed to the group because he wasn't part of it. "Wrong, wrong, wrong!" Nolan cried. "My brother is a piece of slime! Tim is a piece of slime!" While one of his two older brothers had simply begun making friends with neighborhood blacks, the other was "a race mixer. He done picked up this little piece of dirt from down the street." While the first brother had "his parties and junk with the boneheads," this second was sleeping with his black girlfriend in the house. The young woman's family disapproved as much as Nolan's, but nothing could be done.

The brother had been going with the young woman for only two days, "but they was making googley eyes at each other before that." Nolan kept insisting that it simply could not work. "There's a little saying, first you have love, then you have marriage, all of a sudden here comes old high yellow in the baby carriage." He giggled and said, "And every time I wake up in the morning, get myself a cup of coffee, I always think about them two having a kid. The kid would be the same color as my coffee in the morning." He giggled again.

"I mean, you got a kid who if you put a little open jar of jelly on him, he'd look like a peanut butter and jelly sandwich."

He admitted that this was assuming that they were going to have children, "which I'm almost sure they probably will."

I asked, "But suppose they didn't have any kids. Would it upset you that he's sleeping with her?"

He said it would, and I pressed him to tell me what his feelings were. This took much urging.

He answered finally: "Hatred."

He could not explain why. He was angry and shaken, and he became even more unrestrained as we continued.

I summarized a speech of his by saying that he was saying we should deport the black people. He agreed to that summary. Further, I suggested to him, he was saying that we should deport the Jews, but not shoot them. I noticed at that point that he was smirking. "Damn!" I said. "Now you're grinning! I'm in more trouble than I thought!" He mumbled. "OK," I said, "tell me the truth. Is there a part of you that that would tickle?"

"What?" he evaded.

"Tell me the truth. Is there a part of you that it would tickle?"

"To kill the Jews?" he asked. "Oh, let's see." He calmed down a little. And entered into an answer that had only a tinge of humor and teasing, and a considerable air of seriousness: "All right, I would, I know I'd probably kill the Zionist Jews. All right, because they're the worst."

For members of the racist world, "Zionist Jew" means those Jews who identify with the world Jewish conspiracy to achieve universal domination. This tends to mean most Jews.

The Jews do have, he went on, "a right to live," so the Nazis would have to "find some little island or something to stick them on."

I suggested that Alcatraz might be a good island for the purpose.

That sounded pretty good to Nolan at first, but then he pointed out that it was too close to the United States. Nevertheless, he said, he would "definitely get rid of the Zionist Jews. The other ones, I'd stuff somewhere."

I asked what percentage of Jews he thought would be "Zionist Jews," but he could not answer. Might there be half? I asked. "Maybe." How would we be able to distinguish who was a Zionist and who alternatively was to be deported? I asked. How were we going to tell? He responded with what he recalled of a lesson he had been taught at one of the indoctrination weekends on Miles's farm. (I had heard the same speech.) "How we going to tell? I know we ain't going to get power anytime soon. I'm not saying we're not going to get to power. But over the time it takes, we're going to take down names—we get names and stuff of Jews. We get names and stuff of Zionists. And see what kind of business they get into. How they help destroy us and stuff."

This took him forward. "All right. After we kill all known Zionist Jews, we put the Jews somewhere they couldn't get to the other people of the world. That way, that way, if there is one Zionist left, he just spread throughout his little community of Jews so it ain't going to get to the rest of the world. Like I said, if we miss a couple, they'd be concentrated in one area. We can keep an eye on them.

"All right," he said, "so that takes care of the Jews. Now the Puerto Ricans—" Now Nolan was in full cry. His buddy Michael was sitting in, giggling away, tickled by Nolan's audacity. "The Puerto Ricans, I'd kick them out of here so fast. I'd just send them back to where they had come from, make sure they never get back here again. Same thing with the Cubans. Cubans, they'd want to live in Cuba after we blow up Castro. After we wipe that guy out and get rid of communism down there, I think they'll all want to live there.

"So, Mexicans, shove them back into Mexico and put up a brick wall all along there or something, just something to keep them over on their own side.

"And then, we'd have Blackie back in Africa. Unless he didn't want to go. Then we'd use him for fertilizer."

In this little speech, Nolan, talking with passion and exaggeration, wanted to be as outrageous as he could. He got a lot of appreciation from the others for these performances. He had no idea that the joke was obscene.

The transcripts of the interviews with Nolan have astonished me. Almost nothing I was saying in those conversations reached him. It was stunning to see how little data or thought lay behind his attitudes, his nonchalant contempt for black Americans, his superstitious conceptions of Jews. When pressed for detail on any subject, he really had none. He was perfectly at home mouthing and acting on extreme beliefs with no justification. There was virtually no base in experience, other than a couple of incidents from his youth, which probably were distorted in memory.

It was clear enough that Nolan's racism was valued for what it allowed him to be. He could be one of a group who carried out exciting actions at rallies. He could vandalize property with his marking pen and his stickers. He could shock his companions by the amusing ferocity of his monologues.

He liked all that. The enlistment into the group had given him entry to a new form of theater, had let him into a new gang. He became a turned-on, mouthy teenager who had to be listened to. Enacting the role of the militant racist was the reward; there were no visible costs.

Nolan was not a mean person. He was a fairly ordinary young man with a generally sunny nature. He was spirited and lively. He truly liked hard work.

Nolan was quite isolated within his family and within the community. We hear nothing useful coming from the siblings, from an extended family, or from community institutions. There were only the amusements the big city offered the alienated youth of its streets: the rock concerts, the bars, the house parties, and—for these particular kids—the racist gang.

Nolan had been ripe to fall out of school at the first opportunity. He took a chaotic first day of tenth grade as the signal that it was okay to go, and his family (that is, his mother) was unaware that he had done so. The community and the school made no effort to draw him back in—or he recalls none—and he had set himself up for a lifetime of underemployment.

A year or two after these interviews, Nolan drifted away from the Death's-Head Strike Group. He enlisted in the National Guard and took a summer's active duty, during which he finally took and passed the GED. After the summer, he and several friends took a cellar apartment and devoted themselves to alcohol. He told some people that they were starting a new white power group, but no one saw any evidence of this.

I talked a few years later to Nolan's buddy Michael. Nolan had just hit the newspapers, Michael told me: Nolan had been arrested and was out on bail. Nolan, who "had too many weapons around him," had gone out into the street to shoot one of his semiautomatic weapons into the air. It happened that Nolan lived directly across the street from the police station. Michael had just called Nolan up and told him that he was a damn fool. "You can't even shoot off a firecracker out there," Michael said. "He was just showing off to some damn girls."

EIGHTEEN

Reflections

Scared, stranded white youths in the changing city are one of the reservoirs from which the white supremacist movement draws recruits, and the Death's-Head Strike Group is an instructive sample. These are, for the most part, fairly normal people, although poverty has left serious marks and the families are weak and isolated. But you can't say, in most cases, that these youths are "sick." They are not sturdy psychologically, but they are not peculiar. The members we met in the preceding chapters have mostly drifted on to loneliness, alcohol, or other groups; Paul has found people much like them as replacements.

The racism of the young men in the Strike Group is crude. Its most overpowering element is the flat conviction that blacks and whites are utterly distinct. I have spoken of this before in relation to the national white racist leaders; it is just as true with these young people: A person *is* a black or white—absolute categories—just as a truck is a truck, a lawnmower is a lawnmower.

This absolute conviction reflects what has been said among family and in the neighborhood, but also what the young people see as they walk in streets: The worlds of white and black *are* distinct. Dissenting voices—teachers, media—seem duplicitous against this backdrop.

Race is an absolute category, and the presumed characteristics of a member of the racial group are taken as God-given and unalterable. Blacks, they believe, are people who do not want to work, who gain money through bullying or cheating, who rob and who are violent. Blacks want to hurt whites—to assault and rob white males, to rape white females. Pressed for detail, white racists will estimate that eighty percent of black people are of this sort.

White racist group members are afraid of black people. When we drove through black neighborhoods, even in daylight, Paul and the others were nervous that the car might break down.

In all our discussions, the group members spontaneously, with no prompting, spoke about race mixing: cross-racial sex, cross-racial childbearing. The images upset them, and I strained to grasp how real the emotional disturbance was.

I wanted to discover the degree to which anxiety about sexuality underlay the racial antagonism. White racial violence in the South after Reconstruction was a means of social control: Whites preserved white superiority through violence and the threat of violence. In the century after Reconstruction, somewhere between three thousand and five thousand black people were lynched by whites. These lynchings were meant to terrorize the black population and keep it quiescent and under white control. Many of the victims were burned alive, chained to iron stakes that had been driven into the ground; others were hanged. The lucky ones were shot soon after the burning or the hanging began; there are many accounts, however, of desperate men crawling from the flames and being pushed back in. The newspaper accounts are grueling, the cruelty astonishing. Bodies were slashed; fingers were cut off. Often the victim's testicles or penis were cut off.

This hideous work can be seen simply as the furthest extent of the statement of superiority, the mob's ultimate statement of the degradation of the black. It may also be fueled by the aggressor's fears about his own sexuality.

What accounts for the Strike Group members' focus on interracial sexuality? Are the roots similar to those that lead to mutilation of a lynching victim? Is it perhaps a milder form of terror, a sense that one is weak, low in potency in the world—that fear I have spoken of, that one readily will blow away in the wind? Is that terror now expressing itself in a shuddering fear of a black sexuality that seems more potent? In their fantasies, the group members make it clear that black men are stronger than they themselves are, with a greater capacity for vigorous sex; the imagined partner of the black is being violated by a stronger force. There is a hint of the group member's fear that he himself might be violated by the black male. And, not surprisingly, the young men in the group bristle with hatred and aversion toward the male homosexual community; gays are right at the top of their list of people to be hated and feared.

The national leaders in the white racist movement, as we saw earlier, use racism as a tool in their individual quests for power. Each leader selects, from the bundle of white racist ideas (or, ideas-with-emotion), those best suited to his own personality, those that best let him exercise his individual style. In the same way, Strike Group members emphasized those parts of the bundle that best served them. Nolan, thus, used the ideas that let him play his role of the brat, while Raymond worked with the problems of governing a province.

These crude young racists are strikingly ill-educated and unsophisticated.

One day I asked a member named Phillip what sort of thoughts he had in his head about Jews. "It's weird," he said, "I can't explain it, it's so strange. . . . It's weird," he said again. "It's like someone from another planet."

"What do you mean?"

"It's weird. Jews look like white people. It's like someone has taken a white person's body and put a Jew in it. I can be walking down the street," he said, "and this person will be walking toward me, and he can look just like a white person, and I would be wondering whether that person might be a Jew, and I would be wondering what he would think of me if he knew I was a Nazi."

Things were getting better, he added; he was beginning to be able to recognize Jews from seeing who opposed them at rallies. Jews tended to be different. "This one dude," he said, "I could look and just tell he was Jewish by his features. He had these glasses on. He had a big nose. And he leaned back when he walked and he waddled. I knew a lot of Jews walk like that."

There is no way to overestimate the amount of ignorance in the racist movement. Many of the players are working with only the scrappiest of educations. What they do know is jumbled chaotically in their heads. They have put information together from haphazard sources in unorganized fashion; they really don't have any structured conception of reality, any organized body of knowledge that would allow them to recognize absurdity. Anything is possible in their worlds.

The white racist press is filled with foolishness. The editors know their readership. I was looking at issues from the early eighties and found an article with word of a new "scientific discovery." A scientist had found out, it told us, that certain substances in semen could be transmitted into the blood supply of a man's sexual partner and create long-lasting effects. The scientist reported that a white woman who made love even one time with a black man might well find herself permanently changed as a result; she herself might change in her features, and she might well find herself, *three years later,* giving birth to a black child.

So watch out, race mixers!

The credulity and the ignorance came up repeatedly. There was almost nothing that these people knew for sure; there was almost nothing that they were not willing to believe.

The ignorance showed itself at times as charming naïveté. Late one night as I recorded through a long session, Phillip asked, "Why do we got to talk about our childhoods?" And later, as I was changing tapes, he suddenly asked me, "Would you take me to the Jew church one day, so I can see what it is like?"

Most of us wish for our children a life of vibrancy and rich sensuality, a spirit that ranges freely, tasting experience with intensity and drawing meaning from it.

I am writing with the office window partly open; I smell the April rain and the wet earth; I see the bits of green at the tips of a few trees as spring inches toward us.

How to convey, in contrast, the *flatness* of the Strike Group member's spirit, the *lack?*

When I sat and talked with poor black people in Detroit, gathering material for a previous research project, their language was terrific.

The interviews had lively rhythm; they soared and they plunged. The speakers knew themselves and paid attention to their feelings and their fears and their dreams; they talked about all that. Not these urban white youths. Theirs is an impoverished language—their culture or their lives have given them few words, and expression is not important. And they know little about their feelings. You pull statements out of them one at a time; you pull reflections out as if with pliers. Playful images in your questions leave them puzzled; playful suggestions go past them.

The stories of the black respondents were jammed with people—individuals—colorful characters the speaker outlined for you, characters who had reasons for their actions. The stories of these whites have no one in them who is a single individual. There are stock figures with labels on them. It is a dull, unpopulated world.

And it is a world with no possibilities. No playful, chance opportunities leap up, pull you forward. There is today, a dull day; tomorrow is going to be the same.

The Strike Group members don't like to have a lot of exciting possibilities in their heads. It's a small, dull world, a predictable one, since nothing happens. Perhaps that's necessary—children of alcoholics don't like surprises.

They have chosen a gray perceptual world. Their flattening of individualities and particularities gives them a simple world. It doesn't seem like much fun, but they're not long on play.

The piece of time they live in is also small. A member would talk with me about a new development, and I would think from his language we were talking about a transition that developed over a long stretch of time—only to find that we were talking about a couple of days at the most. The subject was almost always *now*. This partly had to do with one's sense of being able to have an effect. We don't think about things we cannot affect, especially if they are threatening. It is only as we start to imagine a situation in which we can have some impact that we invest the picture with any detail. It is the deep sense of *hopelessness* that paralyzes the imagination of the Strike Group members. They are a frightened group of young men who live in a world with little possible change, little imagined future, and very few people.

The supremacist folklore offers scraps of past for them, and now and then one would speak of feeling that his membership made him kin to a Roman or Viking ancestor. And of course, the white racist movement as a whole has been violently resentful of the Jewish claim to a history: Who is this "chosen people" who have played so self-conscious a role over such centuries? It is no accident that Christian Identity has seized that history and claimed it for its own.

The Death's-Head Strike Group's newsletter is a primitive collection of photocopied news articles and photos of the group in uniform; the content expresses the focus on action and image. In contrast, news-papers from the left feature closely printed columns on abstract the-ory. The fixation on ideas radically distinguishes the extreme left from the extreme right. "Theory" on the extreme right consists ba-sically of a single sentence: "There is a conspiracy."

Words and ideas have less importance for the extreme right. This came home to me in an early conversation with the young Strike Group member named Michael. He was showing me a bundle of fliers the group had been supplied by a high Klan leader in New York. The Strike Group would use a stamp pad to put their name and post office box number on one corner of the flier and go off to leave them on porches.

I was pretty amazed. A left-wing group would consume months in argument attempting to craft an acceptable handout: Words are very important, and you have to mean exactly what the words say. And here, on the other hand, were folks who simply received someone else's material, stamped their name on it, and passed it around!

I looked at the material Michael was showing me. One of the items was a vicious drawing, showing a strange, hook-nosed, slit-eyed crea-ture in a skullcap; this caricature of a Jew, festooned with a star of David and a hammer and sickle, was identified in the caption as a parasite working to destroy the white race.

I looked over at Michael, a hardworking youth who hung out with louder guys and giggled a lot at the outrageous things they said. "This is quite an attack on Jews, isn't it, Michael?" I said to him quietly.

He looked surprised. "I don't know, Rafe. I never thought about it."

Most of the leaflets were vile; most attacked black people. Pornographic drawings of black men and women, depicted as cannibals and gorillas, went with text calling on whites to save themselves from the beasts. Michael probably had not thought about this, either. He didn't really care about details of the message; the messages were interchangeable.

The messages all fit his general stance, which was to express opposition to and contempt for the designated enemies of the white race. He didn't think about the impact of the message on individual blacks or Jews; his imaginings seldom reached beyond his immediate life.

Distribution of the leaflet had value as an action that expressed his state of membership. There was not really any goal other than that. Racism for him was a *state of being*, valued for the declaration "I *am*."

I had always assumed that there was a close relationship between the words on a leaflet and the character of the person who handed it to you. But Michael had never looked with any thought at the leaflet he handed to strangers. I had assumed that people took words and images seriously. This was a limited view, and Michael was extending my education. For him, the action was important; the words were secondary, the exact ideas secondary. The overall idea mattered: *Our acts show the bad nature of our enemies; I am doing something to advance my side.* The action was what counted.

This relationship to ideas matters if you ask whether a member like Michael could be led away from the Strike Group. If you take the leaflet's detail as a statement about Michael, you must believe that the man is hopelessly stuck in this place and could never be imagined in another setting. But his very loose relation to the leaflet leads us us to a different and more hopeful conclusion. Michael is comfortable with ugly racist ideas; he is not deterred by the vulgarity of his leaflet; he will probably always be comfortable with the gutter thoughts of white America. The act of distribution, however, does not mean that he is driven to public expression of these ideas. He is driven to the act of proclaiming solidarity with his group of comrades and with his imagined larger family of whites. That kind of action, that expression of solidarity, could take many alternate forms; so-

cially positive endeavors could yield the same pleasure of membership, comradeship, and defiance.

I have not said clearly enough that the Strike Group members had
only weak connections to women and could not fulfill the role of
father. We have seen this with Paul; it was true of his followers, who,
like Raymond, left their women and any babies they had sired. Group
members went with various young women, never very seriously, except for two men, Rick and Stefan, both of whom ended up becoming
quite serious with their girlfriends and simultaneously leaving the
group. It seemed to work out that way: One could not be really
serious with a woman and remain a good Strike Group member.

For Rick, the story is rather cheerful. Our first meeting featured
him telling me that in wearing a Klan robe or a swastika he expressed
his real essence, "the real me"; but when he began living with his
woman friend a year later he became less and less available for rallies.
After another year he scarcely showed up. After yet one more year,
I visited him and his woman friend at their apartment and found that
he had gotten himself work with a future: He was employed full time
as a driver for a service that brought food to elderly citizens in their
homes and had an additional half-time job at night in a nursing
home. He was working seventy hours a week and had just acquired
Blue Cross coverage. He and his partner were talking about marriage;
he mentioned casually in our interview his fairly matter-of-fact in-
terdependence at work with black co-workers. He found himself with
good feelings for them, and he had some friendships growing. Rick
was on his way to being an adult man with commitments to a
woman, and probably would be able to rear children. This did not
mix with continued activity in the Strike Group.

Stefan's story is less clear. Where Rick was nineteen when I met
him, Stefan was already twenty-six. At our first meeting, he told me
that for several years all his friends had been black. Stefan lived for
athletics. He had played basketball in the parks for several years as
part of a black crowd. He had told them that he was Puerto Rican
and that his name was Pablo. His basketball buddies believed him.
Then Stefan abruptly broke those ties, left his black friends, and
joined the Death's-Head Strike Group. He liked talking to the guys

in this new friendship circle but remained intensely shy with women. He had never really had a girlfriend. He was singled out by a high-school girl who dated one of the other older Strike Group members; Joetta soon began to go with Stefan and rather quickly became pregnant. Stefan insisted on their becoming married. Meanwhile, his ties with the group were becoming strained. He began listening harder and harder when I talked with him about other ways of perceiving the world. Joetta soon gave birth; Stefan quit coming out to most group activities; he found a grungy job at a warehouse, loading trucks. Stefan, Joetta, and the baby entered into a stormy year before the marriage collapsed. Joetta was bored by childcare; Stefan was maddened by the loss of his previous athlete's life, which looked better and better to him from this distance.

Joetta fooled around with a fast-living set of acquaintances from high school, handing the child off to her mother when possible. Stefan fumed at his new restrictions and at her apparent faults. He struck her on several occasions. The couple separated a number of times; soon they were parted. The little boy was at Stefan's house periodically, but Stefan had no idea how to care for him. Stefan spoke repeatedly of his losses—his losses of the carefree life—it sounded as though he were speaking of a loss of innocence.

Throughout this time Stefan had moved further and further from the group. He lived still in his mother's house, where I had first met him; he had an apartment in her attic. The house is tucked away in a neighborhood of Arab immigrants, with whom he had friendly, if shallow, acquaintanceship. I was amazed to find that he had taken down his cut-out pictures of Hitler from the attic walls and replaced them with propaganda photos of Soviet women, muscular female industrial workers in heroic poses. He began to speak somewhat glowingly of communism, and I wondered whether "Pablo" who had become a Nazi was now going to become a Red. I had also heard, however, that he had ties to another neo-Nazi group that was beginning to surface, and soon heard from his old friends that he was now leading that little group, probably in partnership with a local Klan organizer. Stefan had been fairly jealous of Paul's role as leader, and I was less surprised by his aspirations than by his persistent link to Nazism. The child remained in the care of Joetta's mother, a capable woman married to quite a competent skilled worker.

Stefan's wandering through identities fascinates me, but the critical point is his inability to be a father. Many of the members were so very young that their self-absorbed lives are not surprising, but the older men like Stefan, Raymond, and Paul were just as limited. The world of real jobs, real marriages, and real parenting is replaced by flags, boots, fights, and boasts—a perpetual male adolescence.

Around midnight one evening I rode into Ann Arbor after an evening with a collection of Strike Group members at Paul's place. As I neared my neighborhood, my eyes fell on the day-care center for single parents where a former student of mine, Maureen, worked. As a child, Maureen had been the victim of a brutal father. As a young adult, she had helped organize a shelter for abused women. She now taught at the day-care center, paying particular attention to mothers who felt insecure, helping them relate to their children. Maureen had made her experience a resource; she did concrete things to help specific people.

I looked at the day-care center, and I thought of the evening I had just spent, listening to the childish cries and postures of the Strike Group members—the sneering and exulting, the loud cries of "Power!" as they watched a video of some old rallies. I thought of the years they spent in costume and playacting, forcing a public to respond so that they can continue a moratorium on personal development and economic struggle.

I thought of the emptiness and the futility, and compared it to the life of Maureen, who deals in detail with real events, behaves responsively with individual people, has entered open-ended involvements. As I looked at her life, the isolated nature of the lives in the Death's-Head Strike Group stood out, the irrelevance of their lives stood out.

The waste is profound.

EPILOGUE

Organized white racism is about a mood—lonely resentment—and several ideas—white specialness, the biological significance of "race," and the primacy of power in human relations. These ideas and the feeling of being cheated (not unique to racists) are powerfully motivating in the absence of ideas that might lead to more positive action. People will find some way to make their lives meaningful, and if nothing richer is at hand, racism (or religious fanaticism or nationalism or gang membership) will do. The appeal of white racist ideologies reflects the absence of competing sets of thought, emotion, and experience, competing faiths that say "This is how the world is constructed" and "This is how you can become a person who matters and whose life matters."

Formal and informal education about racism tend to undervalue the importance of experience. You can't sell people a new idea backed only by your authority. You have to have respect for the lives the people have led to this point and begin with them there; their experiences have led them to their assumptions and conceptions. As you identify and legitimate those experiences, you can help people identify their own primary needs in society. Then they can begin to imagine other people as having parallel needs. You can begin to think together about what each of you needs in the world in order to get along, and you can begin to think together about what others need. Education about racism should be education about personal identity; we have to begin with our own lives. We must begin with respect for the lives of one another.

I've often encountered a related problem in courses I've taught. Students often want to say, "I am color blind; I don't see black and white." This is a way to say "I am a good girl/boy" in a subculture where racism is not chic. Students feel a push to declare their non-racism. The words used come from a misconception that racism is a thing out there in the environment that one could pick up or reject. The students don't understand. Racism is a way of perceiving the world and a way of thinking. To a certain degree it is part of everyone who lives in a racist society. Imagine growing up next to a cement factory, and imagine the cement dust inevitably becoming a part of your body. As we grow up within a society that is saturated in white racism, year after year we pass through interactions in which white racist conceptions are an unspoken subtext. We make lives in institutions in which this is true. We cannot live from day to day without absorbing a certain amount of white racism into our thoughts. (We similarly absorb homophobia and sexism.) It is foolish to say, "I am not racist." Part of one's mind (if one is white and perhaps if one is a person of color) has necessarily absorbed racist ways of thinking. It is important to discover the subtle ways our culture's racism has affected our thinking: to identify those habits of thought and learn how to keep them from influencing us. We can get tripped up by ideas we don't allow ourselves to acknowledge.

But I don't want racism to be part of me, you might say.

Know yourself, must be the reply. You have no choice. Whether you like it or not, part of your soul includes elements of racism. This is not evil: You did not choose to be born in this society. To use an analogy, you did not choose to be born to your particular parents, but if you do not identify the preconceptions you have unwittingly absorbed from them, you may behave inappropriately in current relationships. In the same way, if we do not identify the elements of white racism that we have unconsciously absorbed, we may harm ourselves as well as others who matter in our lives.

In one of his songs, Leadbelly tells us how to deal with the blues: When you wake up in the morning with the blues, you got to say "Good morning, blues," you got to sit down and talk with your blues, got to get to know them, got to talk it over. Whites (and maybe sometimes people of color) have to get well acquainted with the subtext of racism in our lives. Not in order to feel guilty, but in order to be sure the way we act more accurately reflects our intentions.

It doesn't matter whether or not you or I can call ourselves good folk. Our actions are what matter. Real people get hurt badly in our society by poverty and racism. We can alter the institutions that do the damage. We need to be fully conscious of our influences; we need to know ourselves. The militant racists let us see the racist parts of our souls with few filters; we should observe and learn.

I think preventive work can do a lot to cut down the number of people ready to be recruited into racist groups, and that prevention probably lies mainly in trying to establish ways for kids of middle-school age or younger to find mentorship and membership in constructive alternatives. I think education needs to be much more interactive, and it must avoid preaching. And I think social control matters. I've seen enough to know that it helps when the police set clear, firm limits; we have seen weakness by the state and the police in Germany opening the way for neo-Nazi violence. At the same time I think citizens must ensure that police agencies stick to constitutional guidelines. Racist groups make a tempting target these days—no one wants to be their champion—and police agencies need good publicity when they are competing for appropriations. Nevertheless, the health of the Bill of Rights matters more than police convenience.

Readers may ask how dangerous white racists are. They carry out less violence nowadays than they did when local authorities commonly collaborated with them before the civil rights movement. The white racist movement is stronger, on the other hand, when respected leaders pander to racism (the Willie Horton ads in the Bush campaign, for example) or encourage the white population to conceive of people of color as welfare cheats and criminals. The white racist movement is part of America, not an alien presence; it grows and wanes as general American racism grows and wanes.

The country today is pretty scared, and with good reason. The economy is in bad shape and recovery is not going to benefit many. The unskilled have no place in the emerging world, and the semiskilled may not do much better. Even the middle class is in trouble: the ranks of middle management must shrink markedly and stay smaller, if American businesses are to compete on the world market.

Jobs and benefits are shaky. It's a frightening environment. Scared people turn inward. Damaging white racist distortions in our institutions are most likely in such a climate; vigilance is called for—many racists wear suits, not sheets.

Research reports usually conclude by saying ". . . and so more research is needed." Surprisingly little research has been funded on organized racism, and practical difficulties of access limit the sampling researchers can do. Moreover, there are so few studies done that one has trouble estimating their value: How accurate are a writer's perceptions, how valuable a writer's inferences? This is hard to estimate when you look at a single small-sample study such as this one; it would get easier if you could compare several small-sample studies of the same phenomenon.

Yet our greatest need, I think, is for research on prevention and on the connection between the movement and mainstream society. How do we effectively reduce the vulnerability of youth to recruitment in white racist organizations? What programs have been tried, and with what results? It is time for evaluation studies on prevention. And if we look at the world of movement members and the world of everyday citizens and the world of influential people of power, how do ideas, sentiments, and actions in one of those worlds affect ideas, sentiments, and actions in the other two?

I will close with an image I will remember the longest, an encounter in Metairie, Louisiana.

The man was thin, a little over sixty-five, brave enough to speak up to the stranger, but kind of worn. His wire-frame glasses jiggled as he wrinkled up his nose; his small brown eyes glinted through the lenses.

Everyone is so mad, he told me; everyone is so disgusted; people are not going to take it, there is going to be a revolution. He had listened to "that young fellow" David Duke for years, he told me, and that little fellow never told lies. "I never had a new truck in my life," he told me, pointing to the old brown pickup by the side of the house. "I bought that thing with eighty thousand miles on it.

Never had a new house in my life. Raised four children, the wife and I." His wife had just come home from ten days in the hospital. "I'm retired now," he continued, "from the telephone company. But I'm going to have to get a part-time job now. To pay the bills.

"There will be a revolution," he said, here on his porch, by the plain gravel road lined with other working-class homes. David Duke's run for governor was two weeks off, and I was knocking on doors where people had Duke signs on the lawn—would they come out on the porch and tell me what it was about? "People are so mad," he explained. "We've been turned into second-class citizens. Forced integration. Forced busing. There shouldn't be forced integration. There should be an all-black school and an all-white school and a mixed school, and people could choose. Choice.

"But *I* never got a thing," he continued. "Don't you think I would have wanted to have help? Like all that help these welfare people get? I put four children through parochial school. But my taxes paid for the schools I couldn't use. Don't you think I would have loved for them to go to Tulane or Loyola? But I couldn't hardly afford the price to send them to a damn little-bitty little college over here. And even there I got turned down on every application I made for aid; they said I made too much money. Thirty thousand!

"And this *affirmative action.* Promoting people who weren't there but five years." He squinted at me. "Don't you think *I* would want to be a supervisor, working there all my life? But no, here come these niggers!"

We had talked about immigration, and he had told me that the problem was that some people don't do it right. You were supposed to bring your heart to America when you came here, but some left it in the place they came from. Who did he mean? I asked, pretending innocence. "Well, these Jewish people," he replied. "Their hearts are for Israel. They come here and they see this country as a cow to be milked for Israel."

We talked some more. I knew from the comments on Jews that he probably read literature from white supremacist organizations such as Duke's National Association for the Advancement of White People. He agreed that he read their paper some but said it wasn't a Nazi group. We spoke of abortion. ("The only choice is *before* you get pregnant.") He emphasized his hatred of having his tax money spent on programs he did not want. What would those be? I asked. All the things that welfare people got, he said. And foreign aid. And hey, had I seen all those Supreme Court justices on television at the hearings on Clarence Thomas—all those high salaries?

On he went. Three times he summarized by saying, with a twisted face and flat nasal voice: "Liberalism is *e-v-i-l*." His voice was slow and emphatic as he said the word *evil*. But the heart of our talk was the very last line. Reciting one more time all the things that had been denied him, squinting his eyes one last time, peering down his nose through the tiny lenses of the wire-frame glasses, he intoned, *"I want everybody to get what I got: Nothing!"*

APPENDIX:
SUGGESTED READING

Excellent current material is continually available from the major organizations that monitor the racist movement:

Center for Democratic Renewal
P.O. Box 50469
Atlanta, Georgia 30302
(404) 221-0025

Southern Poverty Law Center
(attn: Klanwatch)
400 Washington Ave.
Montgomery, Alabama 36104

American Jewish Committee
165 E. 56th St.
New York, NY 10022
(212) 751-4000

Anti-Defamation League of
the B'nai B'rith
823 UN Plaza
New York, NY 10017
(212) 490-2525

North Carolinians Against Racial
and Religious Violence (NCARRV)
P.O. Box 240
Durham, NC 27702
(919) 668-5965

Northwest Coalition Against
Malicious Harassment
P.O. Box 16776
Seattle, WA 98116
(206) 233-9136

Coalition for Human Dignity
P.O. Box 40344
Portland, OR 97240
(503) 281-5823

Following are some highly useful sources on the subject of racism.

BASIC SOURCES

Center for Democratic Renewal. *When Hate Groups Come to Town: A Handbook of Model Community Responses.* Montgomery, Alabama: Black Belt Press, 1992.
CDR's superb manual is a synthesis of its years of proactive community organizing.

Center for Democratic Renewal. *They Don't All Wear Sheets*. New York: National Council of Churches of Christ in the USA, 1987.
   Indispensable pamphlet, periodically updated, surveying the white racist movement.

Zeskind, Leonard. *The "Christian Identity" Movement: Analyzing Its Theological Rationalization for Racist and Anti-Semitic Violence*. Atlanta: Center for Democratic Renewal, 1986.
   A definitive study of Christian Identity.

ACADEMIC WORKS

Aho, James A. *The Politics of Righteousness: Idaho Christian Patriotism*. Seattle: University of Washington Press, 1990.
   Careful, quantitative, scholarly study of the Idaho sections of the movement. Highly provocative findings.

Barrett, Stanley R. *Is God a Racist? The Right Wing in Canada*. Toronto: University of Toronto Press, 1987.
   An extremely useful anthropologist's examination of the Canadian white racist movement.

Chalmers, David. *Hooded Americanism: The History of the Ku Klux Klan*. Durham, NC: Duke University Press, 1981.
   A fine history of the Klan.

Hixson, William B., Jr. *Search for the American Right Wing: An Analysis of the Social Science Record, 1955–1987*. Princeton, NJ: Princeton University Press, 1992.
   Thoughtful review of the major analytic frameworks in which American social scientists have studied the political right wing.

Powell, Lawrence N. "Slouching Toward Baton Rouge: The 1989 Legislative Election of David Duke." In Douglas D. Rose (ed.), *The Emergence of David Duke and the Politics of Race*. Chapel Hill: University of North Carolina Press, 1992.
   A deft scholarly analysis of the demography of Duke support.

Schuman, Howard, Charlotte Steeh, and Lawrence Bobo. *Racial Attitudes in America: Trends and Interpretations*. Cambridge, MA: Harvard University Press, 1985.
   The best scholarly summation of survey data on American racial attitudes.

Wade, Wyn Craig. *The Fiery Cross: The Ku Klux Klan in America*. New York: Simon & Schuster, 1987.
   A careful, current history of the Klan.

FIELD REPORTS

Coates, James. *Armed and Dangerous: The Rise of the Survivalist Right*. New York: Noonday Press, 1987.
   Examines most branches of the white racist movement.

Corcoran, James. *Bitter Harvest: Gordon Kahl and the Posse Commitatus: Murder in the Heartland.* New York: Viking, 1990.
   The collision of the farm crisis, law enforcement, and radical racism.

Finch, Phillip. *God, Guts, and Guns.* New York: Seaview/Putnam, 1983.
   Excellent fieldwork, provocative reflections; an examination of the white racist movement more than a decade ago.

Flynn, Kevin, and Gary Gerhardt. *The Silent Brotherhood.* New York: Free Press, 1989.
   The rise and fall of the Order and Robert Mathews.

Ginzburg, Ralph. *100 Years of Lynching.* New York: Lancer Books, 1962.
   Newspaper accounts of lynchings. Indispensable for understanding the reality.

Langer, Elinor. "The American Neo-Nazi Movement Today." *The Nation,* vol. 251, Nr. 3, July 16/23, 1990, pp. 82–108.
   Perceptive, timely overview; sound insights.

Martinez, Thomas, with John Guinther. *Brotherhood of Murder.* New York: McGraw-Hill, 1988.
   A former associate of the Order tells his story.

Newton, Michael, and Judy Ann Newton. *The Ku Klux Klan: An Encyclopedia.* New York: Garland Publishing, 1991.
   A fine first reference.

Ridgeway, James. *Blood in the Face: The Ku Klux Klan, Aryan Nations, Nazi Skinheads, and the Rise of a New White Culture.* New York: Thunder's Mouth Press, 1990.
   A fine survey of the white racist movement.

Sims, Patsy. *The Klan.* New York: Stein and Day, 1978.
   Extraordinary firsthand reporting; the personnel have changed, but the insights are still right on target.

Thompson, Jerry. *My Life in the Klan.* New York: Putnam, 1982.
   An undercover reporter's observations.

KLAN BUSTING

Dees Morris, and Steve Fiffer. *Hate on Trial: The Case Against America's Most Dangerous Neo-Nazi.* New York: Villard Books (Random House), 1993.
   How Dees and associates brought Tom Metzger to account for his role in the Portland Skinhead murder case.

Kennedy, Stetson. *The Klan Unmasked.* Boca Raton, FL: Florida Atlantic University Press, 1954.
   Detailed recounting of several major anti-Klan cases.

Stanton, Bill. *Klanwatch: Bringing the Ku Klux Klan to Justice*. New York: Grove Weidenfeld, 1991.
  Earlier work by Dees and associates.

CONNECTIONS WITH THE MAINSTREAM

Bellant, Russ. *The Coors Connection: How Coors Family Philanthropy Undermines Democratic Pluralism*. Boston: South End Press, 1991.

Bellant, Russ. *Old Nazis, the New Right and the Republican Party*. Boston: South End Press, 1991.
  Bellant provides careful research on linkages between "extremists" and the mainstream. The second, in particular, is indispensable.

HOLOCAUST DENIAL

Lipstadt, Deborah E. *Beyond Belief: The American Press and the Coming of the Holocaust, 1933–1945*. New York: Free Press, 1986.
  Invaluable. A tracing of the presentation (or obscuring) of the news of the Holocaust in the American press—how public response was not mobilized despite reports having come through.

Lipstadt, Deborah E. *Denying the Holocaust: The Growing Assault on Truth and Memory*. New York: Free Press, 1993.
  Superb discussion of the denial movement.

Shapiro, Shelly. (ed.). *Truth Prevails: Demolishing Holocaust Denial: The End of "The Leuchter Report."* New York: The Beate Klarsfeld Foundation, and Albany: Holocaust Survivors and Friends in Pursuit of Justice, 1990.
  A careful exposé of the deceptions that constitute Holocaust denial arguments.

Stern, Kenneth S. *Holocaust Denial*. New York: The American Jewish Committee, 1993.
  Superb discussion of the denial movement.

FOR THE BEST IN PAPERBACKS, LOOK FOR THE

In every corner of the world, on every subject under the sun, Penguin represents quality and variety—the very best in publishing today.

For complete information about books available from Penguin—including Puffins, Penguin Classics, and Arkana—and how to order them, write to us at the appropriate address below. Please note that for copyright reasons the selection of books varies from country to country.

In the United Kingdom: Please write to *Dept. JC, Penguin Books Ltd, FREEPOST, West Drayton, Middlesex. UB7 0BR*.

If you have any difficulty in obtaining a title, please send your order with the correct money, plus ten percent for postage and packaging, to *P.O. Box No. 11, West Drayton, Middlesex UB7 0BR*

In the United States: Please write to *Consumer Sales, Penguin USA, P.O. Box 999, Dept. 17109, Bergenfield, New Jersey 07621-0120*. VISA and MasterCard holders call 1-800-253-6476 to order all Penguin titles

In Canada: Please write to *Penguin Books Canada Ltd, 10 Alcorn Avenue, Suite 300, Toronto, Ontario M4V 3B2*

In Australia: Please write to *Penguin Books Australia Ltd, P.O. Box 257, Ringwood, Victoria 3134*

In New Zealand: Please write to *Penguin Books (NZ) Ltd, Private Bag 102902, North Shore Mail Centre, Auckland 10*

In India: Please write to *Penguin Books India Pvt Ltd, 706 Eros Apartments, 56 Nehru Place, New Delhi 110 019*

In the Netherlands: Please write to *Penguin Books Netherlands bv, Postbus 3507, NL-1001 AH Amsterdam*

In Germany: Please write to *Penguin Books Deutschland GmbH, Metzlerstrasse 26, 60594 Frankfurt am Main*

In Spain: Please write to *Penguin Books S. A., Bravo Murillo 19, 1° B, 28015 Madrid*

In Italy: Please write to *Penguin Italia s.r.l., Via Felice Casati 20, I-20124 Milano*

In France: Please write to *Penguin France S. A., 17 rue Lejeune, F–31000 Toulouse*

In Japan: Please write to *Penguin Books Japan, Ishikiribashi Building, 2–5–4, Suido, Bunkyo-ku, Tokyo 112*

In Greece: Please write to *Penguin Hellas Ltd, Dimocritou 3, GR–106 71 Athens*

In South Africa: Please write to *Longman Penguin Southern Africa (Pty) Ltd, Private Bag X08, Bertsham 2013*